THE MASTER & MARGARITA

A Critical Companion

THE MASTER & MARGARITA

A Critical Companion

Edited by Laura D. Weeks

Northwestern University Press

The American Association of Teachers of Slavic and East European Languages

Northwestern University Press

Evanston, Illinois 60208-4210

Printed in the United States of America.

Library of Congress Cataloging-in-Publication Data

The Master & Margarita : a critical companion / edited by Laura D. Weeks.

p. cm. — (Northwestern /AATSEEL critical companions to Russian literature)

Includes bibliographical references.

ISBN 0-8101-1212-4 (paper).

1. Bulgakov, Mikhail Afanas'evich, 1891–1940. Master i Margarita.

I. Weeks, Laura D. II. Series.

PG3476.B78M3353 1996

891.7342—dc20 95-45958

CIP

The paper used in this publication meets the minimum requirements of the American National Standard for Information Sciences—Permanence of Paper for Printed Library Materials, ANSI Z39.48–1984.

Contents

III. PRIMARY SOURCES

IV. SELECT BIBLIOGRAPHY

Acknowledgments

I would like to thank Ellendea Proffer and Mary Ann Szporluk of Ardis Press, and Diana Burgin, co-translator of *The Master and Margarita*, who generously shared their insights as well as a manuscript version of the new Ardis translation of the novel with me. Warm thanks are also due to the contributors of the new material that appears in this volume: Andrew Barratt, J. A. E. Curtis, Thomas Epstein, Alexander Griniakin, and Ronald D. LeBlanc. Quite aside from their outstanding contributions, they worked gracefully under deadline pressure and responded to my editorial revisions with humor and patience. Barry Scherr, general editor of the Northwestern/AATSEEL Critical Companions, was extremely helpful and encouraging while slogging through the early drafts. Special thanks are due to Susan Harris, Editor-in-Chief of Northwestern University Press, for the seemingly endless time, energy, and devotion she gave to the project.

Every enterprise inevitably incurs some personal as well as professional debts. I would like to thank my Portland colleagues Sandra Rosengrant, Judson Rosengrant, and Martha Hickey for supplying reference material at any and all hours, Stanley W. Durland for supplying material on the Jesus Seminar, Tatiana I. Durland and Mary and Thomas Gotwals for the gift of time in which to write the first draft, and John D. Weeks, truly a man of infinite resource and sagacity.

The following essays were previously published, in somewhat different form, and appear here by permission: V. Lakshin, "M. Bulgakov's Novel *The Master and Margarita*," *Soviet Studies in Literature*, vol. 1, no. 7 (Winter 1968–69): 3–65, by permission of M. E. Sharpe, Inc., Armonk, N.Y.; Ellendea Proffer, "Bulgakov's *The Master and Margarita:* Genre and Motif," *Canadian Slavic Studies* 3 (Winter 1969): 615–28; Andrew Barratt, "Beyond Parody: The Goethe Connection," from *Between Two Worlds: A Critical Introduction to "The Master and Margarita"* (Oxford: Clarendon Press, 1987), © Andrew Barratt, 1987, by permission of Oxford University Press; David Bethea, "History as Hippodrome: The Apocalyptic Horse and Rider in *The Master and Margarita*," *Russian Review* 41 (1982): 373–99, by permission of Ohio State University Press; Edythe C. Haber, "The Mythic Structure of Bulgakov's *The Master and Margarita*," *Russia Review* 34 (1975): 382–409, by permission of Ohio State University Press; Marietta Chudakova, "Chapter Five from the First Version of *The Master and Margarita*: 'An Interlude at Griboedov's Hut,'" *Literaturnoe Obozrenie* 1 (1991); selections from Bulgakov's correspondence from J. A. E. Curtis, *Manucripts Don't Burn. Mikhail Bulgakov: A Life in Letters and Diaries* (London: Bloomsbury, 1991).

I INTRODUCTION

"What I Have Written, I Have Written"

LAURA D. WEEKS

That Bulgakov should be remembered in world literature for a piece of prose fiction, and a novel at that, is highly ironical. A native of Kiev, where he was raised in a large, boisterous happy family by a professor at the Kiev Theological Academy and a teacher at a girls' private boarding school, he entered literature through the side door. He was trained as a doctor at the University of Kiev, did a stint in a rural clinic during the first stages of the Civil War (1918–1920), returned to Kiev to set up private practice as a venereologist, and finally abandoned both his medical profession and his native city to begin life as a writer in Moscow.[1]

At the time he began writing *The Master and Margarita* he was thirty-seven years old, married to his second wife, Liubov' Evgen'evna Belozerskaia, and had already made a name for himself. He had spent his first years in Moscow working for the newspapers *Gudok* (The whistle) and *Nakanune* (On the eve), where he specialized in the writing of feuilletons – savagely funny sketches written in a witty, urbane style, sometimes descending to the level of street speech, that deal with a wide variety of bizarre or tragicomic incidents in the daily life of Moscow in the twenties.[2] He would later boast that he had become so skilled in the writing of feuilletons that a single sketch took no more than eighteen to twenty-two minutes, including time out for smoking and whistling. (Retyping, "including coy digressions with the typist," took another eight).[3] His collection of short stories entitled *Diaboliada* appeared in print in 1925, and in that same year his quasi-autobiographical novel *The White Guard*, based on his family's experiences during the Russian Revolution of 1917, began serialization in the prestigious journal *Rossiia*.

But *The White Guard* was never published in full in the Soviet Union in Bulgakov's lifetime.[4] *Rossiia* fell victim to the growing repression in the arts and was closed, never having published the sixth issue for the year 1925, the one that contained the conclusion of the novel. In any case, the novel was better known to the Moscow public in its staged form, as the phenomenally successful *Days of the Turbins* which was produced by the Moscow Art Theater, premiered on October 5, 1926, and ran for more than eight hundred performances in Bulgakov's lifetime.[5] *Days* was followed in rapid succession by two other successes – *Zoika's Apartment* (*Zoikina Kvartira*), produced by the Vakhtangov Theater, and *The Crimson Island* (*Bagrovyi Ostrov*), produced by the Kamernyi Theater. Thus it was primarily in the theater that Bulgakov made his mark, and when his fortunes turned sour, beginning in 1929, he sustained himself by remaining attached to the world of the theater, serving as a consultant for the Moscow Art Theater, reading and evaluating scripts for TRAM (Theater for Working Youth), and writing libretti for the Bolshoi. When he died, it was by and large the people of the theater, not literary types, who mourned him.[6]

The Master and Margarita occupies a privileged status among Bulgakov's works. The bulk of his output was in the shorter genres – the sketch (including the above-mentioned newspaper sketches and his *Notes on the Shirt-Cuff*),[7] the short story (including *Diaboliada* and the stories that make up *The Country Doctor's Notebook*),[8] the drama and the novella (including his *Fatal Eggs*, which appeared in the collection *Diaboliada* and separately in the almanac *Nedra* in 1924, as well as the wickedly funny *Heart of a Dog*).[9] *The Master and Margarita*, on the other hand, represents one of only three novels produced in his lifetime. In addition to *The White Guard* was his unfinished *Theatrical Romance* (rendered in English as *Black Snow*),[10] which gives a satirical account of his experiences in the Moscow Art Theater. *The Master and Margarita* is his last and finest piece of work, his "sunset novel," as he christened it, and from the care he took in the writing and revising of its multiple texts, it is clear that he intended it to be his last will and testament, the piece by which he would be remembered.[11]

In this he was correct, for it is with the publication of *The Master and Margarita*, twenty-six years after his death, that Bulgakov rose to the status of a cult figure in Russia and gained a place in world literature. All Bulgakov's work is to some extent topical. Both in style and subject matter, his work, to be fully appreciated, requires a certain degree of familiarity with the Russian context that gave it birth. The play *Zoika's Apartment*, for example, relies heavily for its humor on the economic and social circumstances surrounding Lenin's New Economic Policy (NEP), introduced in the early twenties to rescue a floundering national economy. The fate of the characters in *Flight*, a play written in 1926–27 and banned before production, is truly moving if one has some knowledge of the plight of the remnants of the White Army at the end of the Civil War.

But *The Master and Margarita* combines the best of both worlds. It is certainly topical, that is, it reflects the purely Russian conditions of the twenties and thirties – the housing crisis, the state-controlled economy, the early years of terror under Stalin. Bulgakov's particular brand of humor is also purely Russian in origin. His love of meaningful names (in *The Master and Margarita* we encounter Mr. Homeless [Ivan Bezdomny], Mr. Barefoot [Nikanor Ivanovich Bosoi], Mr. Evildoer [Stepa Likhodeev], and Mr. Blasphemer [the writer Bogokhulsky], to name a few), his heavy use of synechdoche and alogism, his playfully intimate asides to the reader, and his flair for dramatic situations show him to be a true student of his acknowledged masters – Gogol and Saltykov-Shchedrin.[12] His delight in verbal play and his use of a structure involving the collision of multiple planes of reality show him to be an experimentalist in the manner of Andrei Bely, a Symbolist poet from the Silver Age of Russian literature and a novelist of astounding virtuosity, with whom he enjoyed relations of mutual respect.[13]

At the same time, the novel very consciously takes its place as an artifact of the greater Western European culture Bulgakov so loved. With its self-conscious manipulation of Goethe's *Faust*, its treatment of such universal themes as cowardice and sin, retribution and redemption, love and immortality, it transcends the purely Russian context. Its blend of the lyrical and the fantastic harks back to the German romantics – Tieck, and especially E.T.A. Hoffmann.[14] Finally, its unorthodox metaphysics and its fragmented presentation of reality mark it as a specifically modern classic.

The Master and Margarita is also an enormously influential novel. The Christ-Pilate chapters, themselves in the tradition of Dostoevsky's *Legend of the Grand Inquisitor*, have generated a host of imitators. The most commonly cited of these is *The Executioner's Block* by the Kirghiz writer Chingiz Aitmatov, whose hero Avdii is clearly modeled after Bulgakov's Yeshua, while certain scenes in the novel exactly parallel those of *The Master and Margarita*, such as Avdii's meeting with a drug runner that replays Bezdomny's meeting with Woland. More recently, Salman Rushdie has cited *The Master and Margarita* as a structural influence on his *Satanic Verses*.[15]

For Russians, then, Bulgakov's novel is something of a watershed marking the transition from Soviet to post-Soviet culture. It is at once a link with the great prerevolutionary philosophical tradition and the post-Symbolist novel par excellence. In the West, and for Americans especially, Bulgakov's novel is a Russian import with as great a significance as the works of Solzhenitsyn and Pasternak, in whose company he is frequently mentioned.[16]

Reception

As Bulgakov lay on his deathbed, already slipping in and out of consciousness, his wife made him a solemn promise that she would take it upon herself to see that his novel was published.[17] But it was not until 1966 that the opportunity presented itself. *The Master and Margarita* appeared in the literary journal *Moskva* in two installments. Part 1 appeared in the November issue of 1966; part 2 appeared in the January issue of 1967. All 150,000 copies of the November issue sold out within hours, and both issues quickly became a bibliographic rarity, proving once again that even in the controlled economy of state-mandated literature, free market forces prevail.

The novel's appearance hit the reading public with the force of a revelation, first for what it said about the author. Bulgakov was by no means an unknown name, but no one could have predicted this from the playwright-satirist. Even the publication of *The White Guard* (also in 1966) did not prepare readers for the phenomenon that is *The Master and Margarita.* Second, there was the literary backdrop against which it appeared. To an audience fed a steady diet of socialist-realist production novels, with their resolutely upbeat realism, an audience, as Bethea says, "starved for myth and romance,"[18] *The Master and Margarita* was a much longed for treat. Because it had lain so long "in the desk drawer," a fact that added to the subversive quality of its satire, it also had the appeal of forbidden fruit.

Vladimir Lakshin's article, presented in abridged form in this volume, was part of a measured critical response to what was clearly a momentous literary event.[19] First came an article by Liudmila Skorino entitled "Faces without Carnival Masks," published in the June 1968 issue of *Voprosy Literatury*, which roundly condemned Bulgakov's antisocial recluse of a hero and his glorification of the fantastic and the supernatural as if other forces were at work in men's lives besides those derived from positivist, materialist philosophy. Her arguments were refuted in the same issue of *Voprosy Literatury* by Igor Vinogradov, who maintained that Bulgakov's use of the fantastic was in the best literary tradition that includes Gogol and E.T.A. Hoffmann. Vinogradov drew attention instead to Pilate's crisis of conscience that lies at the heart of the Jerusalem chapters of the novel. Into this fray Lakshin entered as the "heavy artillery," the chief representative of the liberal school of critics dominating the journal *Novyi Mir.* His approach exemplified the progressive, de-Stalinizing trend of the sixties; accordingly, he produced a reading of the novel that centered on the role of creative artist as victim in Stalin's Russia. Lakshin was, in turn, subjected to a frontal attack by the hard liner Gus, who spoke of nonconformism, ideological subversion, and the moral mandates of the Communist Party of the Soviet Union (CPSU). The debate was brought to a close by an article by Motiashov in the December 1968 issue of *Voprosy Litera-*

tury in which he reminded readers of the Soviet writer's responsibility to the party, the state, and to humanity at large. Thus ended the debate in the Soviet Union, while in the West reviewers greeted the appearance of the novel with surprise, delighted at its obvious political satire but with a nagging feeling that Bulgakov's attempt at metaphysics promised more than it delivered, that "his reach exceeded his grasp."[20]

Lakshin's article, published in the June 1968 issue of *Novyi Mir*, is long, wide-ranging, and written in an impressionistic, discursive style. By the standards of modern criticism it seems almost too vague – it does not elaborate any particular paradigm nor advance any particular thesis, yet in many ways it is an excellent appraisal of the novel. He covers various formal aspects, such as genre (Menippean satire, allegory, Faustian parody), language, and narrative voices. He also touches on all the major themes (cowardice, the role of the artist in society, the problematical issue of Woland's identity), as well as some of the major symbols, notably the sun, the moon, and the twin cites of Moscow and Yershalaim.

But perhaps Lakshin's main accomplishment is to carve a niche for Bulgakov and his novel in the canon of Soviet literature. He establishes Bulgakov's place in the prerevolutionary tradition by mentioning his illustrious predecessors to whom he was obviously indebted (Gogol, Saltykov-Shchedrin, Chekhov, Pushkin), and he brings up the miraculous fairy tale as an indigenous source for his use of the fantastic. In approaching the Soviet context, he uses a two-pronged attack. First he castigates the academics, guardians of the official canon, who can only evaluate Bulgakov in the light of officially approved Soviet writers. Then, even as he apologizes for the "subjectivity of his [i.e., Bulgakov's] social criteria," he places Bulgakov in the group of recently reappraised victims of Stalin's excesses along with Isaac Babel and Marina Tsvetaeva. Bulgakov's Master is included in similarly illustrious company. He is awarded a place alongside other martyrs in the cause of truth such as Joan of Arc, Giordano Bruno, and the members of the terrorist group

The People's Will who were responsible for assassinating Tsar Alexander II. (!)

Today we can debate to what extent Bulgakov's novel is weighted toward the thirties, which saw the worst excesses of Stalin's terror, and how much toward the twenties, dominated by NEP.[21] But at the time, Lakshin's reading of the novel as an allegory of the writer's fate in the Stalinist state was enormously influential, causing critics in both the East and the West to view the novel primarily in political terms, to the detriment of other readings.

The "Bulgakov Fad," to which Lakshin refers in the introduction to his article, has blossomed into a veritable cult of Bulgakov. In addition to the publication in 1973 of what was for years the definitive version of *The Master and Margarita* (Mikhail Bulgakov, *Romany* [Xudozhestvennaia Literatura, 1973]), the seventies saw Iurii Liubimov's highly successful production of the novel adapted for the stage at the Theater on the Taganka which premiered in April 1977. A movie adaptation of the novel planned in the eighties by Klimov has now actually been achieved by Iuri Kara with Vertinskaia as Margarita, Gaft as Woland, and Ulianov as Pilate. Bulgakovmania manifests itself in scholarly symposia, readings, informal gatherings, and in that most ubiquitous of modern art forms – graffiti. In an article published in *Slavic Review* (vol. 47, no. 3 [1988]) John Bushnell described the evolution of the graffiti on the wall of stairway 6, apartment building No. 10, Bolshaia Sadovaia, where Bulgakov lived during his first years in Moscow, and that was transformed into the "sinister apartment" occupied by Woland and his suite. By analyzing the changing graffiti over four years (1983 to 1987), Bushnell was able to draw interesting conclusions about the novel's reception. In particular, his analysis demonstrated the extent to which Bulgakov's felicitous turns of phrase (such aphorisms as "Manuscripts don't burn" and "If there are no documents, there is no such person") have been absorbed into the popular culture. Some recent anecdotal evidence confirms Bulgakov's status in the cultural consciousness of Russian-speaking countries. A group of exchange students coming from different republics but virtually identical in their educational background (all third-year students in pedagogical institutes) interviewed by the present writer in the spring of 1994, when asked about their current (or favorite) reading, universally responded, "*The Master and Margarita*."

The most recent manifestation of the Bulgakov fad returns Bulgakov the prose writer to the arena where he first made his name. The 1994 theatrical season at the Theater of the Nikita Gates (Teatr Nikitskikh Vorot) saw a successful staging of several of his short stories, as well as a piece entitled "The Unusual Adventures of the Master Mikhail Afanas'evich and His Margarita Elena Sergeevna."

In the West the initial reaction to *The Master and Margarita* was soon supplanted by serious scholarship which in recent years has become a major industry. In addition to a number of important monographs on the novel, it has engendered several biographies of Bulgakov, including those by Ellendea Proffer (*Bulgakov* [Ann Arbor, Mich.: Ardis, 1984]), A. Colin Wright (*Mikhail Bulgakov: Life and Interpretations* [Toronto: University of Toronto Press, 1978]), Nadine Natov (*Mikhail Bulgakov* [Boston: Twayne Publishers, 1985]), and Lesley Milne (*Mikhail Bulgakov: A Critical Biography* [Cambridge: Cambridge University Press, 1990]). Several major periodicals have had issues devoted exclusively to Bulgakov, including *Russian Literature Triquarterly* (Ann Arbor, Mich.), no. 15 (1978), edited by Carl and Ellendea Proffer; *Canadian-American Slavic Studies* (Tempe, Ariz.), vol. 15, nos. 2–3 (Summer–Fall 1981), edited by Nadine Natov; *Atti del Convegno "Michail Bulgakov,"* (Milan: University of Milan, 1986) in two parts, edited by Eridano Bazzarelli and Jitka Kresal'kova; *Soviet Literature* (no. 7 [1988]), which contains translations of Bulgakov's *Autobiography*, *The Heart of a Dog*, *The Last Days* (Pushkin), and his letters to Pavel Popov; and *Transactions of the Association of Russian-American Scholars in the U.S.A.* (Richmond Hill, N.Y.), vol. 24, [1991], edited by Nadine Natov.

"So . . . That's Enough, Perhaps": The History of the Writing of *The Master and Margarita*

The writing of *The Master and Margarita* was a long and tortuous process that occupied Bulgakov for roughly twelve years, from 1928 until his death in March 1940.[22] The process began very simply: Proffer records a remark Bulgakov made to his close friend Popov sometime in 1926, that if his mother served as the impetus for the creation of the novel *The White Guard*, the figure of his father would be the starting point for another work he now had in mind.[23] His friend Pavel Markov records a comment Bulgakov made in a different context, namely, that he was obsessed with the enigma of the Passion story.[24] By 1928 he had put down in a notebook fifteen chapters that followed more or less the sequence of events in the novel as we now know it. A poet and an editor meet at Patriarchs' Ponds to discuss the former's antireligious poema, or long narrative poem. They are joined by a mysterious stranger, who gives his own version of the Passion story, after which the editor is beheaded by a tram. The poet tries to warn his brothers-in-literature that the devil has appeared in Moscow, for which he is promptly sequestered in a psychiatric clinic. The mysterious stranger proceeds to give a performance at the Variety Theater, where he wreaks havoc among both audience and staff.

At this point the double-novel structure of the text was already evident, and the cities of Moscow and Yershalaim, those two poles in time and space between which the narrative would vibrate, were already identified by their respective narrative voices – the one garrulous, racy, intimate, conversational; the other sombre, sonorous, elevated, replete with convoluted syntax – and by their respective heroes, Woland and Yeshua. The Moscow chapters clearly bore the marks of Bulgakov's early training as a writer of feuilletons, whereas the Jerusalem chapters more nearly resembled his novel *The White Guard.* The tentative titles Bulgakov gave to the manuscript all point to the overwhelming importance of Woland in the novel: "The Consultant with a Hoof," "A Black Magician," "The Road Tour of Woland," "The Engineer's Hoof." His own shorthand way of referring to the novel, however, was simply as his "novel about the devil."[25]

In revising this first version in 1929, Bulgakov did not change the overall shape, but he did substantially expand the Jerusalem chapter, which was given the enigmatic title "The Gospel according to the Devil." Significantly, at this point the entire Passion story, including the murder of Yuda of Kerioth, was contained in a single chapter. In the fall of 1929 Bulgakov began regaling a select circle of acquaintances with readings from the novel. These were usually given at the home of his close friend, Nicholas Liamin.[26] Bulgakov was a superb reader, bringing to his readings all his flair for dialogue, his theatrical instincts, and his love of mystification.

At this stage in the novel's development there were two fat notebooks containing much of what readers know as part 1 of *The Master and Margarita.* Then came what Bulgakov himself called his "year of catastrophe." Both *The Days of the Turbins* and *Crimson Island* were banned from the stage; *Zoika's Apartment* was removed from the repertoire at the Vakhtangov Theater; the play *Flight*, which was already in rehearsal, was also banned; and a vicious campaign was launched against him in the press. In the spring of 1930 he took his notebooks containing the manuscript and ripped them diagonally from top right to bottom left. He fed the torn sheets to the woodstove, leaving the binding with its ragged remnants as proof that the novel had existed. He then composed a letter to the Soviet government (a "letter on high" as it is called in Russian) painting his predicament in the starkest terms and requesting either to be allowed to emigrate or to be given some kind of position in the theater. On April 18, 1930, the Bulgakovs received a call from Stalin himself. He inquired whether Bulgakov really wished to emigrate. When Bulgakov replied that as a writer he was unthinkable outside the Soviet Union, Stalin advised him to apply again at the Moscow Art Theater, that there might be work for him. He did and there was.[27]

He had now restored some kind of order to his professional life, but his personal life was in disarray. A year before the "year of catastrophe," that is, in February 1928, he had met Elena Sergeevna Shilovskaia, wife of a career military man and professor at the Military Academy, at a party given by mutual acquaintances. The relationship began with the two couples visiting back and forth, but the attraction between Elena Sergeevna and Bulgakov quickly grew into a full-fledged affair. Bulgakov's wife resolved stoically to wait out the infatuation; Elena Sergeevna's husband was not so sanguine. After a highly melodramatic scene culminating in the two men threatening each other with pistols, Shilovsky demanded that Bulgakov and Elena break off any further contact. This they did, and it was only a year and a half later, in September 1932, that they met again and resolved never to separate. Readers of *The Master and Margarita* will savor the description of that second meeting, which has been oh-so-slightly altered both in her diary accounts and in his text: she walked out onto the street, alone for the first time in years (having promised her husband never to leave the house alone). She was carrying flowers, and the first person she met was Bulgakov, "and the first thing he said was, 'I can't live without you,' and I replied, 'Me neither.'"[28] They were married on October 4, 1932, and at this point the all-important "novel about the devil" acquired two new characters who would ultimately give the novel its name.

Bulgakov returned to his novel with renewed vigor in 1933. Working at a stiff pace, he produced, by November of that year, seventeen chapters spread over three and a half fat notebooks. To these he added a fourth notebook, entitled "Conclusion," in which he developed earlier fragments and incidents previously noted in outline form over the course of the next year (from December 1933 to October 1934). This was the third version of *The Master and Margarita*, commonly considered to be the first complete version. It contains some major changes, among them the splitting of the Passion story (now entitled "The Gospel according to Woland") into several chapters, and an increased role for the poet, referred to alternately as Bezdomny or Bezrodny. But above all, it incorporates the story line of a hero, referred to as "the poet," and once even as

"Faust," and his lover Margarita. The story line includes his arrest and detention, her flight, Satan's Grand Ball, and the death by poison and resurrection of the lovers. Between 1934 and 1936 Bulgakov would return sporadically to the novel, revising and expanding the role of the Master and toying with different titles, among them "The Great Chancellor," "Satan," "Here I Am," "A Hat with a Plume," "He Has Appeared," and "The Foreigner's Horseshoe."[29]

In the summer of 1936 Bulgakov made two attempts to revise the novel, beginning, as was his habit, from the very beginning. But these efforts were abandoned early on, the first after five chapters, the second after thirteen. In the autumn of 1937, despite his other projects, he began intensive work on what would be the sixth or second full version of the novel, which he now christened *The Master and Margarita.* Between May and June of 1938 he subjected this version to extensive revision, while simultaneously dictating it to be typed by his wife's sister Ol'ga Bokshanskaia, secretary extraordinaire to the director of the Moscow Art Theater, Nemirovich-Danchenko. Bulgakov's caustically witty description of their working relationship is recorded in the letters he sent his wife during this period, some of which appear in section 3 of this volume. This prodigious effort effectively demonstrates how determined he was to finish the novel. We know from his friends' memoirs and those of his wife that he continued to give readings from the novel, which invariably had a profound effect on the audience. Two especially significant readings were given on April 8, 1938, and on April 27, 1939, and an account of them from Elena Sergeevna's diary are also included in this collection.

From 1939 until his death on March 10, 1940, Bulgakov feverishly continued to revise the novel. He was by this time suffering from the symptoms of acute nephrosclerosis, the kidney disease that had killed his father at roughly the same age as he now was. Blind and in agony from headaches and hypersensitive skin, he had Elena Sergeevna read to him from the manuscript, and he in turn dictated revisions that she recorded both on the manuscript and in a separate notebook. Early in February 1940 she prepared to read to him again.

As she reached the description of Berlioz's funeral (part 2, chapter 1), he stopped her, saying, "So . . . that's enough, perhaps." Thus ended the eighth version of *The Master and Margarita*.[30]

The Novel's Status as Unfinished Text

Following Bulgakov's creative process from the original conception through the various versions reveals the enormous amount of growth that has taken place. Gone are the blatantly crude bits of humor, such as the use of the acronym OBSHCHPIS (which could perhaps be rendered as COMMURINE or MASSPISS) for the Soviet Writers' Union. Gone are the details that Chudakova so charmingly labels "Rabelaisian," such as the phallic vase that comes erect at Margarita's touch. Gone is the Mack Sennett-style chase around Moscow, as Ivan, who in earlier versions steals Berlioz's body and drives madly through Moscow, ultimately ending up, corpse and all, in the Moscow River.

We have included in this volume a reconstruction of the first version of chapter 5, "The Affair at the Griboedov," which is particularly important because it was one of the first episodes Bulgakov read to his friends, and because the second version of it was submitted for publication to the almanac *Nedra* in May 1929 under the title "Mania Furibunda."[31] As noted, Bulgakov destroyed this version in 1930 by ripping the notebooks containing the manuscript, leaving in most cases only one-third to one-half of a page of text. The reconstruction was done by the foremost Bulgakov scholar in Russia, Marietta Chudakova, who is well known for her research into Bulgakov's archives, her re-creation of his reading library, and her imposing biography, *Zhizneopisanie.*

The methods Chudakova used in reconstructing the damaged text are covered in her article "An Attempt at Reconstructing Bulgakov's Text" ("Opyt rekonstruktsii teksta M. A. Bulgakova," *Pamiatniki Kul'tury* [Moscow: 1975], 93–106). First, chapters 1–4 of the first version are revised and expanded in the notebook for the second version, which contains some whole, undamaged pages. Thus Chudakova was sometimes able to reconstruct the first version by consulting the second, although, as she points out, this results in a contamination of the two. Second, she sometimes made educated guesses based on subsequent versions of the novel. Third, she relied on her own encyclopedic knowledge of Bulgakov's particular lexicon, including frequently repeated words and turns of phrase. Fourth, because Bulgakov's handwriting is neat and easily decipherable, with no blanks, mistakes, or abbreviations, she was often able to reconstruct the first half of a word simply from seeing the last half on the next line. Finally, thanks to Bulgakov's penchant for dramatized situations heavy on dialogue, much of the reconstruction clearly consisted of words denoting reported speech ("he remarked," "he interjected," etc.).

We can see from this early excerpt, one of the earliest "finished" episodes in the novel, that Bulgakov is still relying heavily on his training as a writer of feuilletons. Not only does he hide behind the obtrusive, self-conscious narrative voice, he even begins the chapter in the manner of a feuilleton: "Moscow, my dear comrades, is an unusual city." In the course of the novel's development, this narrative voice becomes less personal, more worldly, and puts a certain degree of ironic distance between itself and the object of its narration.

Other striking features wherein this early version differs from the final product are characterization (Bulgakov provides more detailed descriptions of each of the writers dancing at the restaurant, and Ivan is more closely identified with the tradition of the holy fool) and the nature of the Griboedov. Having been sensitized to the significance of food and the act of eating from Ronald LeBlanc's article, we feel the absence of the crucial dialogue between Ambrosii and Foka celebrating the joys of the palate. The Griboedov itself has not yet evolved into a first-class restaurant but is here a humble Russian tearoom smelling of rancid oil and overcooked cabbage, serving such low-brow Russian fare as borshch and pickled herring in sour cream.

Comparing it to the chapter as we now know it, readers will observe that the broad farce or slapstick quality of the first version has given way to a greater economy of style. Bulgakov uses fewer phrases and fewer visual "gags," without in any way diminishing the comic impact of the scene. There is also a greater ironic distance between the narrator and his subject. In the final version Bulgakov relies much less on the obtrusive, naively endearing, archly self-conscious narrator as well as on the time-honored Russian technique of *skaz* – a written reproduction of spoken speech that is deliberately deformed, humorous, chatty in tone. As for the Jerusalem chapters, which were originally recounted by Woland in the first person, they have been elevated to the status of third-person omniscient impersonal narration.

The publication of *The Great Chancellor* (Mikhail Bulgakov, *Velikii Kantsler* [Moscow: Novosti, 1992]) marks another significant advance in the history of *The Master and Margarita*. Under this rubric the well-respected scholar and archivist Lev Lossev has gathered primarily the third version of the novel, which, as noted above, is generally considered the first full version.[32] He has also fleshed out the text with the additions from the fourth version (additions made sporadically between 1934 and 1936) and included in an appendix more complete versions of certain chapters from the sixth, or second full version. It is striking that through all these layers upon layers of revisions, key episodes of the novel (the meeting at Patriarchs' Ponds, the melee at the Griboedov, the appearance of Berlioz's uncle from Kiev, the disappearance of Stepa Likhodeev, and the show at the Variety) remain virtually the same.

But the creative history of the novel also reveals some serious problems with the text. Thanks to Bulgakov's constant corrections and revisions, it is virtually impossible to call even the final notebooks the "definitive version," especially since so many of the final corrections are not in his own hand. It also appears that when preparing the novel for posthumous publication in the 1960s, Elena Sergeevna took it upon herself to make further editorial changes in keeping with what she assumed were Bulgakov's wishes. Because he died without subjecting part 2 of the novel to the rigorous revisions of part 1, in the minds of many critics the novel remains an unfinished work.[33] This is particularly true of those critics who find the ontological solutions of part 2 largely unsatisfying and unsuccessful, even downright disappointing. But the writer of these truthful lines, who has yet to experience this disillusionment with part 2 of the novel, believes that problems and apparent discrepancies encountered in the text can be resolved by placing the novel in the proper critical framework.[34] A number of frameworks proposed in the past are given below. Whereas monistic interpretations of the novel are rapidly losing ground, the growing consensus being that no single interpretation of *The Master and Margarita* exists, no one key that can unlock the novel,[35] these approaches are still valuable in helping readers form a coherent picture of the text, especially first-time readers.

Approaches

CARNIVAL

When *The Master and Margarita* first appeared in print, critics were at a loss to define it in terms of genre. Here, it seemed, was something of a completely new and unrealized form, not cut from whole cloth but pieced together from a variety of familiar genres – satire, romance, fantastic realism in the manner of E.T.A. Hoffmann, fragments of a conventional historical novel. One solution, which was suggested by the carnival atmosphere of the Moscow chapters, was to characterize the novel as carnival, using the definition worked out by the Russian formalist critic Mikhail Bakhtin.[36] The genesis for his definition was the medieval mystery plays given on church feast days and invariably accompanied by an atmosphere of horseplay, crude humor, farce, and revelry. The collision of the eternal (the Passion story, often presented in starkly realistic detail) and the ephemeral allowed carnival goers to air their social and economic grievances and, most important, to set the prevailing social and moral order on its head. The analogy between this ritual and Bulgakov's novel, where the Passion story is set off by the antics of Korov'ev and Behemoth, hardly needs to be spelled out. Among Western critics this approach was first set forth by Nadine Natov[37] and was later used very successfully by Lesley Milne in her monograph *The Master and Margarita: A Comedy of Victory*.[38] It continues to be a valid reading of the novel, especially for those who feel that as of the epilogue nothing has changed, at least on the Moscow level. No lasting retribution has been meted out by Woland and Company, no real growth has been achieved by any character. In this sense the novel functions much like Bakhtin's carnival, as "a temporary liberation from the prevailing truth and from the established order."[39]

MENIPPEAN SATIRE

Another approach advanced early in the history of Bulgakov criticism, by the Russians Vulis and Lakshin[40] and in the United States by the eminent Bulgakov critic Ellendea Proffer, was to view the novel as Menippean satire. (An excerpt from Proffer's article is included in this volume, and the reader is invited to turn to it.) Briefly stated, Menippean satire, which takes its name from the third-century cynic philosopher Menippus, is an exotic mixture of seemingly contradictory elements: history and myth, philosophy and fantasy, the serious and the comic, high- and low-narrative levels. In this mixture, time and space are warped, alternate states of reality (dreams, sickness) are prominent, and irony abounds. Above all, Menippean satire allows the writer to target society's institutions and authority figures without fear of retribution. In Bulgakov's Moscow, the targets worthy of satire were many, and he hit them all – the state-planned economy and its mania for foreign currency; the housing shortage and people's ingenious solutions to it; state-mandated literature and the trash it produced; Marxist-Leninist materialism and the self-satisfied philistines it bred.

ROMAN-A-CLEF

The level of satire in *The Master and Margarita* is so strong that it led to early readings of the novel as a roman à clef, "a novel in which actual persons and events are presented under the guise of fiction."[41] Coupling the objects of satire in the novel with a knowledge of Bulgakov's treatment at the hands of the literary establishment, critics began identifying every feature of Bulgakov's fictive universe with its real-life counterpart. Some of these counterparts are transparently obvious: MASSOLIT is a thinly veiled version of the Russian Association of Proletarian Writers (RAPP), the predecessor of the Writers' Union, so despised by Bulgakov and his close associates; the Griboedov is the House of Writers on Herzen Street; Perelygino is the writers' colony of Peredelkino outside Moscow; the critic Latunsky is Leopold Averbakh, who trashed Bulgakov's *Diaboliada* when it appeared in print; the poet Bezdomny's name (Mr. "Homeless") is chosen to remind readers of other "proletarian" poets who wrote under similar pseudonyms, such as Demyan Bednyi (Mr. "Poor") and Oleksandr Bezymenskii (Mr. "Nameless");[42] the poet Riukhin is manifestly the great bard of the socialist state, Vladimir Mayakovsky, with whom Bulgakov enjoyed relations of mutual and undisguised hatred.

ALLEGORY

From the level of satire it is only a short step to the level of political allegory, and *The Master and Margarita* has been read as an elaborate allegory of Stalin's Russia. This approach was most thoroughly worked out by Elena Mahlow, for whom the entire novel is an allegory of Russian intellectual history in this century, with Margarita representing the prerevolutionary intelligentsia, Pilate representing the dictatorship of the proletariat, Yeshua representing the true proletariat, and so on.[43] Even more elaborate schemes have been worked out involving a one-to-one correspondence between the novel's characters and contemporary Russian reality. Woland stands in for Stalin, and his suite represents Stalin's famous henchmen – Molotov, Voroshilov, and Kaganovich. The murder of Yuda of Kerioth is the murder of Kirov. The removal of Stepa Likhodeev to Yalta is the removal of Trotsky to Alma Ata in January 1928.[44] More than one critic has fastened on Bulgakov's peculiar relationship to Stalin (Stalin was a great fan of Bulgakov's *Days of the Turbins*, and after his personal intervention in Bulgakov's life, the latter was considered something of an expert on writing appeals for those who had been arrested) and has automatically assumed that the relationship of Stalin, Bulgakov, and Elena Sergeevna was reproduced in the Woland-Master-Margarita triangle.[45]

As Barratt has pointed out, this approach enjoyed quite a vogue when the novel was first published, especially in the West, where readers knew of the appalling conditions under which the novel was written and delighted to find in it the author's posthumous revenge.[46] But, as Barratt also points out, this approach is ultimately a dead end for some very cogent reasons. In addition to some serious problems with chronology, such a reading cheapens the novel. It implies that after the first thrill of recognition as each character's identity is guessed, most of the marrow has been sucked from the bone, whereas that is clearly not the case. As for the level of satire, that approach is also limiting, since, to refer again to Barratt, the novel is so supersaturated with satire as to render it harmless. Barratt's third, and to my mind, most important point is that the horseplay that occasions most of the satire in part 1 of the novel drops off considerably in part 2. Thus, approaching the novel as political satire does nothing to increase the reader's appreciation of the novel's unity, and it does nothing to resolve the critical problem with which we began this survey of possible approaches, namely, the enormous difference readers have felt between parts 1 and 2 of the novel. What Jung says of Goethe's *Faust* is also true of *The Master and Margarita*: parts 1 and 2 exist in entirely different realms. Without part 2, part 1 would still exist as literature, but the presence of part 2 adds a completely different dimension to the novel.[47]

FAUSTIAN PARODY

The analogy drawn here between *The Master and Margarita* and *Faust* is quite deliberate, because the one has so often been read as a parody of the other. The first detailed account of the connections between the two texts was that of Elizabeth Stenbock-Fermor.[48] In addition to identifying crucial characters and key episodes borrowed from *Faust* and the Faust legend (thus Woland is Mephistopheles, who goes by the name Junker Woland on Walpurgis night; Margarita is Goethe's eternal feminine in all its manifestations [Jungfrau, Mutter, Königen, Göttin]; Korov'ev is Faust, now Mephistopheles' in this novelservant, thanks to the joke he made at their first meeting; the demon Vitzli-Putzli mentioned by Berlioz is borrowed from the Faust puppet plays; Margarita's slip is Helena's garment by which Faust was to be saved from Hades), she examines the coincidence of moral issues common to both.

More recently, Andrew Barratt has performed an invaluable service by demonstrating that *The Master and Margarita* is not so much a parody of Goethe's *Faust* as a creative reworking of the inherited text. Since an excerpt from Barratt's chapter on the *Faust* connection is included in this volume, the following will serve as a summary of the omitted sections. The list of parallels between the two texts is long and striking. There is, first of all, the epigraph, "Say, who are you then? A part of that force, which wills forever evil, and does forever good." Then there is the opening scene at Patriarchs' Ponds, which echoes Mephistopheles' and Faust's encounter with the drunkards in Auerbach's Cellar. The scene at the Variety Theater echoes Mephistopheles' and Faust's performance at the emperor's court, which includes the production of false money and the giving of gifts that later disappear. Satan's Grand Ball echoes the Walpurgisnacht on the brocken, and Woland even draws attention to the parallel by recounting to Margarita how his knee was damaged by a witch on the brocken, some five hundred years before their meeting.

But as it turns out, these analogies are misleading because Bulgakov is constantly undermining the reader's expectations. A good case in point is the identity of Woland, on which so much of the novel's theology hangs. When Woland first enters, all the props would seem to identify him as Mephistopheles – the poodle's head on his cane, the limp, the fact that he poses as a traveling foreign scholar, the giving of different brands of cigarettes (at Auerbach's Cellar, Mephistopheles gives each of the drunkards his favorite brand of wine), and the seemingly senseless "conjuration" by the stars and planets that parodies Mephistopheles' performance with the court astrologer at the emperor's court. As we continue to read, however, we realize that Woland is not at all Mephistopheles. For one thing, he does not cause the death of innocents (Gretchen and her family); for another, his relationship to the Master and Margarita bears no resemblance to the Mephistopheles-Faust-Gretchen triangle. Woland's final appearance as executor of God's will contrasts sharply with Mephistopheles' participation at Faust's death, where he clearly feels cheated of his prey. Other obvious problems arise when we try to identify the two texts too closely. Bulgakov's Margarita is no innocent adolescent, and his Master is no crusader, insatiable in his thirst for knowledge of good and evil. These problems can be resolved, Barratt suggests, if we temporarily ignore the surface dissimilarities and concentrate on the novel's deep structure, where the two casts of characters function analogously. Woland serves as a catalyst who forces the Master and Margarita to fulfill their Faustian potential: "Through his agency, Margarita, like Gretchen before her, has come to embody the redemptive power of love, while the Master has at last achieved the commitment to striving which is synonymous with the Faustian principle."[49] Of crucial importance in both authors' worldviews is the active female principle, the source of selfless love and mercy, and for both Goethe and Bulgakov, the source of salvation.

In recent criticism some new approaches to the novel have sprung up, the most interesting perhaps being the psychoanalytical viewpoint. Riitta Pittman uses the schizophrenia afflicting the poet Bezdomny as a key to unlock the split consciousness of the novel's protagonists as well as the novel's split planes.[50] Judith Mills also concentrates on the figure of Bezdomny, concluding that the entire novel is a metaphor for his fate in Soviet society.[51] Both these approaches are covered in this volume in Barratt's survey of recent criticism, so I will conclude by describing one last approach that is particularly helpful in gaining understanding of the novel's Russian origins. The fantastic or supernatural features of Bulgakov's novel – the use of witches, magic, the extensive demonology – have long attracted attention, but they gain special coherence in the framework of the Russian fairy tale.[52]

MIRACULOUS FAIRY TALE

The first extended analysis of *The Master and Margarita* as a subspecies of Russian fairy tale was Sona Hoisington's "Fairy-Tale Elements in Bulgakov's *The Master and Margarita*" (*Slavic and East European Journal*, vol. 25, no. 2 [1985], 44–55). Using the theory of the Russian Formalist Vladimir Propp – which classifies all the elements of the folktale, notably characters and plot movements, in terms of their function in the narrative – she identified the disappearance of the Master as the "act of villainy" that sets the tale in motion.[53] She then found that most of the major fairy-tale functions (the quest, the punishment of the villain, and so on) are performed by Margarita. Her analysis is interesting for what it says about Bulgakov's universe, since it is the "prince" who is spirited away and the "princess" who must go in search of him.

More recently, Stefania Pavan-Pagnini[54] identified *The Master and Margarita* as a miraculous fairy tale, one of the three subcategories into which Russian fairy tales are generally divided.[55] The main features of the miraculous fairy tale have been summarized by Pavan-Pagnini as follows: the characters are real but the action is fantastic; the reader knows that the action is highly improbable but gets a sense of satisfaction out of the supernatural character of the tale; the discrepancy between content and style gives rise to humorous effects; the action is dynamic, even "nonstop," but frequently lacks motivation; there is only one main hero or heroine and all the other characters act in relation to that individual, who frequently remains nameless; all the characters are either good or evil.[56]

As a general framework for understanding the novel's peculiar blend of the real and the fantastic, this approach strikes us as appropriate; however, in actual application we encounter some serious problems. The main problem seems to be in identifying characters with their functions. As mentioned above, the fairy tale concentrates on a single hero or heroine, and Pavan-Pagnini is forced to distribute the essential functions among the various characters. Thus the initial stages (preparation, removal, and interdiction) all have to do with

Ivan Bezdomny, whereas the later stages (testing, battle, ultimate retribution) all fall to Margarita. Pavan-Pagnini circumvents this obstacle by viewing all the characters as fragments of the Master's shattered psyche, a not unreasonable approach, but one that ultimately leans more toward the psychoanalytical. Perhaps the greatest hurdle this approach fails to clear is the most obvious. Hoisington concludes that within the context of the fairy tale Woland's actions are comprehensible, even acceptable because the reader senses the underlying order at work.[57] Pavan-Pagnini puts it even more succinctly: in the fairy tale "all the characters are either good or evil."[58] The fact is, no one in this novel (except Yeshua) is unambiguously good or evil. Furthermore, the contradictory nature of the agents who dispense justice is the novel's main premise, from the opening epigraph to the bittersweet epilogue.

For those who sense a form of justice at work in the novel, none of these formal approaches is fully satisfactory. For those haunted by the images of Rimskii's shaking head and white hair, Baron Maigel's burning body, and Berlioz's severed head, this is no Bakhtinian "temporary liberation" from the prevailing social and moral order. For those puzzled by the exact location of the Master and Margarita, as well as the rightness of their final reward, this is no Soviet satire run amok. What I am suggesting is that any search for formal solutions to the novel's structural peculiarities invariably ends up in the realm of the novel's theology and, to an even greater degree, in the realm of its metaphysics. What follows are examples of how the novel might be analyzed by combining the two approaches, the formal and the theological.

THE DOUBLE NOVEL

For many years after the novel's appearance, readers and critics alike were distracted by viewing *The Master and Margarita* as a three-ring circus. This is an apt visual metaphor for the novel's three distinct story lines, each with its own setting, cast of characters, and distinctive narrative voice. There is the satirical Moscow story dominated by Woland and Company, the serious Jerusalem story that focuses on Pilate and Yeshua, and the lyrical romance of the Master and Margarita. A variation on this paradigm was to divide the novel into three planes of experience: "everyday" reality, fantasy, and history. Furthering this line of investigation, Vida Taranovski-Johnson demonstrated that the narrative voice is similarly divided into three distinct modes: a "humorous and ironic third-person narrative, marked by conversational, even substandard, language; a neutral, transparent third-person narrative, narration phraseologically unmarked; and a rhetorical first-person narration, lyrical in tone and elevated in style."[59] The trouble arises when one tries to unequivocally assign a narrative voice to each of the story lines. Whereas the Jerusalem chapters are truly set off by their impersonal narrative voice and their long sonorous sentences, careful scrutiny reveals that the Master and Margarita story is not entirely independent of the Moscow-Woland story line. Like the Woland line it swings back and forth between the starkest reality (the Master's arrest and interrogation, Margarita's adultery) and the truly fantastic (Margarita's flight, Satan's ball, the final moonlit ride). The narrative voice is also inconsistent. The story itself is told first in retrospect, by the Master to Ivan in the clinic; then in the present tense, by the narrator directly to the reader; and, finally, by narrative sleight-of-hand, by the Master to Ivan – posthumously! The narrator's attitude toward the protagonists likewise varies from the hysterico-lyrical mode worthy of Gogol to the intimately ironic. In one or two instances the Master and Margarita are subjected to the same condescending irony as the other victims of Woland and Company's shenanigans. In short, although the Master and Margarita may be set off from their fellow Muscovites by their greater moral stature, their greater receptivity to the knowledge imparted by Woland, and their greater ability to intuit the truth, they are still part of the larger story. This leaves a more satisfying impression of a double novel – two separate narrative strands, the historical novel and the Moscow farce, the one embedded in the other. This is where Bulgakov criticism currently stands.[60]

TOWARD A UNIFIED READING OF THE NOVEL

The double novel approach also makes sense from a number of other perspectives. For one thing, it avoids any critical confusion that results from trying to bridge part 1 to part 2 of the novel. Of the supposed three strands, the Moscow farce appears almost exclusively in part 1, leaving only the scrap of the Master's history that he narrates to Ivan in the clinic (chapter 13, "Enter the Hero"). Conversely, part 2 of the novel is almost entirely devoted to the Master and Margarita story, leaving only two chapters devoted to the final antics of the "inseparable pair" Korov'ev and Behemoth (chapter 17, "The End of Apartment 50," and chapter 18, "The Final Adventures of Korov'ev and Behemoth"). It also accounts for the overwhelming structural parallelism between the inner and the outer narratives, which has been elegantly set forth by Colin Wright.[61]

But although this approach has much to recommend it, it does not resolve all formal problems. A major problem still exists, which can be crudely described as one of authority. What is the source of each of the double strands? The Jerusalem chapters are presented as being narrated by Woland, dreamed by Ivan, and read by Margarita from a fragment of the Master's novel. The voice narrating the Moscow level is fraught with even greater difficulties. Is this a fully dramatized narrator, a character on a par with other characters in the story, and if so, on what basis does he claim to possess the authoritative account of events? Even more puzzling, how can he relate events both in the present tense as an eyewitness and, retrospectively, to "set the record straight"?[62] All these problems are resolved if we view the entire text as originating from a single source. One possible source that has been suggested is Woland. After all, the novel began as "the novel about the devil," and the Jerusalem chapters in particular were to be "the gospel according to the devil." We also know that in the early versions of the novel Woland follows Bezdomny to the psychiatric clinic to narrate the second of the Jerusalem episodes (see the preternaturally huge poodle that flashes by the clinic windows at the end of the reconstructed early version of chapter 5 included in this volume). As Neil Cornwell has recently suggested, "If we are looking for a hidden author or narrator, one who is present on all levels with a knowledge of all events – who has greater omniscience than Woland?"[63]

Another possible source is the poet Bezdomny, newly resurrected as Professor Ponyrev, historian at the Institute of History and Philosophy. This approach has recently gained some credibility, as indicated in the above-mentioned work by Mills, and it refutes the long-held opinion that the Master's lost novel is in fact *The Master and Margarita*. That opinion was largely based on Proffer's discovery that the final words of the Master's lost novel, as told to Bezdomny, and the final words of *The Master and Margarita* are the same.[64] But there are serious problems with viewing the Master as the author of the entire text, especially with the ending, in which he would have to narrate his own death, and even more so with the epilogue, which he could not have written, unless we assume that Bezdomny is somehow an adept at automatic writing(!).[65] Ivan, on the other hand, is privy to all kinds of information that no other character has. This includes the original conversation at Patriarchs' Ponds (hence he can narrate both as eyewitness and in retrospect), the original antireligious poema that only he and Berlioz saw, and the layout of all the novel's interiors: the Griboedov, Stravinsky's clinic, and Berlioz's apartment. His transformation from proletarian poet to professor of history leads us to believe that as a character he absorbed many of the features of Fesya, a shadowy character from the first version of the novel who was subsequently eliminated. A talented youth with an aptitude for foreign languages, Fesya became a professor of history but was persecuted after the revolution and lost his post at the university.[66] Because of his superb erudition and his "suspect" class background, Chudakova sees him as a foil for Berlioz's superficial erudition and a symbol of the prerevolutionary intelligentsia.

The case for Ivan's authorship of the entire text rests primarily (but not exclusively) on two pieces of textual evidence. It has been repeated ad infinitum that the first of the Pilate chapters belongs to Woland, yet it is received in a dreamlike state and is addressed specifically to Ivan: "Yes, it was about ten o'clock in the morning, worthy Ivan Nicolaevich." Moreover, we know the exact moment of its transcription:

> Having tormented himself with these two Berliozes, Ivan crossed out everything and decided to begin with something very striking in order to quickly attract the reader's attention, and he wrote down how the cat boarded the trolley, then returned to the episode with the severed head. The head and the Consultant's prediction turned his thoughts toward Pontius Pilate, and for greater persuasiveness Ivan decided *to retell the story of the Procurator in full, from the moment when he, in his white cloak with a bloody lining, came out onto the colonnade of Herod's Palace.* (emphasis added)

Here, in embryonic form, are the first three chapters of the novel, the most finished being the first of the Pilate chapters. Since we are told that the nurse's aide, Praskov'ia Fedorovna, gathers up all Ivan's handwritten sheets after they are scattered by the wind, there is good reason to believe they are not lost. The second of the four Pilate chapters is also Ivan's, along with the final vision in the epilogue, both created under identical conditions (drug-induced dream) and at identical times (just before dawn). This leaves only the two chapters from the Master's manuscript as external to the text as a whole. These, the Master tells Ivan, had been published and are therefore presumably accessible to Ivan after he is released from the clinic.[67]

Another, more playful clue to Ivan's authorship is the obtrusive narrator's claim, in part 2, chapter 1, that he can lead the reader to Margarita's gothic townhouse: "An enchanting spot! Anyone who wishes to can take a look at the garden and see for himself. Let him ask me and I'll give him the address and show him the way – the house is still standing to this very day." At first blush, this would seem to be nothing more than a throwback to Bulgakov's own master, Gogol, from whom he learned so much of his narrative technique (a similar statement is used by the narrator in the first tale of Gogol's *Mirgorod* cycle). However, all irony aside, the second thing Ivan does in the epilogue is to lead the reader to Margarita's gothic townhouse.

Seeing Ivan as the source of both the "inner" and the "outer" texts lends greater consistency to the nested narrative in the case of those oft-repeated motifs and phrases, such as "gods, gods of mine," which is uttered not only by Pilate but by the Master, the narrator, and Ivan. With the exception of Pilate's exclamation in chapter 26 (which belongs to the Master's fragment), three of these four sources derive from a single root.

Perhaps the most conclusive proof of Ivan's authorship is the epilogue itself, which Bulgakov added very late, in May 1939, probably in a fit of disillusionment at the reaction of his audience to a reading of the novel.[68] Bearing in mind the well-known adage that "three can keep a secret if two are dead," we observe that of the three possible sources for the novel, two have disappeared in the penultimate chapter – Woland to the abyss, the Master to his final resting place. Even if they could somehow communicate the contents of the epilogue, it is doubtful that either one could transcribe them or disseminate them as part of the novel.[69] Hence only Ivan as author solves the dual riddle of authority and dissemination so aptly put by Avins.[70]

Another view argues in support of a unified reading of the novel. Let us suppose that Bulgakov wanted us to envision his fictive universe as a single continuum. Certainly, the overwhelming amount of parallelism between the two levels would seem to indicate this to be so – the symbols (the sun, the moon, the roses, just to name the most commonly cited ones); the time frame, which is the same in both stories (from midweek through Sunday of Passion Week); the weather, which is the same in both Moscow and Yershalaim; and the two cities themselves, which have similar architecture and imagery.[71] The answer to this parallelism lies at the intersection of physics and metaphysics. We know that among the primary sources Bulgakov consulted time and again while writing the novel was *The Imaginary in Geometry* by Pavel Florensky, a theologian turned mathematician who wrote in the early twenties and thirties. *The Imaginary in Geometry* was published in 1922, and we know from Chudakova's work that Bulgakov's copy was heavily marked, especially the part beginning at page 45.[72] The influence of the book on Bulgakov's thinking was first examined by Beatie and Powell in their seminal article "Bulgakov, Dante, and Relativity" (*Canadian-American Slavic Studies* 16, 2–3 [1981], 250–70). Here I will only introduce that part of Florensky's theory that effectively explains how two different planes of reality can exist in a single universe:

> The region of the imaginary is real, reachable, and in Dante's language is called the empyrean. We can imagine all space as double, composed of real and of imaginary Gaussian coordinate surfaces coinciding with the real ones, but the transition from the real surface to the imaginary one is possible only through the breaking of space and the turning inside out of a body through itself . . . Thus, tearing apart time, the *Divina Commedia* unexpectedly turns out to be, not behind, but ahead of our contemporary science.[73]

Florensky's application is particularly useful because he took as his example another literary model of the universe – Dante's *Divina Commedia.* Readers had always envisioned Dante's hell as a series of concentric rings of diminishing diameter, which makes for a cone-shaped hell with Satan at the tip of the cone. But Florensky interpreted Dante's journey down through hell and back up to purgatory as a straight line, taking his description of the turning (at the tip of the cone) quite literally to mean that he turned or flipped head to toe.[74] Since we know how thoroughly Bulgakov studied Florensky's book, especially the analysis of Dante's journey, can it be coincidence that Margarita, about to enter the fifth dimension of Woland's apartment,[75] also flips head to toe:

> Margarita gave the broom another upward prod, and the mass of rooftops fell away, replaced by a lake of quivering electric lights. Suddenly, this lake rose up vertically, and then appeared above Margarita's head, while the moon shone beneath her feet. Realizing that she had turned a somersault, she resumed her normal position, and when she turned to look, she saw that the lake was

> no longer there and that back there behind her there remained only a rosy glow on the horizon. A second later and it, too, had vanished, and Margarita saw that she was alone with the moon, which was flying above her to her left. Margarita's hair continued to stand up like a haystack, and the moonlight whistled as it washed over her body. Judging by how two rows of widely spaced lights below had merged into two unbroken fiery lines and by how rapidly they vanished behind her, Margarita surmised that she was traveling at monstrous speed and was amazed that she was not gasping for breath.

Here we have an elegant illustration of Florensky's theory of traveling from the one plane to the other, which occurs when bodies travel at the speed of light (see Margarita's "monstrous speed" above) and requires a bend or turn. What Florensky effectively did was to transform the concept of Dante's universe from a geometric shape to a Möbius strip.

> His (Dante's) journey was a reality; but if anyone should begin to deny this (assertion), then in any case it must be acknowledged as a poetic reality, that is, one accessible to imagination and thought, which means that it contains within itself the givens for explaining its geometrical postulates. And so, proceeding all the while forward along a straight line and having turned over once en route, the poet arrives back at his point of departure in the same position in which he left.[76]

Like Dante's, Bulgakov's universe has been viewed geometrically as three nested narratives – three concentric rings, with Moscow on the outside containing apartment building 302, which in turn contains Woland who is the source of the Jerusalem chapters. But if we view the novel's locations arranged linearly, that is, along the Möbius strip, then the ancient and eternal city of Yershalaim lies only a little way distant from modern Moscow – at the bend in the road. The all-important bend or twist needed to transport the reader from Moscow to Yershalaim and back is a turning operation performed by the reader. A similar operation was described by Andrei Bely in his article "The Line, the Circle, the Spiral – of Symbolism":

> The run-on line that forms the surface of the page is the uniting of circular movement to linear movement; in moving from line to line the eye describes a circle. The uniting of one page to another combines circular and linear movement and forms a spiral. The truth of the book is spiral; the truth of the book is the eternal changing of unchanging positions. That truth does not lie either in volution or in the unchanging nature of repetitions. That truth lies in the reincarnation of *that which has been posited once and for all.* But that which has been posited once and for all is Eternity.[77]

The bends in the road are marked by Bulgakov with his customary accuracy. They are those haunting phrases and fragments of phrases that usher us in and out of this non-Euclidian space: "In a white cloak with a blood-red lining"; "The darkness which had come in from the Mediterranean." Since they universally occur at the end of a chapter and are repeated at the beginning of the next, the reader literally has to turn the page (or at the very least rotate his eyes upward) at each transition. The phrase "follow me reader, and only me" jolts the reader especially hard because it alone of all the transitions is uttered and repeated in real time, not historical time, thus marking the biggest transition of all – from part 1 to part 2 of the novel.

Theology

CHRISTIAN ICONOGRAPHY

The proposed reading of *The Master and Margarita*, in which both inner and outer texts form part of a single continuum, still leaves something to be desired. It does not prepare readers for the supernatural events in part 2 of the novel, especially the ending, in which, it seems, the inner text has invaded the outer text. Matthew the Levite appears on the roof of the Pashkov House in present-day Moscow, and Yeshua personally gives orders concerning the Master and Margarita. Clearly, any reading has to address the novel's theology, which is its most active level, and consequently has engendered the liveliest critical debate. Upon seeing the chapter title "Pontius Pilate," immediately followed by a description of the palace of Herod the Great, readers are prepared for a heavy dose of religious imagery. They may be less prepared, however, for an equally dense amount of religious imagery in the outer text, so I will begin there.

Margarita. Each of the main protagonists bears an enormous semantic load of Christian iconography, much of it derived from the Russian Orthodox tradition. This is especially true of Margarita. To begin with the purely Russian context, she is a classic example of the strong woman from Russian nineteenth-century literature. The strong woman is a heroine like Turgenev's Elena (*On the Eve*) or Tolstoy's Natasha (*War and Peace*) – a woman stronger than the man she loves, a woman dominated by emotion, full of purpose and direction, and characterized by a quality of wholeness. She is the active force, whereas her beloved is passive, weak, undirected, dominated by a single intellectual trait.[78]

In her above-mentioned article, Stenbock-Fermor identifies Margarita as Goethe's eternal feminine, Jungfrau, Mutter, Königen, Göttin, and so on. She is all of these, but in their specifically Russian manifestation. Russian Orthodox iconography never concentrated on the aesthetic appeal of the adolescent Virgin Mary, but rather on Mary's celestial role as Queen of the Universe and her more compassionate role as Mother of God.[79] These are, in fact, the roles Margarita is called on to fill. She is Queen Margot to Woland and Company (an oblique allusion to her being a descendent of Queen Marguerite de Valois, wife of Henry IV of France) and at the Grand Ball she serves parodically as Queen of Hell.[80] Her motherly compassion emerges in her care of the little boy in Latunsky's apartment building and in her relationship to Ivan Bezdomny. Twice she is even portrayed as two of the most beautiful iconographic representations of Mary in Russian Orthodoxy. After she has been poisoned by Azazello's wine, her face is transformed, losing its witchlike squint to register simply sorrow: "The dead woman's face brightened and finally softened, and her smile was no longer predatory, but more that of a woman who had gone through a lot of suffering."[81] This motif is repeated when the Master and Margarita pay their final visit to Ivan in the psychiatric clinic: "She looked at the youth and in her eyes sorrow (*skorb'*) could be read." In Russian Orthodoxy, Mary is sometimes known as the "Mother of Sorrows" (*Mater' Skorbi*). In that same scene, Margarita bends low over the poet while he puts his arms around her neck and looks at her "with sadness and with a kind of quiet tenderness" (*umilenie*). This is a beautiful portrait of the Mother of Tenderness (*Bogomater' Umileniia*), traditionally depicted with Mary bent slightly over her child, and the child looking up at her, with his arms around her neck and their cheeks touching.

In *The Apocalyptic Vision of Mikhail Bulgakov's The Master and Margarita*, Edward Ericson presents even more parallels. In his analysis, Margarita functions both as Mary (the "unmarried bride") and as the Church, the compassionate body that suffers for its "head" (Christ), just as Margarita suffers for the Master.[82] In her odyssey there are a number of parallels and parodies of Orthodox Christian ritual, both before and during her service at Satan's Ball (the black mass or witches' sabbath being itself a parody of the Eucharist). The rubbing of Azazello's cream over her body parodies the Orthodox rite of Chrismation. This is followed by baptism (her dip in the river outside Moscow) and the drinking of the eucharist (the blood turned into wine that she is given at the ball). During the ball she is revived by being "washed in the blood" (as Christians are washed in the blood of the lamb), and the heavy chain with the poodle ornament she is given to wear is reminiscent of the huge crucifix worn by the Orthodox priest.[83] Margarita's performance at Satan's Ball has often been compared to the apocryphal Orthodox story of the Virgin's descent into hell in which Mary, accompanied by the archangel Michael, visits hell on the night of Good Friday and obtains temporary relief for the prisoners. In her final appearance as part of Ivan Bezdomny's apocalyptic vision, Margarita resembles the woman clothed in the sun with the moon at her feet, from the Revelation of St. John.

Ivan Bezdomny. Like Margarita, the poet Ivan Bezdomny originates in a purely Russian context. His dishevelled appearance, his awkwardness, and his habit of "stumbling on the truth" mark him as "Ivanushka the Fool," archetypal hero of Russian fairy tales.[84] "Ivanushka the Fool" is typically the youngest of three brothers, socially inept but pure of heart, and he inevitably rises above adversity to marry the princess and become king. Bezdomny is also a parody of the Russian tradition of "*iurodivy*," or "fools in Christ."[85] These "holy fools," as they are sometimes called, are traditionally homeless "half-wits" who dress poorly and survive on charity. Symbolically, they represent man at his furthest remove from God (man having renounced reason of his own free will) and at his closest to Christ (man having taken on the humiliation and suffering that falls to such vagrants).[86] In Russian literature, such fools have often been a marvelous medium for speaking the truth without fear of retribution (see Dostoevsky's *The Idiot* or Pushkin's *Boris Godunov*). This feature of Ivan's character was more pronounced in earlier versions of the novel, as we see from the excerpt included in this volume. As a literary "type," Ivan has also been called a parody of Dostoevsky's Ivan Karamazov.[87]

But it is Bezdomny's role as "disciple" that is most central to the novel and that is most clearly marked with iconographic imagery. His appearance at the Griboedov Restaurant is a masterful parody of John the Baptist. "Homeless" appears clothed in rags after his "baptism" in the Moscow River, to warn his colleagues that Satan is among them. The crowd's reaction ("It's a clear-cut case – D.T.'s") parodies the prophecy that John the Baptist "shall be great in the sight of the Lord and shall drink no wine nor strong drink" (Luke 1:15). Once in the psychiatric clinic, Ivan renounces his former life as a poet three times: once when Dr. Stravinsky recognizes him as a famous poet, again when the Master asks him what he does for a living, and for a third time when the state investigator expresses the hope that he will soon write poetry again – an implicit parody of Peter's denial of Christ. Ivan's relationship to the Master is reminiscent of John, the disciple beloved of Christ. As the Master's disciple and the scribe who records the Master's story (see the Master's injunction, "You write the sequel") Ivan parallels the figure of Matthew the Levite from the Jerusalem chapters, himself a parody of the evangelist. If we accept the hypothesis of Ivan as the author of the entire novel, another parallel emerges: John the evangelist, himself a historian and of all the evangelists the one most preoccupied with the placing of Christ in history.[88]

However, it is precisely in his role as disciple that Bezdomny has generated the most controversy. At present two distinct camps exist: one viewing him positively as the Master's true disciple, a man of greater moral integrity than most Muscovites, who emerges from his brush with higher reality armed with an expanded consciousness and a willingness to fulfill the Master's last command;[89] the other sees him as a failed disciple, a man who grasped the truth but let it go, who has accepted Soviet reality and made his compromise with evil.[90] The crux of the controversy is the state of the text itself. If the Master's novel has been burned (not once but twice!) and Ivan does not write the sequel, as many readers and critics have assumed, then he fails entirely to transmit the Master's message entrusted to him.[91] Both interpretations hinge on a reading of the epilogue. If the epilogue is read literally, then Ivan is a failure who remembers nothing of his past except what he recalls in a drug-induced dream. If read with a heavy dose of irony supplied by Ivan himself, the epilogue is a delightful act of collusion between narrator and reader, of the kind that regularly occurs in Gogol. "Ivan knows," says the narrator. What does Ivan know? He knows exactly what any Soviet reader knows: in order to obtain his release from the clinic, he has been forced to adopt the double life common to all members of the Soviet intelligentsia. By day he will do his research at the Institute of History and Philosophy; by night he will write fantastic literature couched in Aesopian language.[92] In a word, schizophrenia, as had been predicted.

But whether viewed positively or negatively, Ivan's structural significance for the novel is indisputable. He is the figure that opens and closes the novel, the only character to feature prominently in both parts 1 and 2, and the person who occupies more narrative space than any other Muscovite, including the Master himself. As Pittman says, "Ivan Bezdomny emerges as the pivotal character and the lynch-pin of *The Master and Margarita*, since the novel's narrative structure revolves around him."[93] Barratt points out that Ivan also functions as a bond with the reader, since his reaction to Woland and his search for the truth resembles that of the first-time reader more nearly than that of any other character.[94]

The Master. As a character, the Master is at once more all-encompassing and more frustrating than either Margarita or Bezdomny. Oddly enough, it is with him that the Christian iconography begins to break down. Because of the intense parallelism between the inner and outer texts, the reader's first impulse is to see in him a Christlike victim, the Moscow equivalent of Yeshua.[95] Certainly, from a structural standpoint, this holds true. Early on, Leatherbarrow noted that the Master's metaphorical death at the hands of the literary establishment parallels the actual crucifixion of Yeshua.[96] Further evidence along this line can easily be found: the Master is one of three men "murdered" by Woland's suite, the others being Berlioz and Baron Maigel. Hence, on both levels, we have an innocent crucified between two scoundrels. Other parallels brought out by Leatherbarrow are that both heroes die during a storm and both leave behind a loyal disciple.[97]

More convincing than any structural parallels is the kenotic kinship that links the two figures. In addition to their undeserved suffering, both the Master and Yeshua embody certain of Christ's qualities. These have been beautifully brought out by Edward Ericson in his analysis of the Master's enigmatic character.[98] Both the Master and Yeshua are homeless (Yeshua tells Pilate he has "no regular dwelling"; the Master tells Ivan he has "no place to go"). Both are accused of madness (Pilate's scheme for rescuing Yeshua from the hands of the Sanhedrin is to declare him insane; the Master is an "incurable" patient in the psychiatric clinic). Both achieve a high degree of anonymity (Yeshua cannot supply a family name nor can he tell Pilate anything about his parents; the Master simply says, "I have no surname. I renounced it."). Ericson cogently argues that these very qualities elevate the man to a universal symbol of suffering.[99]

The analogy breaks down at an obvious point. Yeshua at no time renounces his vision of the truth, and he gives his life for it. The Master, on the other hand, retreats under the savage attack by the philistines, burns his manuscript, and renounces his role as the voice of truth. He is, then, at best, an imperfect victim. Yet it is his very status as victim that frustrates another avenue of comparison, that between the Master and Faust. In Barratt's discussion of the "Faust Connection," we saw that *surface* parallels between the Master and Faust yield very little. As Stenbock-Fermor put it, it is difficult to recognize in the passive Master "the restless, daring, striving Faust."[100] For all his intuition of the truth, the Master never makes any pact with the devil, and after his first encounter with the world at large, he quickly renounces any further striving, preferring the safety of the psychiatric clinic. "And you know, I find it's not so bad here," he tells Ivan. "There's no need to formulate any grandiose plans." Critics have often observed that of the two, Margarita shows more of Faust's unstoppable determination. As for the Master, the best that can be said of his "questing nature" is that he resembles a noble-minded but ineffectual romantic – a Don Quixote in modern dress.[101]

Pursuing the thread of the Master's status as victim has often lead critics to view him as a symbol of the persecuted artist in the Soviet state – the voice of conscience crying in the wilderness of state-mandated mediocrity. Yet even here he is a flawed symbol of suffering. Faced with attacks from the critical establishment, his resistance crumbles and he is consumed with shame for his act of cowardice (the burning of the manuscript). Critics have also dwelt at length on the close analogies between his and Bulgakov's own story. The details in support of this view are many, from the strange psychic illness that afflicts the Master (Bulgakov experienced a long period during which he could not venture outside his apartment alone) to the little black skull cap with the letter *M* embroidered in yellow silk that Elena Sergeevna sewed for her husband. Whereas this is a rich area for investigation, reading the novel as a form of autobiography effectively deflects readers from considering the Master's significance as a composite symbol of the artist. As J.A.E. Curtis has so ably demonstrated, Bulgakov was much preoccupied in his last years with the nature of creativity and the role of the artist. His portrayals of the artist's relationship to society at large, to authority, and especially to reality are heavily influenced by the Romantic heritage.

> The Romantic artist, however, is also frequently portrayed as the victim of an uncomprehending society, persecuted in the idealistic pursuit of his vision, and doomed for the sake of his art. His sacred ideal is often in the end unattainable, which is why so many portrayals of Romantic heroes seem to verge on the ironic. The Romantic concern is with noble failures rather than heroic successes.[102]

To conclude this section on Christian imagery, I would like to return to the final vision of Margarita as "the woman clothed in the sun with the moon at her feet." This is an image from the final book of the New Testament, and as readers get to the finale of *The Master and Margarita*, they sense the same buildup of momentum in which not only the characters, but the elements play a part – storms, winds, earthquake, fire, darkness covering the sky and the moon turning to blood, voices resounding like trumpets uttering the cry, "It's time! It's time!" And over all floats the symbol of the four horsemen – four dark horsemen against the night sky. So densely packed with apocalyptic imagery are chapters 31 and 32 that David Bethea has called them "not only the most 'elaborate' but the most *explicit* parody of the Book of Revelation in Russian literature."[103] Aside from Bethea's magisterial work *The Shape of the Apocalypse in Modern Russian Fiction*, the most extensive work done on Bulgakov's manipulation of both the symbols and the sense of apocalypse is Edward Ericson's *The Apocalyptic Vision of Mikhail Bulgakov's The Master and Margarita*, which is covered in Barratt's survey of recent criticism.

Despite the density of the Christian imagery on the Moscow level of the novel, it cannot be viewed out of context, that is, independently of the Jerusalem chapters. This is especially true when we consider how much of Christian ritual and symbolism is presented parodistically. What is Bulgakov's intent here, and what conclusions can be drawn about his worldview? Here we will have to respectfully part ways with Andrew Barratt's contention that "the Jerusalem narrative, no matter how great its overall importance, remains strictly subservient to the Moscow story in narrative terms."[104] The centrality of the Jerusalem narrative is demonstrated first by the act of reading—on subsequent readings, the Jerusalem narrative is foregrounded, whereas the Moscow story recedes—and second by the act of writing. Proffer notes that "precisely these chapters contained the fewest changes from draft to draft of the novel . . . they formed the keystone of the novel from its inception."[105] The Jerusalem narrative assumes centrality by virtue of genesis (cf. Markov's comment that Bulgakov was obsessed by the Passion story). The novel began as Bulgakov's version of the Passion.

Readers well acquainted with the Gospel accounts cannot help but be startled and moved by Bulgakov's rendering of the Passion story. Like his treatment of Goethe's *Faust*, this would seem to be a creative reworking of what we assumed was a canonical (hence immutable) text. Barratt has identified three levels on which Bulgakov estranges or defamiliarizes the well-known story.[106] One level of estrangement takes place on the level of language. Bulgakov gives places and people their Aramaic names, or a close phonetic rendering of them (hence Yeshua, Yershalaim), and he uses the correct terminology for the Roman occupation forces. This, together with his phenomenally accurate descriptions of the layout of ancient Jerusalem, gives his narrative an added quality of authenticity. He further estranges the story by omitting certain features and changing others. Yeshua is twenty-seven, not thirty-three; he is an orphan from Gamala and does not know who his parents were. He does not enter Jerusalem on the back of a donkey to the adulation of the crowd, and he has but one disciple – the rather sullen Matthew the Levite. The final level of estrangement is the result of Bulgakov's unrelieved realism. No reader has yet failed to react to the crucifixion scene, with the masses of flies swarming over Yeshua's face, armpits, and groin, and the cracked voice of Gestas, who had already gone mad from torment, singing tunelessly on his post. This stark realism is in keeping with the Russian tradition. In Dosteovsky's *The Idiot*, Prince Myshkin and his alter ego, Rogozhin, are powerfully attracted by a copy of Holbein's *Descent from the Cross*, with its morbid physicality, the body of Jesus already assuming a greenish-yellow hue.

The overall effect of Bulgakov's rendering of the Passion is to strip Jesus of all the attributes associated with his role as Messiah: no donkey, no Hosannas, no miracles, no robe, no crown of thorns, no resurrection. Bulgakov's Yeshua sidesteps his divinity as neatly as he sidesteps the single ray of sunlight that penetrates the colonnade during his interrogation. The absence of the resurrection would have been felt particularly strongly by Russian readers, because in the Russian Orthodox tradition the Easter celebration is the high point of the church year, so much so that the Russian Orthodox Church is called the Church of Resurrection. By calling into question the principle doctrine of Christianity and the canonical texts on which it is based (the Gospels, here represented by Matthew the Levite's highly unreliable parchments), Bulgakov effectively calls into question the Christian worldview.

Further evidence that Bulgakov's worldview differs from the traditional Christian one is his treatment of good and evil. In its formative stages, Christianity absorbed a heavy dose of Persian dualism, which means that good and evil do not coexist in the creation but are forever battling it out, until the final reckoning. This eschatological momentum contrasts sharply with Bulgakov's cosmology, where good and evil coexist, each having its proper place, like light and darkness in this passage, perhaps the most quoted passage from the entire novel:

> You pronounced your words as if you refuse to acknowledge the existence of either shadows or evil. But would you kindly ponder this question: What would your good do if evil didn't exist, and what would the earth look like if all the shadows disappeared? After all, shadows are cast by things and people. Here is the

> shadow of my sword. But shadows also come from trees and from living beings. Do you want to strip the earth of all trees and living things just because of your fantasy of enjoying the naked light? You're stupid.[107]

This passage first attracted critical attention because of the respective speakers involved. Here it is Woland, presumably Satan, and therefore intent on destroying the creation, who must instruct Matthew the Levite, evangelist and emissary from Yeshua, on the necessary balance of powers within the universe. In fact, the entire scene, which takes place on the roof of the Pashkov House as Woland and Company prepare to leave Moscow, was the first evidence critics offered that Bulgakov is proposing an alternative to traditional Christian theology. His Satan, if that is Woland's true identity, far from playing the role of "adversary," actually takes orders from above; moreover, he fulfills his role both *knowingly* and *willingly.* That he serves in a kind of "heavenly hierarchy" is further supported by the scene in which Margarita grants mercy to Frieda, and Woland remarks that mercy "is not in his department." As an agent of divine justice, Woland resembles the Satan of the Old Testament,[108] but here again the picture is not entirely consistent, since he seems equally comfortable meting out reward or punishment. It is true that a number of critics see him as a source of evil,[109] yet his effect on those he encounters can be positively benign, as it is in the case of the Master and Margarita. Perhaps the most perplexing aspect of Woland's complex nature is how he can be the author of a gospel. How can Satan, regarded in Christianity as the "Father of lies," be a purveyor of truth?

GNOSTICISM

The search for alternative religious worldviews that might more closely approximate Bulgakov's has led critics to Gnosticism, a heretical offshoot of Christianity that flourished in the second and third centuries A.D.

> Ancient gnostics were religious people who sought true knowledge (gnosis) in a wide variety of traditions. They regarded attain-

> ment of knowledge as the key to a salvation that emphasized the mystical awakening of the self, the god within. Many gnostics were dualists in that they contrasted the divine world of light above with the fallen, created world of darkness below.[110]

There are many points of contact between Bulgakov's cosmology and the Gnostic worldview, foremost among them being the pronounced dualism common to both. Gnostics divided the universe into two distinct planes: one transcendent, divine; the other fallen, material – a division that is echoed in the polarization of Bulgakov's universe into positive and negative qualities: light-shadow, truth-lie; sun-moon; courage-cowardice.[111] Gnostics believed that at death the spirit is liberated from the body where it has been emprisoned and joins the divine realm. A similar belief colors the Master's and Margarita's release-in-death and final flight. To quote Meier's description of the Gnostic view of death:

> Physical death does not spell destruction for the initiated who have "found the interpretation" of Jesus' sayings and who therefore do not experience death. Physical death is simply final release from the evil material world.[112]

Such a vision also colors that haunting passage (another late addition) that opens chapter 32:

> Gods, my gods! How sad the earth is at eventide! How mysterious are the mists over the swamps. Anyone who has wandered in these mists, who has suffered a great deal before death, or flown above the earth bearing a burden beyond his strength knows it. Someone who is exhausted knows it. And without regret he forsakes the mists of the earth, its swamps and rivers, and sinks into the arms of death with a light heart, knowing that death alone can soothe him.[113]

(Incidentally, although many gnostics considered themselves Christians, they did not believe in the resurrection of the body. This would explain why Bulgakov does not include a resurrected Yeshua appearing to Matthew the Levite.) Above all, we recognize in Bulgakov that intense feeling of alienation and entrapment in a world that was debased and corrupt from its inception. In Gnosticism this is said to be the condition common to those who have insight into the truth, and it certainly applies to the Master, and in our positive reading, to Bezdomny as well.

The body of critical literature examining connections between Bulgakov's worldview and Gnosticism is steadily growing, and has amassed some impressive evidence. Galinskaia has demonstrated the influence on Bulgakov of the eighteenth-century Ukrainian philosopher Skovoroda (himself espousing a markedly Gnostic worldview).[114] Barratt has added an important new dimension to this discussion by emphasizing the *process* of recognition through which each of the protagonists acquires insight. He also compares the enormous amount of hostility encountered by the "alien" messenger, who, in Gnostic belief, periodically comes to earth to impart knowledge to a chosen few, to the Muscovites' reception of Woland. Barratt concludes that the alien messenger is Woland, whose message is only received by the three protagonists (the Master, Margarita, and Bezdomny), the other Muscovites being much too busy trying to deny the message and destroy the bearer.[115] The most thorough examination of the Gnostic worldview in the novel is George Krugovoy's *The Gnostic Novel of Mikhail Bulgakov: Sources and Exegesis*, in which Woland is clearly identified with the inferior, material plane of existence, and the Master and Margarita are his willing dupes. A detailed description of Krugovoy's work is included in Barratt's survey of recent criticism.

MANICHAEISM

Another theology that has been proposed as a better fit for Bulgakov than the Christian worldview is Manichaeism, itself heavily influenced by Gnosticism. Elements of Manichaeism in the novel had been noted early on by T.R.N. Edwards in his *Three Russian Writers and the Irrational*.[116] More recently, Gareth Williams has found certain specific elements of Manichaeism in the novel, to wit, the distribution of Mani's five qualities of the divinity (love, faith, loyalty, courage, and wisdom) among the novel's protagonists, and the five elements belonging to the world of evil (poison or infection, darkness, mist, storm winds, and devouring flames) associated with Woland and his suite.

Like Gnosticism, Manichaeism posits two planes of existence. Originally these were separate, but after the conquest of man by Satan, the world of light became contaminated by the darkness. Mankind then became the battleground for the struggle between the two forces.

> The visible world is a sort of machine for extracting the good, light elements out of the chaotic mixture left by the struggle. The main parts of the world machine are the sun and the moon. According to Mani, the moon constantly extracts particles of ethereal light from the earthly world and gradually transfers them to the sun, whence, completely purified, they go to the heavenly regions. The angels have withdrawn from earth, which the princes of darkness rule. Not all men may go to heaven, only those in whom there is a particle of light. The rest go to hell. There is no resurrection.[117]

Thus it is primarily on the basis of Bulgakov's use of sun and moon imagery that Williams gives his exegesis of the novel's Manichaean worldview. Specifically, the moon's role in the above-mentioned process of purification is used to interpret the function of the moon in the novel, especially the moonlit path, Pilate's ultimate redemption, and the final appearance of Master and Margarita on the path.[118]

History

In the face of this daunting array of metaphysics, I would like to propose that the discipline of primary importance to an understanding of *The Master and Margarita* is not theology so much as history. At first blush, it is not immediately obvious that one takes precedence over the other. The notion of apocalypse (as seen in the final two chapters) and the notion of history are synonymous, inasmuch as the apocalypse is the symbol of the eschatological notion of history espoused by Christians. The very meaning of apocalypse implies a conflict between history as men experience it and see themselves participating in it, and History as directed by some external authority. This issue, as Bethea says, "is central to the apocalyptic conception and structure of *The Master and Margarita* – namely, the direction and meaning of human history, its end as divine plot, and the ultimate purpose of historical study."[119]

But other clues indicate that the writing of history was foremost in Bulgakov's mind as he suffered over the drafts of the novel. I have already mentioned the phenomenal accuracy of the geography and architecture of ancient Jerusalem in Bulgakov's inner text. The details were largely gleaned from a monograph written by his father's colleague Makkaveiski entitled *The Archaeology and History of the Suffering of Our Lord, Jesus Christ.*[120] Similarly influential (albeit from a thematic point of view) was an article by his own father, who analyzed various civilizations in the history of mankind that fell because a high level of intellectual and material development was not accompanied by moral development and spiritual enlightenment.[121] He concluded that a similar "denial of spiritual values and wholehearted devotion to the material would lead to catastrophe in his own time once again."[122] As Edythe Haber has demonstrated, Bulgakov seems to have shared his father's concern for the materialistic, rationalistic, spiritually deficient "post-Christian" culture in which he lived. In the novel he uses Berlioz as a symbol of the modern man whose considerable erudition is not accompanied by any spiritual enlightenment whatsoever.[123]

In an earlier article I have argued that Bulgakov wrote *The Master and Margarita* in part as a polemical response to the prevailing Marxist-Leninist vision of history. We know that Bulgakov was "greatly skeptical of the historical optimism professed by Marxism, concerning man's discovering history's laws and 'taking the future into his own hand'"; moreover, Lesley Milne has demonstrated in some detail how the opening debate between Berlioz and Woland follows the classical Marxist-Leninist version of the Hegelian "negation of the negation," making the first two chapters of the novel a "diabolically elegant mockery in which dialectical materialism is stood on its head."[124] We might also note that about the same time as Bulgakov is rumored to have conceived his "novel about the devil," he became friendly with the writer Eugene Zamiatin, and the two spent many hours discussing their radically opposing views of history, one being, in Milne's words, "a conservative apologist for evolution, the other the arch apostle of endless revolution."[125]

Bulgakov's intense interest in history coincided with the upsurge in militant atheism that followed the relaxed years of NEP. Publications discrediting Christianity were rife, among them a tract entitled *A Chrestomathy of Antireligious Readings*, which Zerkalov claims contains a verbatim extract of Berlioz's arguments in chapter 1 of the novel.[126] The publishing house Ateist (The Atheist) issued Russian translations of major texts of the so-called mythological school, including Arthur Drew's *The Christ Myth* and John Robertson's *Christ and Mythology*. Briefly stated, the mythological school advances the argument that all the elements in Jesus' story are borrowed from cultural myths that existed long before Christ, hence there was no historical Jesus. We know that Bulgakov owned and had closely read both Drew's and Robertson's works.[127] He also studied attentively a work by Barbus translated into Russian as "Jesus against Christ" (*Iisus protive Khrista*), as well as a stenographic copy of Lunacharsky's discussion of this work with the Metropolitan Vvedensky.[128] Immediately preceding this wave of militant atheism, there had been a resurgence of interest in witchcraft and demonology. Chudakova has pointed to Erenburg's *The Extraordinary Adventures of Julio Jurenito and His Disciples* (Berlin, 1922) in which the devil appears to the hero in a café, and Grin's short story *Fandango* (in *Almanac of Adventures*, Moscow, 1927) as possible influences on Bulgakov's concept, as well as Chayanov's *Venediktov, or the Memorable Events of My Life*.[129] Then there was Chevkin's play *Yeshua Ga-Nozri. An Impartial Discovery of the Truth*, produced in Simbirsk in 1922, which portrays Jesus as a very nonmiraculous doctor, and that Chudakova presumes Bulgakov learned about through the review in *Krasnaia Niva* in 1923.[130]

Amid this hostile hotbed of dialectical materialism and militant atheism, Bulgakov chose to do the unthinkable. He refuted both the Marxist-Leninist vision of history, with its uphill battle between spontaneity and consciousness, and the mythological school's hypotheses by intuiting the defining moment in history, the unique and unrepeatable event that stands forever at the center of history.[131] In depicting Christ before Pilate, he focused on the one moment most elaborated by the evangelists, precisely because this is the moment when sacred and profane histories merge.

> Pilate, particularly as presented in the Gospel of John (ch. 19:11), is completely and in an outstanding way the involuntary instrument of the Christ event, which he brings to its very climax, to the decision on the cross. Thus, the mention of Pontius Pilate in the Apostle's Creed not only corresponds to a definite historical situation of the Church, but also has a theological significance, inasmuch as it shows by way of example how the course of even the so-called secular events stands in relation to redemptive history.[132]

Bulgakov's meticulous attention to the historical context of the confrontation between Pilate and Jesus places him squarely in the tradition of the Quest for the Historical Jesus. Briefly, the Quest involves subjecting the gospel accounts of Christ's life to rigorous scholarship in an attempt to find those elements that are historically verifiable. The Quest began in the eighteenth century in Germany with David Friedrich Strauss's *Life of Jesus*, and it includes some very well known names – Reimarus, Thomas Jefferson, and Albert Schweitzer, from whose monograph the "Quest" gained its name.[133] Questers after the historical Jesus were heavily influenced by Ernest Renan's *Life of Jesus*, which was widely read both in Europe and Russia in the late nineteenth century and which appeared in print in Kiev in 1902–3, and F. W. Farrar's *Life of Christ* (London: Cassell, 1897). Shades of both these texts can be found in Bulgakov's account of the Passion story.

The most recent manifestation of the Quest for the Historical

Jesus is the Jesus Seminar – a group of predominantly U.S. scholars who have evaluated every statement attributed to Christ, using various approaches: cultural anthropology, archeology, and sociology, as well as a profound knowledge of the urtexts (the Source Q and the Gospel of Thomas).[134] The statements have been arranged in hierarchical order ranging from those definitely uttered by Jesus to those likely but not definitely attributable to him, and ending with those most certainly added by the evangelists. Like all scholarship, the work of the Jesus Seminar betrays the times in which it is written; for example, it is a highly politicized account. Jesus is a rebel from the underprivileged, dispossessed classes who is interested in overturning the social order. It also denigrates the written word in favor of the oral tradition (Christ's teachings are portrayed primarily as a collection of sayings [*chreaia*]) and refers to the gospel accounts as "elitist."

Putting aside any reservations, the historical accuracy of the work of the Jesus Seminar is impressive. Equally impressive is the extent to which Bulgakov's portrayal matches that of the Seminar, albeit it precedes the latter by some sixty years. The methodology in both cases is strikingly similar. The Jesus Seminar largely discredits the Gospel narratives; Bulgakov's Yeshua actually disavows the sayings written down by Matthew the Levite. The Jesus Seminar seeks to strip away the features of Jewish Messianism from the historical figure of Jesus; Bulgakov deletes all the features that identify Jesus as the Christ: the entry on the donkey to the shouts of Hosanna, the crown of thorns, the casting of lots for the robe. It is interesting that in both accounts Jesus emerges as a wandering philosopher. Here is a description by one of the Seminar's most prominent members, John Dominic Crossan:

> The historical Jesus was, then, a peasant Jewish cynic. His peasant village was close enough to a Graeco-Roman city like Sepphorus that sight and knowledge of Cynicism are neither inexplicable nor unlikely. But his work was among the farms and villages of Lower Gallilee. His strategy, implicitly for himself and explicitly for his

> followers, was the combination of free healing and common eating, a religious and economic egalitarianism that negated alike and at once the hierarchical and patronal normalcies of Jewish religion and Roman power. Miracle and parable, healing and eating were calculated to force individuals into unmediated physical and spiritual contact with God and physical and unmediated contact with one another. He announced, in other words, the brokerless Kingdom of God.[135]

An even closer comparison reveals that in both cases the defining features of Jesus' mission are the same: "free healing" ("But your sufferings will soon end and your headache will pass"); "free eating" (Yeshua is arrested while eating at Judas of Kerioth's house); "religious and economic egalitarianism that negated alike and at once the hierarchical and patronal normalcies of Jewish religion and Roman power" ("I said that every kind of power is a form of violence against people and that there will come a time when neither the power of the Caesars, nor any other kind of power will exist. Man will enter the kingdom of truth and justice, where no such power will be necessary"); "unmediated physical and spiritual contact with one another" ("The trouble is . . . that you are too isolated and have lost all faith in people. After all, you would agree, one shouldn't lavish one's attention on a dog. Your life is impoverished, Hegemon").

For all its historical accuracy, Bulgakov's portrait is largely intuitive, something we tend to forget in the act of reading. It is a uniquely successful product of painstaking research and blinding insight. Perhaps what is most striking of all is the rhetorical force with which Bulgakov asserts his historical re-creation. "Keep in mind," he says, "that Jesus did exist. And no points of view are necessary. He simply existed and that's all there is to it." The proof is left as an exercise for the reader.

NOTES

1. Readers can consult a large and impressive array of biographies of Bulgakov. The primary source is still Marietta Chudakova's masterful

Zhizneopisanie Mikhaila Bulgakova (Moscow: Kniga, 1988). This was originally published in installments in the journal *Moskva* (part 1, no. 6 [1987], 3–54; part 2, no. 7 [1987], 5–52; part 3, no. 8 [1987], 9–87; part 4, no. 11 [1988], 39–114; part 5, no. 12 [1988], 67–79. It should be noted that there are significant differences between the serial installments and the text that appeared in book form. The other major source in Russian is L. Ianovskaia, *Tvorcheskii Put' Mikhaila Bulgakova* (Moscow: Sovetskii Pisatel', 1983). In English, the list includes A. Colin Wright, *Mikhail Bulgakov: Life and Interpretations* (Toronto: University of Toronto Press, 1978); Ellendea Proffer, *Bulgakov* (Ann Arbor, Mich.: Ardis, 1984); Nadine Natov, *Mikhail Bulgakov* (Boston: Twayne, 1985); and Lesley Milne, *Mikhail Bulgakov: A Critical Biography* (Cambridge: Cambridge University Press, 1990).

2. Bulgakov's stint in the newpaper trade was distasteful to him, yet it garnered him a living and a number of important literary contacts. *Gudok* was the newspaper of the Railwaymen's Trade Union; *Nakanune* was the organ of the "Change of Landmarks" movement, whose main publishing offices were in Berlin. As Lesley Milne notes, the quality of Bulgakov's contributions to *Nakanune* was higher than those he contributed to *Gudok*, and remained higher in Bulgakov's own "retrospective" assessment: "Even at this distance in time his contributions to *Nakanune* retain their charm as a witty running commentary, with a constant shimmer of self-mockery, on the re-emergence of stable patterns of life after a cataclysm" (Milne, *Mikhail Bulgakov*, 31).

3. This anecdote is part of Bulgakov's *Letter to a Secret Friend*, written in 1929, which includes a sometimes self-deprecating, sometimes mock-heroic description of his first years in Moscow. (An excerpt can be found in Proffer, *Bulgakov*, 60–61.)

4. The first thirteen chapters of *The White Guard* appeared in *Rossiia* early in 1925 (nos. 4 and 5). In June 1925 Bulgakov delivered the final chapters, but by then the journal was in jeopardy. The novel first appeared in Riga in 1927 in a pirated version with a concocted ending. The first publication (approved by the author) was by Concorde (Paris) in two installments: chapters 1–11 (1927); chapters 12–20 (1929) (see Milne, *Mikhail Bulgakov*, 71).

5. The stormy history of the "reception" of *Days of the Turbins* is one of the most eloquent commentaries on the conditions under which Bulgakov worked. An instant success, beloved of audiences of all persuasions (Right, Left, Red, White) and singled out by Stalin himself, it nevertheless caused a

major press campaign against Bulgakov, and could not be included in the jubilee booklet prepared for the Moscow Art Theater's fortieth anniversary. Elena Sergeevna writes bitterly, "Well, just think of it. Among the jubilee productions, they did not include *Days of the Turbins,* which has run for thirteen years, more than eight hundred shows!! This is unique among plays by a Soviet author. Not only that, there is no mention in any article either of Bulgakov's name or the title of the play" (Elena Sergeevna Bulgakova, *Dnevnik Eleny Bulgakovoi* [Moscow: Knizhnaia Palata, 1990], 212).

6. Proffer, *Bulgakov,* 502.

7. Like *The White Guard,* Bulgakov's *Notes on the Shirt-Cuff* was never published in its entirety during his lifetime. Sections appeared in *Nakanune* in June 1922, in *Vozrozhdenie* in 1923, and in *Rossiia* in 1923 (Milne, *Mikhail Bulgakov,* 34–35).

8. *A Country Doctor's Notebook,* trans. Michael Glenny (London: Collins, 1975; in Russian, *Zapiski Iunogo Vracha*), contains short stories based on Bulgakov's experiences as a Zemstvo doctor in Saratov. The Zemstvo was a group of regional or county councils created as part of Alexander II's reforms. Their duties included overseeing local transportation and conditions of roads, distribution and storage of harvests, and matters of local health and hygiene. A few isolated stories from *A Country Doctor's Notebook* appeared in print in 1925, but once again the entire collection was not published in Bulgakov's lifetime.

9. *Heart of a Dog* was written between January and March 1925, and was officially refused publication by 1926.

10. *Black Snow. A Theatrical Novel,* trans. Michael Glenny (London: Hodder and Stoughton, 1967; in Russian, *Teatral'nyi Roman*), was written in 1936. The full title in Russian reads *Notes of a Dead Man. Theatrical Romance,* and it was Bulgakov's form of "revenge" when he at last broke with the Moscow Art Theater in 1936. The novel remained only a little more than half written. Bulgakov abandoned it in order to press ahead with *The Master and Margarita.*

11. There is ample evidence that Bulgakov felt that *The Master and Margarita* justified his existence as a writer and as a human being. There is also evidence of his feverish determination to see the novel to completion. Dramatic and poignant, this evidence has now become part of the "Bulgakov canon." Thus on the 1934 manuscript of the fourth version is written: "To be finished before dying"; on the corner of the chapter "Woland's Final

Flight" from the third version (1931) are the words "Lord, help me to finish the novel"; and in a letter to his wife of June 2, 1938, he had written, "The novel must be finished. Now! Now!" (see Part III of this volume). Finally, as he lay dying, he told his wife, "Maybe this is right (after all). What could I have written after 'The Master'?" (Chudakova, *Zhizneopisanie*, 481).

12. The other overwhelming influence on Bulgakov's vision of art and the artist was the great Russian poet Pushkin. Pushkin appears in various guises in Bulgakov's work, both early (a quote from *The Captain's Daughter* forms one of the epilogues to *The White Guard*) and late (in 1934 he wrote a play, *Last Days* (Pushkin). Pushkin exerted an equally powerful influence on his life, especially in his conduct toward authority. Early in his career, while still in Vladikavkaz, we find Bulgakov taking the podium to defend Pushkin from attacks by the new breed of Soviet hack writers. Late in his career we find him falling into a relationship with Stalin that echoed Pushkin's relationship to Nicholas I. For a good discussion of Pushkin's influence on Bulgakov's vision of history, see David Bethea, *The Shape of Apocalypse in Modern Russian Fiction* (Princeton, N.J.: Princeton University Press, 1989), 189–92.

13. Bely autographed a copy of his *Moscow Eccentric* (*Moskovskii Chudak*) "to Mikhail Afanas'evich Bulgakov from a sincere admirer" (see Milne, *Mikhail Bulgakov*, 78). For more on his relationship to Bely, see Chudakova, *Zhizneopisanie*, 232–33.

14. We know that Bulgakov read Mirimsky's article, "Hoffmann's Social Fantasy" ("Sotsial'naia fantastika Gofmana," *Literaturnaia ucheba*, no. 5 [1938], 64–87) and that he found much in it to support his own views on the function of art.

15. Milne, *Mikhail Bulgakov*, 262.

16. The connection between Bulgakov and Pasternak has become increasingly well established. See, for example, Milne, *Mikhail Bulgakov*, 234–39; Bethea, *The Shape of Apocalypse*, 232–36; Carol Avins, "Reaching a Reader: The Master's Audience in *The Master and Margarita*," *Slavic Review* 45, no. 2 (1986), 272–85; and Mikhail Kreps, *Bulgakov i Pasternak kak romanisty* (Ann Arbor: Hermitage, 1984).

17. Marietta Chudakova, *Zhizneopisanie Mikhaila Bulgakova*, 481.

18. Bethea, *The Shape of Apocalypse*, 187.

19. This paragraph has been largely condensed from Andrew Barratt's excellent account of the debate sparked by the novel's appearance in *Between*

Two Worlds: A Critical Introduction to "The Master and Margarita" (Oxford: Clarendon, 1987), 13–25. Attentive readers will note that in her early article (included in this volume), Ellendea Proffer enters into polemics with these same Soviet responses. Thus, with the appearance of the first serious scholarship (following the initial "surprise reaction" and "book review" phase) the dialogue was resumed in the West.

20. See Joan Delaney Grossman, "*The Master and Margarita*: The Reach Exceeds the Grasp," *Slavic Review* 31 (December 1972), 89–100. If not the first, this article was certainly one of the most succinct expressions of disappointment in the novel's metaphysics.

21. The question of the novel's "center of gravity," that is, whether its social satire reflects the economic upheavals of the twenties or the terror of the thirties, remains an active area of debate. In her contribution to this volume, J.A.E. Curtis argues for the latter, effectively cataloguing all the mysterious circumstances and veiled allusions to the purges, show trials, and mass arrests that rose to a crescendo after the murder of Kirov, Chief of Secret Police, in 1934.

22. The standard work on the "creative process" of *The Master and Margarita* has long been Chudakova's "Tvorcheskaia istoriia romana M. Bulgakova *Master i Margarita*," *Voprosy literatury* 1 (1976), 218–53, which has also long been available in English (M. Chudakova, "*The Master and Margarita*: The Development of a Novel," *Russian Literature Triquarterly* 15 [1978], 177–209). To some extent this description has been superseded by Chudakova's later work (the work on *The Master and Margarita* is covered in parts 4 and 5 of the biography), and it has been challenged by Ianovskaia (see note 32 below). Yet it remains sound overall and is an excellent introduction to the textology.

23. Proffer, *Bulgakov*, 525. Milne gives the original source of this quotation as Popov's "Zametki Avtobiograficheskogo Kharaktera," found in the Manuscript Department of the Lenin Library.

24. "Markov recalls that the writer told him during the rehearsals of *Days of the Turbins* (i.e., 1926) that he had long been tormented by the enigma of the New Testament tragedy" (Barratt, *Between Two Worlds*, 43).

25. See, for example, Elena Sergeevna's diary entry for September 27, 1933: "Misha read to Kolia L(iamin) the new chapters of the novel about the devil, written over the last few days, or, rather, nights" (Elena Bulgakova, *Dnevnik Eleny Bulgakovoi*, 39; in English, see, J.A.E. Curtis, *Manuscripts*

Don't Burn. Mikhail Bulgakov. A Life in Letters and Diaries [London: Bloomsbury, 1991], 161). In the famous letter to the authorities requesting permission to emigrate (see note 27 below), Bulgakov also refers to destroying the manuscript of the "novel about the devil."

26. M. O. Chudakova, "Opyt rekonstruktsii Teksta M. A. Bulgakova," in *Pamiatniki Kul'tury* (Moscow: Nauka, 1975), 93.

27. The full text of the letter appears in J.A.E. Curtis, *Manuscripts Don't Burn*, 103–10, and as an appendix in Milne, *Mikhail Bulgakov*, 268–74.

28. See Ianovskaia's introduction to Elena Sergeevna's Diaries, "Elena Bulgakova, ee dnevniki, ee vospominaniia," 24–25. It is fascinating that this scene, replete with melodrama, romance (even elements of the popular American Regency Romances; Barratt refers to "effects one associates with the very worst boulevard romances" [Andrew Barratt, *Between Two Worlds*, p. 251]) takes such a powerful hold on readers. Chudakova relates at length "an encounter with Bulgakov" remembered by one Margarita Smirnova and told to Chudakova that exactly parallels the meeting in the novel. (The reminiscence has been translated in Riitta H. Pittman, *The Writer's Divided Self in Bulgakov's The Master and Margarita* [New York: St. Martin's, 1991], 132–33.)

29. Chudakova, *Zhizneopisanie*, 309–10; in English, Chudakova, "The Development of a Novel," 188.

30. Chudakova, *Zhizneopisanie*, 480.

31. The date of submission was listed as May 8, 1929, and the entry was listed as "a chapter from the novel *The Engineer's Hoof*." It was not accepted for publication. See Chudakova, "Arkhiv M. A. Bulgakova," *Zapiski Otdela Rukopisei* 37 (1976): 63–80; Milne, *Mikhail Bulgakov*, 172; Proffer, *Bulgakov*, 307.

32. *Velikii Kantsler* was reissued in 1993 by Izofaks. An interesting point arises in Lossev's introduction to *Velikii Kantsler* (Moscow: Novosti, 1992), 9–18. Whereas Ianovskaia maintains that there were a total of *six* versions of *The Master and Margarita* and attributes the destruction of the first (1928–29) version to an act of editing on Bulgakov's part (he ripped the chapters he had rewritten and was done with), Lossev defends Chudakova's original count of eight versions. The evidence he submits is both sound and ingenious. First, Belozerskaia and others remember that they heard a finished *novel* in 1929. Second, Bulgakov speaks in 1930 of his destruction of his *novel* (not his manuscript) about the devil. Third, in the final version, the Master

speaks of burning first the notebooks with the rough drafts, then the typescript of his novel.

33. The last round of revisions to the novel were dictated by Bulgakov and written down by Elena Sergeevna either on pages glued into the typescript or in a special notebook bought for that purpose. The epilogue was glued into the already "bound" typescript. Proffer considers that the Possev edition of the novel (see the note on translations in this collection) bears the marks of an amateur editor's hand – that of Elena Sergeevna (Proffer, *Bulgakov*, 636 f.).

34. Lesley Milne has a good discussion of the critical disillusionment with part 2 of the novel (Lesley Milne, *Mikhail Bulgakov*, 251–52). She too concludes that the novel benefits from being viewed within a critical paradigm, such as the Bakhtinian concept of the chronotope.

35. David Bethea, *The Shape of Apocalypse*, 193.

36. See M. M. Bakhtin, *Tvorchestvo Fransua Rable* (Moscow: Khudozhestvennaia literatura, 1965); in English, *Rabelais and His World*, trans. Helene Iswolsky (Cambridge, Mass.: MIT Press, 1968).

37. Nadine Natov, "Structural and Topological Ambivalence of Bulgakov's Novels Interpreted against the Background of Baxtin's Theory of 'Grotesque Realism' and Carnivalization," *American Contributions to the Eighth International Congress of Slavists* 2 (Columbus, Ohio: Slavica, 1978), 536–49.

38. Lesley Milne, *The Master and Margarita: A Comedy of Victory* (Birmingham: Birmingham Slavonic Monographs, 1977).

39. Bakhtin, *Rabelais and His World*, 10, cited in Barratt, *Between Two Worlds*, 94.

40. A. Vulis, "Posleslovie," *Moskva*, no. 11 (1966), 127–30; V. Lakshin, "Roman M. Bulgakova *Master i Margarita*," *Novyi mir*, no. 6 (1968), 284–311. Excerpts from the English translation of Lakshin's article are included in this volume.

41. C. O. Holman, *Handbook of Literature* (Indianapolis: Odyssey, 1972), 459.

42. Among the other antireligious publications that influenced Bulgakov's "Gospel According to Woland," critics now have reason to include Demian Bednyi's "Flawless New Testament." Both Chudakova (*Zhizneopisanie*, 296–97) and Kuziakina ("Mikhail Bulgakov i Demian Bednyi," in *M. A. Bulgakov – dramaturg i khudozhestvennaia kul'tura ego vremeni* [Mos-

cow, 1988], 410) point out the similarities between Bednyi's "realistic Jesus" and the Jesus portrayed by Ivan Bezdomny in his antireligious poema. The discussion is summarized by Pittman in *The Writer's Divided Self*, 143–44.

43. Elena Mahlow, *Bulgakov's The Master and Margarita: The Text as Cipher* (New York: Vantage, 1975).

44. D.G.B. Piper, "An Approach to *The Master and Margarita*," *Forum for Modern Language Studies* 7 (1971): 144–50.

45. Ibid., 136. A. Terts, "Literaturnyi protsess v Rossii," *Kontinent* 1 (1974), 159 f.

46. Barratt, *Between Two Worlds*, 95.

47. One example from among Jung's numerous allusions to the qualitative difference between parts 1 and 2 of Goethe's Faust can be found in his essay "On the Psychology of the Unconscious" (C. G. Jung, *Two Essays on Analytical Psychology*, trans. R.F.C. Hull, 2d ed. [Princeton, N.J.: Princeton University Press, 1953], 34).

48. Elizabeth Stenbock-Fermor, "Bulgakov's *The Master and Margarita* and Goethe's *Faust*," *Slavic and East European Journal* 13 (1969): 309–25.

49. Barratt, *Between Two Worlds*, 288.

50. Pittman, *The Writer's Divided Self*.

51. Judith M. Mills, "Of Dreams, Devils, Irrationality and *The Master and Margarita*," in *Russian Literature and Psychoanalysis*, ed. Daniel Rancour-Laferriere (Philadelphia: John Benjamins, 1989), 303–28.

52. From the very beginning critics recognized the elements of the Russian fairy tale in the novel, this despite the Hebraic provenance of the angels (Abaddon, Azazello) and the Christian subtext (see, for example, Lakshin, in Part II of this volume). Another good discussion of the supernatural in the novel is Elizabeth Klosty Beaujour, "The Uses of Witches in Fedin and Bulgakov," *Slavic Review*, 33 (1974): 695–707. See also Rita Giuliani, "Demonologia e magia nel *Maestro e Margherita* di M. A. Bulgakov," *Ricerche Slavistiche* 29–31 (1982–84): 269–304.

53. Vladimir Propp, *Morfologiia skazki* (Leningrad, 1928); in English, *Morphology of the Folktale*, trans. L. Scott, 2d ed. (Austin: University of Texas Press, 1968).

54. Stefania Pavan-Pagnini, "Morfologiia romana Bulgakova *Master i Margarita* kak volshebnoi skazki," *Russian Literature* 31 (1992): 353–74.

55. The other two subgroups are "animal tales" and "tales of everyday

life" (Iu. M. Sokolov, *Russian Folklore*, trans. Catherine Ruth Smith [New York: Macmillan, 1950]).

56. Pavan-Pagnini, "Morfologiia romana Bulgakova," 353–54.

57. Hoisington, "Fairy-tale Elements," 47.

58. Pavan-Pagnini, "Morfologiia romana Bulgakova," 354. Hoisington also reminds us that "the fairy tales allow for no moral ambiguity" (Hoisington, 44).

59. Vida Taranovski-Johnson, "The Thematic Function of the Narrator in *The Master and Margarita*," *Canadian American Slavic Studies* 15, nos. 2–3 (1981), 272. For a superb discussion of the novel's structure and the use of narrative voice(s), see Barratt, *Between Two Worlds*, 104–10.

60. See especially Barratt, *Between Two Worlds*, 110–16.

61. A. Colin Wright, "Satan in Moscow: An Approach to Bulgakov's *The Master and Margarita*," *PMLA* 88 (October 1973), 1162–72, and his *Mikhail Bulgakov: Life and Interpretations.*

62. See Barratt, *Between Two Worlds*, especially 107.

63. Neil Cornwell, *The Literary Fantastic: From Gothic to Post-Modern* (New York: Harvester Books, 1990), 168. The problem, however, as should be clear from the above discussion, is one of authority, and many critics opt for an extratextual authority. Ericson, for example, feels that no character inside the action could narrate it (Edward E. Ericson, Jr., *The Apocalyptic Vision of Mikhail Bulgakov's The Master and Margarita* [Lewiston: Edwin Mellen, 1991], 142.

64. Ellendea Proffer, "Bulgakov's *The Master and Margarita*: Genre and Motif," *Canadian Slavic Studies* 3 (1969): 615–28.

65. "Whereas Bulgakov performs some amazing sleight of hand with the laws of the physical world as we know it, the laws that govern his fictive universe are quite rigorous with regard to time and space. The narrator never misses an opportunity to point out the inner consistency of this universe" (Weeks, "In Defense of the Homeless: On the Uses of History and the Role of Bezdomnyi in *The Master and Margarita*," *The Russian Review* 48 [1989]: 60). This would make it highly unlikely that Bulgakov would "slip up" in a matter so important as how the manuscript could be transmitted. A portion of the discussion of the character of Bezdomnyi is restated from my earlier article.

66. Marietta Chudakova, "Arkhiv M. Bulgakova. Materialy dlia tvorcheskoi biografii pisatelia," *Zapiski otdela rukopisei Vsesoiuznoi biblioteki im V. I.*

Lenina 37 (1976): 70–71; "Opyt rekonstruktsii teksta M. Bulgakova," *Pamiatniki kul'tury* (Moscow, 1977), 100–101. See pages 306–10 in *Zhizneopisanie.*

67. This is the crucial episode missing from all editions of the novel (Russian and English) before the 1973 *Romany* publication. See the note on translations in this volume.

68. The epilogue was added after the readings noted in Elena Sergeevna's diary: April 27 through May 15, 1939 (Elena Sergeevna Bulgakova, *Dnevnik Eleny Bulgakovoi,* 256–59). As Barratt points out, these readings are crucial to an understanding of Bulgakov's aims in creating the figure of Woland and of the resolution of the novel's metaphysical problems (Barratt, *Between Two Worlds,* 303). The audience's stunned reaction must have troubled Bulgakov deeply. The diary entries of the readings are included in Part III of this volume.

69. Avins demonstrates very effectively that crucial to the survival of the Master's story is someone to transmit it, and an audience capable of receiving it, however imperfectly. As the Master's disciple, and the only person to hear "the Gospel according to Woland" firsthand, Ivan is the crucial link between writer and audience. As long as the "formative figures in his experience during those distant spring days – Woland, Pilate, Yeshua, the Master and his love – remain deep in his consciousess . . . at that subconscious level, which Ivan penetrates once a year, a vestige of the story in which Woland had initiated him lives on" (Avins, "Reaching a Reader," 282). She concludes, however, that Ivan is a failed disciple, that is, he fails to transmit the message entrusted to him: "Unable to meet the demands of a discipleship, he fails not only to carry on the work of the Master but even fully to grasp the lessons of his life and word and to transmit them to others. The influence of the Master and the Jerusalem text on Ivan – that is, the degree of success with which the text has reached an audience – soon diminishes" (281).

70. There seems to be general agreement that the authority which is the source of the Jerusalem chapters is "extratextual," be it Woland, a dream, or the "ur-text" that the Master somehow intuits. We respectfully disagree, however, with Avins's assessment of Ivan as a failed audience for that text. For one thing, Avins twice mentions that Ivan never sees the Master's story in print, whereas the crucial passage from the 1973 *Romany* edition (see note 67 above) makes it clear both that an excerpt of the Master's novel has appeared in print and that Ivan has read it.

71. Two seminal articles are indispensable for an understanding of the

complex parallelism that exists on the novel's two planes, one dealing with the theme of the two cities, the other with symbols, time sequences, and structural parallelism. See Barbara Kejna-Sharratt, "The Tale of Two Cities: The Unifying Function of the Setting in Mikhail Bulgakov's *The Master and Margarita*," *Forum for Modern Language Studies* 16 (1974): 1–12; and Bruce A. Beatie and Phyllis W. Powell, "Story and Symbol: Notes Toward a Structural Analysis of Bulgakov's *The Master and Margarita*," *Russian Literature Triquarterly* 15 (1978): 219–51.

72. Bruce A. Beatie and Phyllis W. Powell, "Bulgakov, Dante, and Relativity," *Canadian-American Slavic Studies* 16, nos. 2–3 (1981): 251. Beatie and Powell are quoting from Chudakova's early important piece "Uslovie Sushchestvovaniia," *V mire knig*, no. 12 (1974).

73. See Beatie and Powell, "Bulgakov, Dante and Relativity," 252.

74. The Italian says just that: "My master with great effort, turned head over heels."

Quando noi fummo la dove la coscia
  Si volge, a punto in sul grosso dell'anche,
  Lo duca, con fati a e con angoscia,
volse la testa ov'elli avea le zanche,
  e aggrapposi al pel com'uom che sale.
[When we had reached the joint where the great thigh
  merges into the swelling of the haunch,
  my Guide and Master, straining terribly,
Turned his head to where his feet had been
  and began to grip the hair as if he were climbing.]

English from Dante Alighieri, *The Divine Comedy. The John Ciardi Translation* (New York: W. W. Norton, 1954), 179.

75. Actually, Dante and Vergil turn upon meeting Satan, whereas Margarita turns just before meeting Satan.

76. Pavel Florenskii, *Mnimosti v geometrii* (Moscow: Pomor'e, 1922), 47, cited in Bethea, *The Shape of Apocalypse*, 203.

77. Cited in Robert A. Maguire and John E. Malmstad, "Petersburg," in *Andrei Belyi, Spirit of Symbolism* (Cambridge, Mass.: Harvard University Press, 1987), 143.

78. The most concise description of the Russian "strong woman" as a type is given in Vera Dunham, "The Strong Woman Motif," in *The Transformation of Russian Society*, ed. Cyril E. Black (Cambridge, Mass.: Harvard

University Press, 1960), 459–83. Klosty Beaujour also sees Margarita as belonging to this tradition ("The Uses of Witches in Fedin and Bulgakov," 698).

79. George P. Fedotov, *The Russian Religious Mind*, vol. 1 (Belmont, Mass.: Nordland, 1975), 360–62.

80. Marguerite de Valois became a legend by saving her husband's life during the St. Bartholomew's Day Massacre. We know that Bulgakov underlined the entry under Marguerite de Valois in the *Brockhaus-Efron Encyclopedia.* The finest and most thorough study of Margarita's symbolic functions is Edward Ericson's *The Apocalyptic Vision of Mikhail Bulgakov's The Master and Margarita* (Lewiston, Maine: Edwin Mellen, 1991) (this citation from page 125). In general, this work is so important for an understanding of the Eastern Orthodox worldview (hence an understanding of the novel's theology) that it is covered in this volume both in Barratt's survey of recent literature and in the annotated bibliography.

81. Mikhail Bulgakov, *The Master and Margarita*, trans. Diana Burgin and Katherine O'Connor (Ann Arbor, Mich.: Ardis, 1995), 313.

82. Ericson, *The Apocalyptic Vision*, 118.

83. Ibid., 120–22, 125.

84. Stenbock-Fermor, "Bulgakov's *The Master and Margarita* and Goethe's *Faust*," 325.

85. Ibid. See also Pierre Hart, "*The Master and Margarita* as Creative Process," *Modern Fiction Studies* (Summer 1973): 169–78.

86. For a marvelous discussion of *iurodstvo*, see Harriet Murav, *Holy Foolishness: Dostoevsky's Novels and the Poetics of Cultural Critique* (Stanford: Stanford University Press, 1992).

87. David Lowe, "Bulgakov and Dostoevsky: A Tale of Two Ivans," *Russian Literature Triquarterly*, no. 15 (1978), 253–62.

88. See the concluding arguments in Weeks, "In Defense of the Homeless," 64–65.

89. Among those who view Ivan positively are Hart, "The Master and Margarita as Creative Process"; Val Bolen, "Theme and Coherence in Bulgakov's *The Master and Margarita*," *Slavic and East European Journal* 16, no. 4 (1972); Weeks, "In Defense of the Homeless"; and Bethea, *The Shape of Apocalypse*. Robert Mann also sees Ivan as the possible author of the entire novel: "The Path of the Bronze Horseman in *The Master and Margarita*," in *Oregon Studies in Chinese and Russian Culture*, edited by Albert Leong (New York: Peter Lang, 1990).

90. The opposing camp, i.e., those who view Ivan as a failure or at best a figure to be pitied, includes Proffer, *Bulgakov*; Avins, "Reaching a Reader"; Barratt, *Between Two Worlds*; Ericson, *The Apocalyptic Vision*; and Pittman, *The Writer's Divided Self.*

91. Avins, "Reaching a Reader" (see note 69 above). Barratt also reaches this conclusion that *The Master and Margarita* is a "literary conception that can never be communicated" (*Between Two Worlds*, 311).

92. This echoes Edythe Haber, who has offered one of the most balanced assessments of Ivan: "On the surface it appears that the former poet, now professor of history and philosophy, Prof. Ponyrev, has been cured of his earlier schizophrenia. In other words, he has become an acceptable member of Soviet society. . . . But his normalcy is more apparent than real. For during the sping full moon Ivan Nikolaevich's reason loses its power; he grows restless and dreams strange dreams. In other words, the schizophrenia is still in force. Indeed, it seems that such an illness is inevitable in one who has visions of higher truth and yet is striving to survive in the earthly sunlit world. In the person of Ivan Homeless, Bulgakov seems to be suggesting that the Pilate-like double life is bound to appear in the Soviet artist or intellectual who tries to live both in the world of his imagination and in the atheistic and oppressive everyday world" (Edythe C. Haber, "The Mythic Structure of Bulgakov's *The Master and Margarita*," *Russian Review* 34, no. 4 [1975]: 407.) Excerpts from this article are included in this volume.

93. Pittman, *The Writer's Divided Self*, 97.

94. Barratt, *Between Two Worlds*, 159–60.

95. The strongest proponent of this analogy is A. Colin Wright, "Satan in Moscow: An Approach to Bulgakov's *The Master and Margarita*," *PMLA* 88 (1973). (We might also mention the early Soviet responses by Skorino and Lakshin covered in Part II of this volume.) An equally strong analogy can be made between the Master and Pilate, two prisoners crucified between conscience and cowardice.

96. W. J. Leatherbarrow, "The Devil and the Creative Visionary in Bulgakov's *Master i Margarita*," *New Zealand Slavonic Journal*, no. 1 (1975), 32 f.

97. Ibid.

98. See Ericson, *The Apocalyptic Vision*, ch. 6.

99. Ericson, *The Apocalyptic Vision*, 101–2.

100. Stenbock-Fermor, "Bulgakov's *The Master and Margarita* and Goethe's

Faust," 311. In an early article that stated succinctly all the problems involved in evaluating the character of the Master and the nature of his final reward, Margot Frank remarked, "The Master, like Faust, is being tested by the powers on high and falls short" ("The Mystery of the Master's Final Destination," *Canadian-American Slavic Studies* 15, nos. 2–3 (1981): 288).

101. For Bulgakov, the figure of Don Quixote was a multivalent symbol encapsulating all the ideals he lived by as a man and as an artist. One of his very late pieces was a stage adaptation of Cervantes' *Don Quixote*, and the words *Don Quixote* were among the last he uttered before dying. In bringing in this allusion at this point, I would like to alert the reader to the "romantic" vision of the master discussed by Barratt (*Between Two Worlds*, 246–51), which includes viewing him as an inspired rebel-romantic out to remake reality, or a "sacred vessel" through which superior knowledge and insight flows. The finest discussion of Bulgakov's preoccupation with "noble failures" and his embodiment of the romantic ideal in his art is contained in chapter 5 of J.A.E. Curtis, *Bulgakov's Last Decade: The Writer as Hero* (Cambridge: Cambridge University Press, 1987).

102. Curtis, *Bulgakov's Last Decade*, 196.

103. Bethea, "History as Hippodrome: The Apocalyptic Horse and Rider in *The Master and Margarita*," *Russian Review* 41 (October 1982): 393.

104. Barratt, *Between Two Worlds*, 174.

105. Proffer, *Bulgakov*, 637.

106. Barratt, *Between Two Worlds*, 178–83.

107. *The Master and Margarita*, trans. Burgin and O'Connor, 305.

108. It does not take more than a brief survey of the literature to convince the reader of the complexity of the figure of Woland. There is general agreement that he is the embodiment of retributive justice in the novel – the otherworldly agent who will set things right among men. Thus Milne characterizes him as "an agent of retribution" who "does not deal in compassion, only in retributive justice" (Milne, *Mikhail Bulgakov*, 242), a view corroborated by Ericson, who christens Woland "the minister of justice" whose "most significant role is that of meting out justice" (Ericson, *The Apocalyptic Vision*, 45). I myself, in an earlier article, identified Woland as the Satan of the Old Testament who performs his function in the divine hierarchy within certain circumscribed limits (although I now tend to think this view an oversimplification). His larger function was to represent the justice of the Old Testament, that is, the Law (see Laura D. Weeks, "Hebraic Antecedents

in *The Master and Margarita*: Woland and Company Revisited," *Slavic Review* 43, no. 3 [1984]: 224–41). The contradictions inherent in his character begin to arise when one considers that as a figure he is not particularly evil. He hands out punishment without any particular malice, and as an agent of justice he partakes equally of the demonic and the divine. Thus Haber refers to "this not at all vile Prince of Darkness" (Edythe C. Haber, "The Mythic Structure of Bulgakov's *The Master and Margarita*," *Russian Review* 34 [1985] 187), and Lakshin even calls him "this thoughtful humanist" (V. Lakshin, "M. Bulgakov's novel *The Master and Margarita*," 28). Yet another layer of complexity arises when one asks to what extent does Woland exercise his own will in punishing wrongdoers and to what extent does he act in accordance with a predetermined plan. Curtis remarks that he is "more of a prophet than an agent of destruction," and concludes that he is a go-between moving constantly between this plane and a higher reality, "a plenipotentiary ambassador from the supernatural realm" (Curtis, *Bulgakov's Last Decade*, 173–74). This line of argument reaches its apogee in Barratt's view of Woland as a gnostic messenger (see his article in this volume).

109. The strongest proponent of this view is George Krugovoy, *The Gnostic Novel of M. Bulgakov: Sources and Exegesis* (Lanham: University Press of America, 1991). See also Margot K. Frank, "The Mystery of the Master's Final Destination," *Canadian American Slavic Studies* 15 (1981): 287–94. Even Ericson concludes that "the contrast between the end of Woland and Company and that of the Master and Margarita, and also Pilate, should lay to rest any notion of Satan as a 'good guy' in this novel. Whatever good he has done has not been of his own will" (Ericson, *The Apocalyptic Vision*, 165).

110. *The Gospel of Thomas: The Hidden Sayings of Jesus*, ed. and trans. Marvin Meyer (San Francisco: HarperCollins, 1992), 12.

111. "Characteristically gnostic also is Bulgakov's implicit division of mankind into two classes on the basis of vision or understanding. The opposition of mundane and extra-mundane consciousness . . . has a counterpart in the gnostic distinction between 'sarkics' – men of mere flesh who are tied to this world – and 'pneumatics,' who have the capacity to receive the truth, conferred by gnosis, about their origin and destiny" (Andrew Barratt, "Apocalypse or Revelation? Man and History in Bulgakov's *Belaya gvardiya*," *New Zealand Slavonic Journal* [1985]: 127). Although this is Barratt's description of Bulgakov's worldview in *The White Guard*, it is clearly even more applicable to *The Master and Margarita.*

112. John P. Meier, *A Marginal Jew: Rethinking the Historical Jesus*, vol. 1 (New York: Doubleday, 1991), 126.

113. Bulgakov, *The Master and Margarita*, trans. Burgin and O'Connor, 321.

114. I. Galinskaia, "Albigoiskie assotsiatsii v *Mastere i Margarite* M. A. Bulgakova," *Izvestiia Akademii Nauk SSSR. Seriia literatury i iazyka* 44 (1985): 366–78.

115. Barratt, *Between Two Worlds*, 172.

116. T.R.N. Edwards, *Three Russian Writers and the Irrational: Zamiatin, Pil'nyak and Bulgakov* (Cambridge: Cambridge University Press, 1982); on Bulgakov, 137–80.

117. Gareth Williams, "Some Difficulties in the Interpretation of Bulgakov's *The Master and Margarita* and the Advantages of a Manichaean Approach, with Some Notes on Tolstoi's Influence on the Novel," *Slavic and East European Review*, 68, no. 2 (April 1990): 242.

118. Williams, "Some Difficulties in Interpretation," 243.

119. Bethea, *The Shape of Apocalypse*, 190.

120. Like the article by Bulgakov's father, this was published in the *Proceedings of the Kievan Ecclesiastical Academy* (see note 120 below); cited in Belza, "Genealogiia *Mastera i Margarity*," *Kontekst* (1978): 161–65.

121. Edythe C. Haber, "The Lamp with the Green Shade: Mikhail Bulgakov and His Father," *Transactions of the Association of Russian-American Scholars in the U. S. A.* 24 (1991): 215–16; originally published in *The Russian Review*, vol. 44, no. 4 (October 1985). His father's article was entitled "O prosveshchenii narodov" (On the enlightenment of peoples), published in the *Proceedings of the Kievan Ecclesiastical Academy*, no. 4 (1904).

122. Haber, "The Lamp with the Green Shade," 216.

123. Ibid., 222.

124. Milne, *The Master and Margarita: A Comedy of Victory*, 6–7.

125. Milne, *Mikhail Bulgakov*, 176.

126. Zerkalov found a near-perfect parallel of Berlioz's speech on pages 511 to 546 of this chrestomathy published in Moscow in 1930 (*Evangeliia Mikhaila Bulgakova* [Ann Arbor, Mich.: Ardis, 1984], 213; cited in Barratt, *Between Two Worlds*, 184).

127. Marietta Chudakova, "M. A. Bulgakov Chitatel," *Kniga. Issledovaniia i materialy* 40 (1980): 167.

128. Ibid.

129. Chudakova, *Zhizneopisanie* 297–99. See also Milne, *Mikhail Bulgakov*, 175, and Pittman, *The Writer's Divided Self*, 28–31.

130. Chudakova, *Zhizneopisanie*, 193.

131. See Oscar Cullman, *Christ and Time: The Primitive Christian Conception of Time and History*, trans. Floyd V. Filson (Philadelphia: Westminster, 1964), 178.

132. Cullman, *Christ and Time*, 189–90.

133. Schweitzer's monograph is entitled "The Quest of the Historical Jesus." As far as the person of Jesus, the Quest seems to have arrived at a rough consensus that he was not divine, but a man possessed of "perfect idealism" and enormous personal magnetism.

134. See Meyer, ed. and trans., *The Gospel of Thomas*. Both the Gospel of Thomas and the Source Q contain Jesus' sayings in supposedly unmediated form: they are not embedded in any narrative framework and contain virtually no references to the life of Jesus.

135. John Dominic Crossan, *The Historical Jesus: The Life of a Mediterranean Peasant* (San Francisco: HarperCollins, 1991), 421–22.

Key to the Map of Moscow
With Significant Locations from the Novel
prepared by A. F. Griniakin

No.	*Location*	*Chapter*
1.	Patriarchs' Ponds (where Berlioz and the poet Bezdomny meet Woland)	1
2.	Malaya Bronnaya Street	
3.	Spiridonovka Street	
4.	Nikita Gate	
5.	Herzen Street (formerly Bolshaya Nikitskaya)	4
6.	Arbat Square	(the chase)
7.	Kropotkin Street (formerly Prechistenka)	
8.	Ostozhenka Street	
9.	Boulevard Ring (Tverskoy and Suvorovsky) (where the Griboedov House is located)	5
10.	Skaterny Lane (where police try to arrest the poet)	5
11.	Sadovaya Street (where Apartment Building No. 302 and the Variety Theater are located)	7
12.	Kiev Railway Station (where Berlioz's uncle arrives in Moscow from Kiev)	18
13.	Aleksandrovsky Gardens (where Margarita meets Azazello)	19
14.	The Arbat (Margarita's flight)	21
15.	Smolensky Market (where the Torgsin Store is located)	28
16.	Pashkov House (where Woland and Company say farewell to Moscow)	29

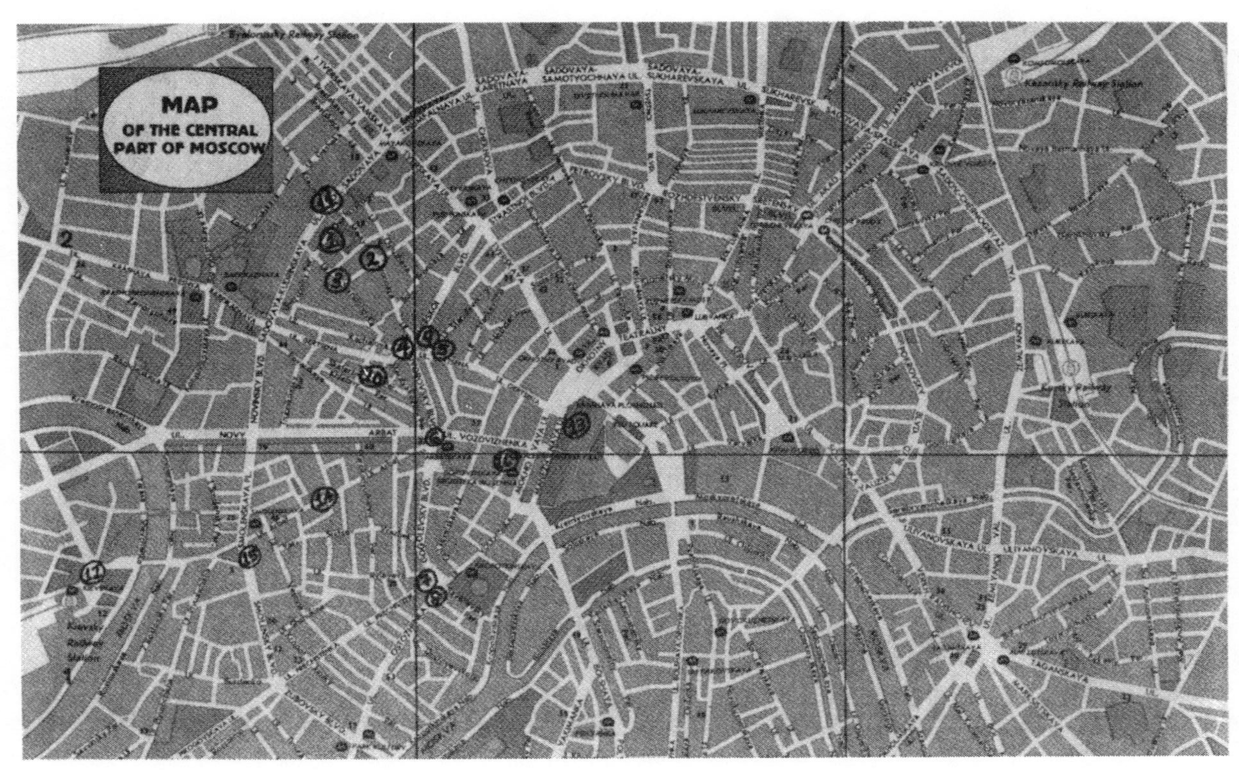
MAP
OF THE CENTRAL
PART OF MOSCOW
SADOVAYA-KARETNAYA
SADOVAYA-SAMOTYOCHNAYA UL.
SADOVAYA-SUKHAREVSKAYA UL.
NOVY
ARBAT
UL.
VOZDVIZHENKA
ZEMLYANOI VAL
ULYANOVSKAYA UL.
TAGANSKAYA
NOVINSKY B-VD
SMOLENSKAYA PL.
GOGOLEVSKY B-VD
PETROVSKY B-VD
ROZHDESTVENSKY B-VD
TEATRALNY
YAKIMANKA
Kazansky Railway Station
Kursky Railway Station
Kievsky Railway Station
1
2

II CRITICISM

M. Bulgakov's Novel *The Master and Margarita*

V. LAKSHIN

One strange and fantastic moonlit night, after the ball at Satan's, when Margarita is reunited with her lover by the power of magic charms, the omnipotent Woland asks the Master to show him his novel about Pontius Pilate. The Master is unable to do this, because he had burned his novel in the stove. "That cannot be," Woland objects. "Manuscripts don't burn." And that instant the cat stood up on his hind legs with a thick package of manuscripts and offered to Woland an exact copy of the destroyed book.

"Manuscripts don't burn." Mikhail Bulgakov died believing in the stubborn, indestructible power of art, when all his own major works lay unpublished in his desk drawer and reached the reader only a quarter of a century later, one at a time. "Manuscripts don't burn." These words served the author, as it were, as an incantation against the destructive work of time and against the solitary oblivion of his last and favorite work, his novel *The Master and Margarita.*

"Manuscripts don't burn." Now that it has been widely read and has led to many debates, interpretations, questions, and guesses, Bulgakov's book has begun to live its own life in literature. A sort of "Bulgakov fad" has even appeared, with all the extremes one sees in these crazes. Crowds of new worshippers of his talent come to evenings in his memory, and the issue of the magazine *Moskva* in which his novel was published is unavailable at any price. No doubt sensation played a role here, but it was also an important artistic success. The book caught the attention of many thoughtful readers. Prominent Soviet writers welcomed the novel's publication. Konstantin Simonov wrote an introduction to the novel. Translations of the book and comments on it have appeared in more than twenty nations: England, Hungary, the German Democratic Republic, Italy, Czechoslovakia, the United States, France, Norway, and so on.

The newspaper *Literaturnaia gazeta* and the magazines *Sibirskie ogni*, *Pod'em*, and others responded favorably to the appearance of the novel.

Only some professors of literature were noticeably disturbed. Bulgakov has still not found a place in their monographs and established textbooks on the literary process, any more than Esenin, Babel, or Tsvetaeva had slightly earlier. The more complex and uncommon the creativity of a writer, the greater the complaints and unpleasantness about him. They coolly undertook to explain to the reader that there are other names in our literature, people with more stable and solid reputations, so that Bulgakov, burdened with many contradictions and prejudices, was clearly inferior to them as an artist.

The worst way to study literature is to compare two talented writers and to reproach one of them with the merits of the other. Even without a survey of Bulgakov's work, nothing could be easier than to point to the one-sidedness of his talent, to the subjectivity of his social criteria and emotions, which noticeably narrowed his artistic horizon, and to his fondness for fantasy, mysticism, and so on. No doubt this is largely valid, but it leaves unexplained the strength of Bulgakov's talent and what he brought that was new to Russian Soviet literature.

In my attempt to comment on the novel, I wish to show what we find truly valuable and remarkable in the writer's legacy, and how so uncommon and complex a novel as *The Master and Margarita* can serve the living cause of our culture.

That the author freely combines the uncombinable – history and a newspaper column, lyric and myth, everyday life and fantasy – creates some difficulty in defining the book's genre. According to M. M. Bakhtin, attempts have already been made to call it Menippean. I will not argue the point. But it could with equal success be called a comic epic, a satirical Utopia, and something else again. Does this bring us any closer, however, to understanding the book itself?

Tolstoy was probably right in holding that significant art always creates its own forms that do not fit into the established hierarchy of genres. Bulgakov's book is yet another confirmation of this. For convenience of language it will do simply to call it a novel. But the free, vivid, and sometimes fantastic form incorporated all the resources of the author's thoughts, moods, and life experience at the time he wrote the book. Inasmuch as he wrote it over a long period and without hope of early publication, warming himself by the very process of writing and seeing the book as his testament, everything the author thought about and experienced was expressed in the novel with great completeness and sincerity. The novel was constructed in the way a snail builds his house, measuring it against himself and leaving no empty places. In *The Master and Margarita* Bulgakov found the form most adequate for his original talent, and thus many separate aspects of his other writings here seem to have merged into one.

The author was particularly concerned with accuracy in presenting the flavor of time and space. I am speaking above all about Bulgakov's Moscow, the Moscow of the thirties. In this novel Moscow, for Bulgakov, is not merely the locale, not merely a city like thousands of others, but his familiar, beloved, fully explored, and now native home. After celebrating the city of his childhood, Kiev, in *The White Guard* (*Belaia gvardiia*), Bulgakov offered poetic tribute to Moscow. He is generally so precise in urban topography that even now it seems one could easily find the very bench in the plaza "right at the crossing with the Bronnaia" where the two writers made their acquaintance with their mysterious consultant; or to follow Ivan over the entire route of his chase after the evil gang – from Patriarchs' Alley to Spiridonovka, then to Nikita's Gates, next to Arbat Square, to Kropotkin Street, and then via an alley to Ostozhenka . . . Moscow is the city that ties the Master to life.

The Master's beloved Moscow and Pontius Pilate's hated, barbarous Jerusalem seem to be unlike in every possible way. But one detail in Bulgakov's urban landscape artfully links the episodes so remote in space and time. All the major scenes of action, conversations, and pictures are accompanied in the novel by two silent witnesses, whose presence the author carefully notes. The light of the moon and sun that washes the pages of the book is not merely an effective illumination of the historical decorations but is somehow the scale of eternity, making it easier to create a bridge from the oppressively hot day of the fourteenth day of Nisan in Jerusalem two millennia ago to the four April days in Moscow during 193- – the two heavenly luminaries, alternately shedding their light on earth, almost become participants in the events, active forces in the novel.

The hot twilight sun over Patriarchs' Ponds, and the bright circle on which Pontius Pilate gazed with despair at the moment of announcing the verdict, the blazing sun over scorched Mt. Golgotha in Jerusalem . . . and the light of the moon, the full moon that splits into pieces for Berlioz, sliding along the streetcar tracks; the moon over the balcony of the Roman Procurator, and in the garden where Judas was knifed; and the moonlit road to the window of the hospital where Ivan Nikolaevich languished; and the endless bright ribbon of the finale along which Yeshua and Pontius Pilate walk in friendly conversation.

The sun – the customary symbol of life, joy, and genuine light – accompanies Yeshua along the Via Dolorosa as the emanation of hot and searing reality. In contrast, the moon is a fantastic world of shadows, enigmas, and illusiveness – the kingdom of Woland and his guests, feasting at the spring ball during the full moon – but it is also the cooling light of calm and sleep. Together, the luminaries of the day and night are the only certain witnesses of what happened no one knows when in Jerusalem and of what took place recently in Moscow. They mark the bonds of time, the unity of human history.

Outwardly it would appear that the chapters on Yeshua and Pontius Pilate, which break into the narration of contemporary events three times, live a distinct and independent life in the novel. In fact, we are prepared to accept them even in that quality, so vivid in their colors and so honest are these scenes, so great are the resources of new ideas and spiritual impressions they carry with them. If, however, we give more rigorous thought to the meaning of these "inserted chapters" in the overall structure of the novel, we begin to grasp their unity with the whole. A philosophical novel – and we are justified in calling *The Master and Margarita* just that – moves not so much by the interest of the action or the plot intrigue as by the development of the author's thoughts, which are supported by episodes outwardly distant from one another. Thus as we follow the duel between Pontius Pilate and the tramp philosopher Yeshua, and later witness the latter's terrible execution, we find ourselves in that circle of problems of good and evil, of the helplessness and power of human will that engaged the author in his story of Woland's Moscow adventures. Here, however, these problems are transferred from the plane of contemporary everyday to the level of the historical and legendary and are developed and complicated by new motifs and nuances of thought.

In these chapters we do not encounter Woland at all, and this cannot be an accident. The author seems to be saving his gloomy hero, lest the role of persecutor of all goodness weigh too heavily upon him.

Yet how tempting it is for a creative writer to present Pontius Pilate's cowardly treachery as Satan's inspiration – the more so because Woland himself affirms definitely that he was present on the Procurator's balcony and in the garden when he and Caiaphas conversed.

Bulgakov tempts the reader's imagination with but a single detail dropped in passing. Awaiting at twilight news of the burial of Yeshua, the Procurator suddenly begins to experience inexplicable fear and for some reason shivers as he glances at an empty armchair on the back of which hangs his cloak: "The night of the holiday was approaching, the evening shadows were playing their game, and the fatigued Procurator probably imagined that someone was sitting in the empty armchair."

Except for this transient detail, which was, in any case, so justified psychologically as to lack any hint of mysticism, we find no trace of Woland's presence in the chapters about Yeshua. Once again this confirms Bulgakov's good intentions toward Woland, which had amazed us from the outset. If Yeshua embodied the idea of good, it must be granted that Woland conducts himself toward his eternal antagonist with rare respect and, I would even say, friendliness. For it is he, the Devil, who attempts to persuade Berlioz that Yeshua actually did exist and it is he who begins to recount the legend, the continuation of which we recognize from the Master's saved notebooks.

However, Woland's absence from the chapters devoted to Yeshua, which is itself noteworthy, is important in yet another sense: Bulgakov cannot permit Pontius Pilate the false justification for behaving contemptibly not on his own volition but as if a demon had nudged him along. He leaves the Procurator face to face with Yeshua, presenting the moral account only to his human conscience and depriving him of all defense before the court of time.

Bulgakov regards Pontius Pilate, on whom moral judgment has, as it were, been pronounced beforehand, as an internally complex and, in his way, dramatic figure. He is no stranger to meditation, human feelings, lively sympathy. He clearly does not wish to destroy Yeshua's life for nothing. The wandering philosopher, with his bold speeches, unfamiliar to the Procurator's ear, attracts and interests him. It is after all interesting to gaze at a man who is free from the internal prohibitions and taboos that always weigh so heavily upon us, who fearlessly and simply says right out loud what usually freezes the soul. Pilate is prepared to hide the other in his own place at Strato's Caesarea, to save him from his compatriots' fanaticism, and to make him something on the order of his house philosopher.

One must admit that this brave soldier, intelligent politician, and man possessed of inconceivable power in conquered Jerusalem has a streak of shameful cravenness. First he displays cowardice before the thought of Caesar; he is afraid of informers, fears he will destroy his career, and then, without being aware of his own emotions, becomes timid in the face of Yeshua, vacillates, becomes confused, wanting but not deciding to save him. After Yeshua has already hopelessly compromised himself with his dangerous attack against the power of the Caesars, Pontius Pilate makes a final attempt to help him and, rising above his own weakness, tries to persuade Caiaphas to have mercy on the harmless dreamer. But religious fanaticism is even more terrible and unbending than the fanaticism of civil power, and the Procurator yields to the High Priest. Knowing he is committing a terrible crime against conscience, he consents to the execution of Yeshua.

This cowardice ranks with treachery, because he sympathized with the unlucky wanderer. And even when everything had ended, and lightning had wiped away the traces of the terrible execution on Mount Golgotha, the author does not release Pilate from the pincers of psychological analysis and extends to infinity this torture of the conscience.

Cowardice is Pontius Pilate's principal misfortune. But is it really possible that a soldier, fearless on the field of battle, a knight of the Golden Spear, was actually a coward? And why does Bulgakov insist so strongly on this accusation? In a dream, Pilate hears Yeshua say: "Cowardice is certainly one of the most terrible of faults." But the author himself unexpectedly intervenes and responds in full voice: "No, philosopher, I refute that: it is the most terrible of faults!" Why did Bulgakov's usual restraint betray him here and compel him, in violation of the convention of narration, to utter a personal condemnation of his character?

The Procurator did not wish harm to Yeshua; cowardice brought him to cruelty and treachery. Yeshua cannot condemn him; to him all men are good. But Bulgakov condemns without mercy or indulgence, condemns because he knows that people who set out to do evil are not so dangerous – there really are not so many such people – as those who are supposedly prepared to help good along but are craven and cowardly. Fear for themselves transforms people – who are not bad and who are physically brave – into the blind tools of evil wills.

This is a paradox of which art has often taken note: a courageous warrior, a hero on the field of battle, is at times weak and pitiful in everyday life, timid and lost as soon as someone raises a voice against him. The point is that in military conflict the warrior does not stand alone; he enjoys the righteousness of common enthusiasm, the supporting hands of his comrades. As the proverb has it: "Together, even death is beautiful." But to be brave alone, to defend one's rights, sustained only by one's own sense of justice, this is something only a person with true strength of spirit and high self-awareness can achieve. Unconscious bravery will not withstand this test.

Cowardice is the extreme expression of an internal sense of submission, an imprisonment of the soul; once one has made one's peace with such lack of courage, it is difficult to free oneself of it. It continues to subject a man to itself even on the threshold of death, when that seems particularly absurd. What was there to stop Pontius Pilate from freely taking that road, from listening to the voice of conscience? The Procurator is quite seriously ill, thinks with longing of a poison that would end his suffering, is ready to close the book on his earthly life; but he is still pitifully frightened in the face of Caesar and out of inertia accepts Ceasar's will above his own.

Thus it is not evil, which of itself is blind and not very powerful, but cowardice that readily subjects a man to evil and makes him a spineless tool in the hands of others – this, in Bulgakov's eyes, is the most severe curse. It is capable of making a man of wisdom, boldness, and goodwill into a pitiful rag; it weakens and defames him. The only thing that can save him is internal staunchness, confidence in his own reason, and the voice of his own conscience.

The crowd of the curious has long since dispersed. The soldiers are exhausted from the heat and boredom. The sun has begun to set behind Golgotha, and Yeshua, who believed so unreasonably in the good, is living out his last minutes on the post where he is spread-eagled and roasted by the sun. With his head in its unwound turban hanging helplessly to one side, tortured by horseflies, he who is dying is not an omnipotent god who will be resurrected in the morning, but a mortal man of no power who has walked the last mile for his convictions, who has accepted the torture of crucifixion for them, and who has thereby given them unconquerable power. The meaning of the image rises and grows constantly in its significance, and behind that shameful execution in Jerusalem we see in the haze of two millennia Giordano Bruno in the flames, Joan of Arc executed, and the five shadows of those hung from the battlements of Petropavlovskaia Fortress: the long line of sacrifices contributed by mankind on its path to justice and truth as ransom for their slow and difficult recognition. These people wanted to remain true to themselves and their ideals, which to their contemporaries appeared too new, bold, or dangerous, and they had to pay for it with their lives, but thereby assured their cause immortal glory.

This is why Yeshua, for all his helplessness, is so powerful and unconquerable. This is why only the memory of him, done to death and forgotten, makes the all-powerful Procurator shake and forever chains him to his "conscience beaten black and blue." No, the author sees in him not merely a religious preacher and reformer. In Bulgakov's hands, the image of Yeshua embodies free spiritual activity in general.

The poet-prophet, held in contempt, insulted, persecuted, uncomprehended, stoned, is an old theme in poetry, which has yielded unfading lines in the lyrics of Pushkin and Lermontov:

> Desert sower of freedom
> I started early, before the stars . . . [1]

In Yeshua, Bulgakov sees just such a prophet, one who went out "before the stars" and whose preaching was ahead of his time.

This is how the problem of spiritual power, as compared to the authority of prejudice and the power of strength, essentially covering the same problem that occupied Bulgakov in his biography of Molière and his play about the last days of Pushkin, appears in the perspective of time.

Today, looking back from the 1950s, we recognize better than ever before that communism not only does not disdain morality but that morality is a necessary condition for communism's final victory, inasmuch as the matter at issue is the triumph of new principles in the minds of every individual making up our society. Social morality is inseparable from personal morality. Social justice itself is, in the final analysis, nothing but a sense of personal justice, a moral ideal, transferred to the scale of an entire society.

This is why Bulgakov's novel, written in the 1930s, proved to be remarkably pertinent to the literature of the 1960s, when the attention to social problems that was typical of our writers began to be accompanied by a particularly sharp interest in the question of moral choice and personal morality.

Of course, Bulgakov's novel bears the distinctive imprint of its time and his personal destiny. The book's artistic philosophy reflected both the author's literary adversities and his doleful thoughts before death. The writer believed that justice would certainly triumph with respect to himself and his work, among other things. He knew that, sooner or later, genuine art has always won recognition. Sooner or later . . . But everyone wants this to happen sooner, and certainly during one's lifetime. If the strain of waiting for tomorrow becomes too great, if faith represses the living reality of the present, an involuntary vexation with life emerges, a sense of the vanity of one's work, apathy, emptiness.

In order to drive away these feelings, which weaken the will to create, Bulgakov hurries time and hastens justice, which for once is required to triumph immediately, if only in his poetic fantasy.

Thus in Russian folktales consolation came by miraculous means, and even when the plot did not promise a happy ending, the tale turned out inexplicably well, rewarding good adequately and punishing evil. This was not mere desire to lull, to calm those for whom the tale had appeal: also present was that unchanging faith in the ultimate triumph of justice which always dwelled in the people.

Let this not sound grandiloquent, because it is the simple truth. We have here a victory of art over dust, over terror at inevitable death, over the very temporality and brevity of human existence. The victory is, in a way, illusory, but it is infinitely important and soothing to the soul.

No less dear, however, is another result: the destiny of the novel, forecast in the book. "Your novel still has surprises in store for you," Woland promises the Master, saying farewell to him after the magical ball. For us readers these words apply to the novel *The Master and Margarita.*

The poetic force of the influence of *The Master and Margarita* on its readers today further strengthens the prophecy made a quarter of a century ago. Life has written a novel about this novel. It has given the book a new fate and thereby has made the idea of justice even more irrefutable in Bulgakov's writings, an idea he believed in so firmly and that he so treasured.

NOTES

This is a condensed version of an essay first published in *Novyi Mir*, no. 6 (1968), and translated in *Soviet Studies in Literature*, vol. 1, no. 1 (Winter 1968–69): 3–65.

1. From Pushkin's short lyric poem of 1823.

The Master and Margarita in Recent Criticism: An Overview

ANDREW BARRATT

To say that Russian cultural life has undergone a series of spectacular changes is to risk the charge of understatement. The publication of such previously banned works as Pasternak's *Doctor Zhivago* and Zamyatin's *We*, the belated discovery of the Russian emigré and Western modernist traditions, the return of Alexander Solzhenitsyn – such events amount to an astonishing reversal, the full implications of which are only slowly becoming apparent. Viewed against this larger context, developments in Bulgakov studies will inevitably appear rather modest. Nevertheless, there are significant highlights to report. First and foremost (and most exciting for the Russian reader), the period since 1987 has witnessed the publication of important works like *The Heart of a Dog* and *Adam and Eve*, which had stood beyond the pale even during the most liberal eras of post-Stalinist cultural policy. The archives are gradually yielding their treasures in the form of previously unpublished letters, memoirs, and diaries. And new scholarly works are beginning to appear, most notably Marietta Chudakova's highly acclaimed *Biography of Mikhail Bulgakov*, a remarkable blend of scholarship and oral history that has already acquired the status of an essential text. As for *The Master and Margarita* itself, the appearance of the first scholarly edition and the gradual publication of the voluminous draft versions of the novel have added considerably to our knowledge. One can only look forward with eager anticipation to the eventual publication of a definitive complete work in which all the relevant material relating to the novel will be combined in a readily accessible form.

It is impossible to predict what effect this gradual accumulation of new scholarship will have on the interpretation of Bulgakov's last novel. But at present it seems reasonable to suppose that post-*glasnost* criticism will not diverge greatly from the lines of enquiry already firmly established. This is not to say, however, that no signs of new directions have appeared, both inside Russia and without. Most encouraging on the Russian scene has been the publication of important work by Western critics (mostly Russians, like Gasparov[1] and Zerkalov[2]) and the growing acknowledgment of the huge international body of literature concerning the novel. As far as English-language criticism is concerned, the novel has enjoyed a positive boom, with the publication of no fewer than three new books and a number of major articles. I will discuss these new works under three broad headings.

The Novel as Theology

The central presence within *The Master and Margarita* of Jesus and the Devil in the transfigured forms of Yeshua and Woland has long attracted the interest of critics. Who is Yeshua? In what relationship does he stand to the Jesus of Christian thought? Who is Woland? Do his actions make sense in terms of any conventional conceptions of the demonic or is he to be seen as an essentially benevolent figure, a Satan with a heart of gold? Is there a consistent vision of divine providence at work in the novel? Such questions have exercised the imagination of Bulgakov's readers from the moment of its first publication. But in two recent full-length studies, by George Krugovoy and Edward Ericson, Jr., they receive their most detailed treatment yet.

Krugovoy and Ericson proceed from the same basic critical assumption, namely, that the many difficulties of interpretation raised by *The Master and Margarita* can be resolved by recourse to a thoroughgoing theological reading. Thus Krugovoy describes the novel as an example of "*gnosis*, laboriously encoded in the complex structural texture of the novel,"[3] whereas Ericson writes: "No one can miss the almost ubiquitous biblical and religious allusions. The challenge is to find the pattern of meaning underlying Bulgakov's use of them."[4] But although each critic embarks on the same hermeneutic task of "decoding" the novel's religious message, their findings could hardly be more different.

Krugovoy's study represents a radical challenge to what might be called the critical mainstream in English-language Bulgakov criticism. It can also lay claim to being the most ingenious sustained reading of *The Master and Margarita* in any language. Like many other critics (myself included), Krugovoy begins by raising the question, "Who is Woland?" His answer, however, is quite different from that found in most studies of the novel. Against those who have argued that Woland is a curiously ambiguous creation, a "devil" who appears in the guise both of scourge and benefactor to the human beings he encounters in Moscow, Krugovoy states that such ambiguity is merely a trap set by the devil himself. In his view, Woland, like Milton's Satan, is a fallen angel, and as such "the principal rival and antagonist of God."[5] As for his purpose in coming to Moscow, it is in every case the same: to tempt the weak and seduce the righteous. And his particular mission, so this argument goes, is to capture the souls of the Master and Margarita.

Whereas others have viewed the novel's hero and heroine as the principal beneficiaries of a "kind-hearted devil," Krugovoy sees them as dupes of his malevolent scheme. In the Master's case, the story goes like this: Woland tempts the hero by having him win 100,000 rubles in the state lottery. But rather than put the money to the pursuit of worldly pleasures, the Master puts his good fortune to the godly task of writing his novel about Yeshua and Pilate. This incenses Woland, who wreaks vengeance on the writer through the medium of the Soviet literary establishment, thereby inducing him to destroy the novel and take refuge in Stravinsky's clinic, an act that is identified explicitly with the renunciation of his artistic calling. This task completed, Woland turns his malevolent attention to Margarita. Tempting her with the promise of the Master's return, he has her transformed into a witch who sells her soul to the devil through her participation in the Black Mass at Satan's Ball. For Krugovoy, the final mark of the hero's and heroine's capitulation to the evil force is the utterly mundane reward they ask of Woland after they are miraculously reunited, which is simply to be returned to the Master's cozy basement apartment. It is from this dire condition that the hero and heroine are finally rescued *against Woland's will* – this is the nub – through the divine intercession of Yeshua.

Questions of providence and theodicy also stand at the center of Ericson's study, yet the divine scheme he discerns is of an entirely different order from Krugovoy's. This is nowhere more obvious than in his discussion of Woland. Whereas Krugovoy finds signs of Woland's insidious intent everywhere, Ericson says of Bulgakov's devil that he has "little, if anything" of the tempter about him.[6] And instead of seeing Woland and Yeshua as antagonists, he suggests they be viewed as the dual executors of God's will: "As Yeshua is God's minister of love, so Woland is God's minister of justice."[7] The most intriguing part of his argument, however, concerns the status of the Master's novel within the novel. In Ericson's opinion (again in complete contrast to that of Krugovoy), this text is the result of the devil's work. Inspired by Woland's promptings, the Yershalaim narrative is severely deficient, presenting a picture of Yeshua that is false insofar as it is incomplete. As Ericson puts it: "The Master's depiction gives us only the humanity of Jesus, not his divinity."[8] And it is this very divinity, he goes on to argue, that the reader (and the Master) is finally permitted to behold at the end of the novel, when Yeshua plays his crucial part in the "absolution" of the Master and Margarita.

In short, then, Krugovoy and Ericson have written studies of *The Master and Margarita* that are detailed and scholarly, and that seek to fix the novel's meaning through the use of an intricate interpretative strategy that combines close attention to the text with an appeal to external systems of thought. Each offers a clear and unambiguous version of the novel's theology. Krugovoy, in particular, displays a fierce determination to dispute the suggestion that the novel draws on a Manichaean conception of evil according to which Yeshua and Woland stand in a relationship of "co-equality."[9] And each study contains many pages that repay careful reading, such as Ericson's third chapter on the Eastern Christian tradition and Krugovoy's discussion of the Master's final refuge and its nature.[10]

Needless to say, however, the findings of both critics are open to challenge in a number of ways. Krugovoy's decision to support his thesis by recourse to numerological theories that assign magical significance to all the numbers used in the novel is likely to be regarded with skepticism by many. (Despite the prevalence of such theorizing in his study, it is not essential to the interpretation advanced in it.) Rather more serious, his reading of Satan's Ball as a pure example of a diabolical black mass means that he has to sweep some inconvenient problems under the carpet. Krugovoy's explanation of why Margarita is not required to have sex with Satan is particularly suspect in this regard. (The contrast with Ericson is again instructive: in his study, Satan's Ball is viewed as a paradoxical event that is simultaneously a diabolical parody of the Christian Eucharist and yet also a true *celebration* of that religious ceremony.[11]) One wonders also what Krugovoy would make of recent evidence to suggest that Bulgakov repeatedly insisted that his Woland had no prototype.[12]

Taken together, the works of Krugovoy and Ericson represent a resurgence of a monistic style of interpretation that has become increasingly unfashionable over the years. In marked contrast to a critic like David Bethea, who has argued that "there is no single interpretation, no single blade capable of severing the Gordian knot of *The Master and Margarita*,"[13] Krugovoy and Ericson insist that a single "key" does exist that will unlock all the novel's secrets. But the quest for such a key means inevitably that the critic must explain away the ironies, ambiguities, and paradoxes that are generated at every turn by this most complex novel. Take Woland, for example. Krugovoy's reading is most interesting here, for he argues that very little Bulgakov's devil says should be taken at face value. And this leads the critic to some of his most controversial claims. Whereas most commentators have accepted Woland's now famous utterances – "Manuscripts don't burn!"; "Every man will be given according to his belief"; "What would your good be doing if there were no evil and what would the world look like if shadows disappeared from it?" – as unambiguous statements of Bulgakov's own views, Krugovoy suggests that in each case Woland's real meaning is quite different and that these are actually false messages to the reader. On other occasions, however, Krugovoy is prepared to read Woland's remarks quite literally. The devil's angry reaction to Margarita's display of mercy toward Frieda is a case in point and one that is especially intriguing given that many critics have suspected that Woland actually *is* playacting in this instance. My point is not to suggest who is right or wrong here, but merely to show that to read this novel is to choose between alternative interpretative positions that may be equally plausible. Woland is a devious character, to be sure; to fix his intentions must always remain a provisional and speculative business.

The same is true of another important matter; the Master's novel about Yeshua and Pontius Pilate. What exactly is the status of this text? As we have seen, Ericson argues that it has been inspired by the devil and thus provides a false perspective on the nature of Yeshua. In so doing, he dismisses the widely held view that the novel is a mysterious intuition of a truth that has been distorted in the Christian record. He also specifically disputes the findings of Laura Weeks, who has put the case for *Ivan Bezdomny* as the author of the text. Once again, none of these readings is totally implausible (Ericson actually says as much of Weeks's proposal) and each requires an act of deduction on the part of the critic; the mistake is to believe that only one of them is correct. To borrow one of Ericson's favorite metaphors, *The Master and Margarita* might be usefully considered a kaleidoscope that has the capacity to generate a multitude of patterns: it depends entirely on the beholder how many of those patterns one decides to observe.

Schizophrenia and Apocalypse

If the works of Krugovoy and Ericson are recognizably (even somewhat defiantly) monistic in their approach to *The Master and Margarita*, two other recent books take a different line, proposing models for understanding the novel while accepting the limits of any such interpretative enterprise.

Riitta Pittman's study views the novel in terms of the disorder that afflicts Ivan Bezdomny – schizophrenia. Drawing on the psychological theories of C. G. Jung, she develops the idea that schizophrenia can be used as a metaphor to illuminate the condition of all the main human actors in the novel. As she explains: "The novel embraces a multiplicity of split personalities, or 'cripples,' who as a result of the devil's appearance in Moscow are made 'whole,' as they are brought to view life in its true, multilateral perspective."[14] As these words suggest, Pittman is less interested in Woland's diabolical form and his place in the divine scheme than in his *textual* function as a "Jungian agent of the unconscious who performs the task of 'informing' the characters of 'things' lodged in the psychic depths which lie beyond reason."[15] As for the major characters themselves, Pittman treats them as pairs, with each partner being viewed as the *shadow* (another Jungian term) of the other. The Master and Ivan Bezdomny constitute one such pair, the two men representing "different regions of creative experience" and their "symbiotic partnership" being the means by which Bulgakov articulates his "deeply personal conception of the artist's predicament in a Philistine society."[16] The same model is also applied to Yeshua and Pilate, so that the former is revealed as the "inadmissible 'shadow' or 'inner voice' of Pilate's consciousness."[17]

Pittman's approach to the novel functions as a powerful and flexible tool. In particular, it enables her to work interesting variations on the long-established critical practice of exploring structural parallels. For example, in her discussion of Ivan Bezdomny and the Master, she notes that both are authors of literary works about the historical Jesus and both "suffer because they have failed to stand up for the truth, as they know it. Both have given in to the critics of Jesus/Yeshua."[18] And she also shows how such a procedure can allow us to phrase the questions we need to ask of the novel. Comparing Pilate's celebrated act of cowardice to the Master's behavior, she writes: "The Master's predicament raises a number of moral questions: Is the Master's attempt to burn his manuscript justifiable? Is his failure to defend the story in face of adverse criticism tantamount to a betrayal of the truth? Is the Master guilty of cowardice?"[19]

The most original part of Pittman's study concerns the novel's final scenes. Unlike Krugovoy, Ericson, and the many other critics who have concentrated on the many problems raised by the various "rewards" that await Pilate, the Master, and Margarita, Pittman focuses instead on the relationship between the Master and his "disciple," Ivan Bezdomny. Juxtaposing their two stories as they are depicted in the novel's conclusion, she suggests that each may be understood in terms of a release from the burden of *memory*.[20] As she goes on to point out, this reading places Bulgakov's novel within an entire tradition of writing about the Stalin age that turns on this same central metaphor. When read in conjunction with an influential article by Carol Avins, Pittman's remarks suggest that further work along these lines might prove most rewarding.

The Russian narrative tradition looms even larger in David Bethea's acclaimed book *The Shape of Apocalypse in Russian Fiction*. Indeed, it is a most ambitious and wide-ranging study in historical poetics. As its title announces, it is the Book of Apocalypse which supplies the model that Bethea applies to a number of key modern texts – Dostoevsky's *Idiot*, Bely's *Petersburg*, Platonov's *Chevengur*, Bulgakov's *The Master and Margarita*, and Pasternak's *Doctor Zhivago*. Unlike Ericson, who seeks to use the same biblical text as a means of "decoding" Bulgakov's novel, Bethea approaches *The Master and*

Margarita as an example of "apocalyptic fiction," which he considers a major subgenre of the modern Russian novel. He defines such fictions as "a kind of sacred text or version of *the Book* through which the characters and the narrator and, by implication, the reader – all in their separate, self-enclosed realms – are made privy to 'secret wisdom' from another space-time."[21]

Bethea's is a highly sophisticated work that both requires and rewards the patient attention of the serious scholar. I shall not attempt to summarize either his broad argument or his specific reading of *The Master and Margarita* (part of which is included in this volume). It will suffice here simply to indicate the main focus of his study, which is to suggest that Bulgakov's is just one of a series of modern Russian novels that both confronts and articulates a central historiological problem of the age. This problem can be described in terms of the relationship between "history" (the events of the world as they are manifested in the here and now of everyday experience) and "History," understood either in the Marxist sense of those unseen forces that determine the course of events or in the religious sense of a transcendent destiny that lies beyond the mundane sphere.[22] In Bethea's view, *The Master and Margarita* stands as a supreme example of the latter conception and, as such, presents a powerful countermodel to the Marxist view as articulated in novels of socialist realism.

Some similar issues are addressed on a smaller scale by Laura Weeks. In an article devoted to the figure of Ivan Bezdomny, she pays particular attention to the significance of that character's final occupation as a historian. Weeks notices many interesting details: that Woland too refers to himself as a historian, that the very word *history* (*istoriia*) – the term has many more meanings in Russian than its English equivalent – is constantly repeated on the pages of the novel. Like Pittman, Weeks uses her approach to great effect in her interpretation of the novel's epilogue. Where Pittman talks of Ivan Bezdomny in terms of the burden of memory, Weeks perceives his situation as that of a man " 'stranded' at the intersection of History and history."[23] This serves as the starting point for the argument, already mentioned above, that the entire novel (that is, the novel we know as *The Master and Margarita*) is the work of the former hack poet, who "retreats from history to become the chronicler of History."[24]

New Directions

Although each of the studies discussed above yields important insights into *The Master and Margarita* and the critical problems associated with its interpretation, none of them represents a truly new direction in the study of the novel. In this final section, I shall deal briefly with three studies that might be said to point the way toward new kinds of reading.

The first is an article by Judith Mills which is, to my knowledge, the first full-blooded attempt at a psychoanalytical interpretation of *The Master and Margarita*. The starting point for this reading is an interesting variation on the problem of the text's provenance. Mills suggests that from the very moment Woland materializes in the park at Patriarchs' Ponds, the entire sequence of events can be seen as a dream or hallucination experienced by Ivan Bezdomny: "Ivan may be dreaming continually, his waking in itself part of the dream proper."[25] (Note that Pittman too considers this possibility.[26]) The stimulus for the dream, so Mills's argument proceeds, is the failure of Ivan's poem to meet with Berlioz's approval.[27] As a result, the entire novel becomes a metaphor of Ivan's own story, "the tale of how he comes to deal with creativity, solves the problem of coping with Stalinist society, reconciles himself to reality . . . and then works out a self-justification for his accommodation."[28] I doubt that many critics will be prepared to follow this reading to its conclusion, which suggests that "*The Master and Margarita* could be read as Bulgakov's tribute to Stalin as the significant creative irrational force that could change Russia's and perhaps even humanity's vision of reality."[29] Yet there is much food for thought here. It should not be forgotten that Ivan Bezdomny was a nom de plume Bulgakov himself used during his early years.[30] Could it not be that Ivan (and not the Master) is the *real* "autobiographical" hero of the novel? (Just consider the fact, often pointed out by critics, that Ivan appears in more chapters of the novel than any other character.) Moreover, Mills's view of the Master and Woland as twin projections of Ivan's troubled psyche is echoed in other critics' findings. (Lesley Milne, for example, suggests that "where Woland is an authorial mask, the Master is an authorial double."[31]) Clearly we have come a long way from the naive autobiographical readings that tended simply to identify (and sometimes even confuse) the Master with his creator.

If Mills attempts to explicate *The Master and Margarita* through the application of psychoanalytic methods, our two final writers seek to place the novel against larger contexts. Neil Cornwell discusses Bulgakov's work in his comparative study of the literary fantastic. Drawing on Tzvetan Todorov's highly influential definition of the fantastic as a mode that obliges the reader to *hesitate* between competing explanations of events (to take an example from Bulgakov, is Woland really the devil, or is he Ivan's hallucination?), Cornwell constantly draws attention to those awkward moments of "hesitation" to which we have already referred. Who, he wonders, is the real author of the text: "If we are looking for a hidden author or narrator, one who is present on all levels with a knowledge of all events – who has greater omniscience than Woland?"[32] And of the Yershalaim narrative he raises the equally thorny question: "Is it all one novel, the Master's novel?"[33] These are hardly new issues, of course. But what *is* new here is Cornwell's acceptance of such "undecidability" as the defining feature of the novel. The same is true of Brian McHale's recent study, which contains some fleeting, yet provocative comments on *The Master and Margarita* against the background of postmodernism. Defining the postmodern condition as one that foregrounds "ontological instability or indeterminacy, the *loss* of a world that could be accepted, 'willy-nilly,' as given of experience,"[34] he associates Bulgakov's novel with that particular strand of postmodernist writing that depicts "an anarchic landscape of worlds in plural."[35] *The Master and Margarita* as an example of the "postmodern fantastic"? Clearly there is still plenty of room for more work, all the more so as both McHale and Cornwell suggest interesting new possibilities for comparative study. (Note, in particular, Cornwell's discussion of John Banville's *Mefisto* and Salman Rushdie's *Satanic Verses*.[36])

The work of Cornwell and McHale suggests that, as Woland says of the Master's novel, Bulgakov criticism may have some surprises in store for us yet. But what of the present? Are there any conclusions to be drawn about scholarship on *The Master and Margarita* today? I think there are. Despite the continuing arguments about all manner of things, large and small, a number of trends are clear. Above all, it is apparent that the current emphasis is very much on *The Master and Margarita* as a *metaphysical* novel that depicts the mundane sphere (be it contemporary Moscow or ancient Jerusalem) as an imperfect place where cruelty and cowardice reign, while offering the vision of a transcendent realm where the spirit of mercy will prevail. This has had a marked impact, in particular, on discussion of the Master. Whereas earlier work on the novel tended to treat him as a suffering hero, the victim of Stalinist literary politics, most recent critics have tended to dwell more on his all-too-human failings.

Equally striking is the continuing tendency among critics to relate Bulgakov's novel to the intellectual tradition of Russia's religious revival of the early twentieth century. Pittman associates Bulgakov's concerns with the issues raised in the famous *Landmarks* collection,[37] whereas Krugovoy, Bethea,[38] and Milne emphasize the importance of Pavel Florensky as an influence on Bulgakov's thought.[39] There is also widespread agreement on the value of comparing *The Master and Margarita* to Pasternak's *Doctor Zhivago* as examples of the post-Symbolist novel.[40] As Milne puts it: "In their novels the two writers stand firmly together, expressing shared cultural assumptions: the significance in European art and literature of the Christian idea and the validity of the ethical paradigm therein enshrined, in the face of an epoch which systematically negated these paradigms in word and deed."[41] Bethea has recently suggested a further dimension to this discussion in his essay on Bulgakov and Nabokov as post-Symbolist writers.[42]

As for the future, we can only wait and see what it will hold. Of two things, however, one can be confident: the status of *The Master and Margarita* as a key text of Russia's modern age is assured and the critical arguments about it are likely to continue for a long time to come.

NOTES

1. Boris Gasparov, "Iz nabliudenii nad motivnoi struktury romana M. A. Bulgakova *Master i Margarita*," *Slavica Hierosolymitana* 3 (1978): 198–251.

2. A. Zerkalov, *Evangelie Mikhaila Bulgakova* (Ann Arbor, Mich.: Ardis, 1984).

3. George Krugovoy, *The Gnostic Novel of Mikhail Bulgakov: Sources and Exegesis* (Lanham: University Press of America, 1991), 292.

4. Edward E. Ericson, Jr., *The Apocalyptic Vision of Mikhail Bulgakov's The Master and Margarita* (Lewiston: Edwin Mellen, 1991), 3.

5. Krugovoy, *The Gnostic Novel*, 16.

6. Ericson, *The Apocalyptic Vision*, 18.

7. Ibid., 63.

8. Ibid., 23.

9. Krugovoy, *The Gnostic Novel*, 212. For a spirited recent argument in *favor* of a Manichaean reading of the novel, see Gareth Williams, "Some Difficulties in the Interpretation of Bulgakov's *The Master and Margarita* and the Advantages of a Manichaean Approach, with Some Notes on Tolstoi's Influence on the Novel," *Slavonic and East European Review* 68 (1990): 234–56.

10. Krugovoy, *The Gnostic Novel*, 234–44.

11. Ericson, *The Apocalyptic Vision*, 121.

12. M. O. Chudakova, *Zhizneopisanie Mikhaila Bulgakova* (Moscow: Kniga, 1988), 462.

13. David M. Bethea, *The Shape of Apocalypse in Modern Russian Fiction* (Princeton, N.J.: Princeton University Press, 1989).

14. Riitta H. Pittman, *The Writer's Divided Self in Bulgakov's "The Master and Margarita"* (New York: St. Martin's, 1991), 17.

15. Ibid., 51.

16. Ibid., 115.

17. Ibid., 151.

18. Ibid., 111.

19. Ibid., 162.

20. Ibid., 113.

21. Bethea, *The Shape of Apocalypse*, 33.

22. Ibid., 119.

23. Laura D. Weeks, "In Defense of the Homeless: On the Uses of History and the Role of Bezdomnyi in *The Master and Margarita*," *The Russian Review* 48 (1989): 45–65, particularly 55.

24. Ibid., 60.

25. Judith M. Mills, "Of Dreams, Devils, Irrationality and *The Master and Margarita*," *Russian Literature and Psychoanalysis*, ed. Daniel Rancour-Laferriere (Philadelphia: John Benjamins, 1989), 304.

26. Pittman, *The Writer's Divided Self*, 52–54.

27. Mills, "Of Dreams, Devils, Irrationality," 307.

28. Ibid., 306.

29. Ibid., 321.

30. Pittman, *The Writer's Divided Self*, 99.

31. Lesley Milne, *Mikhail Bulgakov: A Critical Biography* (Cambridge: Cambridge University Press, 1990).

32. Neil Cornwell, *The Literary Fantastic: From Gothic to Postmodern* (New York: Harvester, 1990).

33. Ibid., 169.

34. Brian McHale, *Postmodernist Fiction* (New York: Methuen, 1987), 26.

35. Ibid., 43.

36. Cornwell, *The Literary Fantastic*, 179–97.

37. Pittman, *The Writer's Divided Self*, 8–26.

38. See, especially, David M. Bethea, "Bulgakov and Nabokov: Toward a Comparative Perspective," *Transactions of the Association of Russian-American Scholars in the USA* 24 (1991): 187–209.

39. The interested reader will find a fairly detailed account of Florensky's ideas in Katerina Clark and Michael Holquist, *Mikhail Bakhtin* (Cambridge, Mass.: Harvard University Press, 1984), 120–45.

40. Carol Avins, "Reaching a Reader: The Master's Audience in *The Master and Margarita*," *Slavic Review* 45 (1986): 272–85; Milne, *Mikhail Bulgakov*, 230 ff.; Pittman, *The Writer's Divided Self*; and Bethea, *The Shape of Apocalypse*.

41. Milne, *Mikhail Bulgakov*, 234.

42. Bethea, "Bulgakov and Nabokov."

Bulgakov's *The Master and Margarita*: Genre and Motif

ELLENDEA PROFFER

In spite of the lack of modern works that contain such heterogeneous elements (satirical comedy, the supernatural, and serious philosophical concerns), there does exist a general category under which *The Master and Margarita* can be considered – the genre of Menippean satire. This term is used by Northrop Frye, Ronald Highet, and others in the West, but it has rarely been applied to Russian literature.[1] In 1929, however, that ingenious engineer of Procrustean beds, M. Bakhtin, published his *Problemy poetiki Dostoevskogo*, in which he deals at great length with the characteristics of Menippean satire in general. Although his definition seems tailored to fit Dostoevsky's works, for the most part it agrees with the definitions of Frye and Highet. For example, they all agree that in Menippean satire the author usually deals in the fantastic; he uses a mixture of the serious and the comic, the dramatic and the narrative.[2] Realistic sections (such as Trimalchio's dinner in the *Satyricon*) alternate with fantastic ones. The authors almost always reveal what tradition they are writing in by quoting from or referring to previous works of satire.[3] Bakhtin's characterization of Menippean satire contains fourteen separate (and numbered) points,[4] but not all of these are logically distinct, so several have been combined in the following summary. In each numbered section a few of the ways in which *The Master and Margarita* fits the definition of the genre are suggested.

1. Menippean satire breaks away from traditional time-space considerations and is not bound by any requirements of

verisimilitude to external reality.[5] *The Master and Margarita* takes place in three days, but the devil stops the clock at midnight for his ball. The Pilate story is told by the devil, dreamed by Ivan Bezdomny, and written by the Master.

2. Heroes are often legendary and can be actual historical figures. Pilate and Christ are both.[6]

3. Mystical[7] and religious elements are often portrayed in a coarse and comic way; the ultimate questions are discussed in the most incongruous circumstances – Woland's religious discussion with Berlioz and the treatment of the figure Yeshua fill this requirement.

4. The philosophical and the fantastic are united. This is true of the story of Pilate and the fate of the Master, and of the devil's role in deciding their fates.

5. There is portrayal of unusual states of mind – dreams and insanity, especially schizophrenia. Ivan is supposedly schizophrenic, and the Master is near madness. Pilate is close to a breakdown. There are several important dreams.[8]

6. Scandal scenes are typical. More than anyone since Dostoevsky, Bulgakov uses such scenes, for example, the various scandals caused by Koroviev, Behemoth, and Azazello,[9] as well as the Variety Theater performance.

7. All types of social and philosophical targets are satirized. Topical satire is evident in the sections dealing with the writers' union, the literary world, foreign currency, Muscovite love of luxury, the taking of bribes, and bureaucracy in general. The communist "philosophy" is satirized in the conversation between Woland and Berlioz.

8. Ironies and paradoxes proliferate. In the novel the devil does good, the Communists are just as susceptible to the charms of money as their prerevolutionary counterparts, Berlioz tells the devil that God does not exist, Pilate the executioner pretends the execution never took place, and Barrabas the murderer is freed while the peaceful Yeshua is crucified. The narrator himself serves an ironic purpose every time he "explains" to the

reader what "really" happened – and in the epilogue when he lamely tries to give a reasonable explanation for everything.

9. There is a mixture of stylistic levels. The style of parts of the Pilate chapters is consciously elevated,[10] and this contrasts sharply to the comic style found in the Moscow narrative where Bulgakov uses funny dialogues, parodies of Soviet jargon, and an interfering "lyric" narrator.

This summary clearly shows how many features of *The Master and Margarita* match the characteristics of Menippean satire, which brings one to the next problem: a work of Menippean satire often appears to lack unity and consistency. Its variety of elements may suggest an absence of careful artistic selection and arrangement. Since internal inconsistencies exist within the novel, it is important to demonstrate that most of these inconsistencies are deliberate. Traditionally, the Menippean satirist "does not believe that the world is orderly and rational, and therefore gaps, interruptions, and inconsistencies in the story scarcely concern him."[11] On the other hand, as Frye suggests, in the Menippean satire there is a "higher" consistency, a different set of laws at work:

> The intellectual structure built up from the story makes for violent dislocations in the customary logic of narrative, though the appearance of carelessness that results reflects only the carelessness of the reader or his tendency to judge by a novel-centered concept of fiction.[12]

These points can be illustrated by an analysis of some of Bulgakov's devices and repeated motifs in *The Master and Margarita*.

One argument for deliberate inconsistency is the manner in which the Pontius Pilate story is presented. It would have been fairly simple to make all the Pilate sections fragments of the Master's novel, fragments that are found and read at various times in the work by the characters of the Moscow narrative. But instead, Bulgakov elaborately contrives to have the story presented in many forms – a dream (Ivan's), the manuscript (the Master's), and a story (Satan's) – thereby making it easy for the reader to notice that although the story of Pilate is told in chronological order and in the same style, the means by which it is introduced into the main narrative are flagrantly "unrealistic" and "inconsistent."[13] The author indicates that he could have explained it away, done it realistically if he had wanted to. The major expression of this is found in the conversation between Ivan and the Master in chapter 13. Ivan relates his adventures with the devil and retells the Pilate story, at which point the Master "folded his hands as though in prayer and whispered to himself, 'Oh I guessed it! I guessed it all!'" (135).[14] Obviously Bulgakov was aware of his "inconsistency" and could also have given a "rational" explanation of Ivan's dream. Since he did not, it is reasonable to conclude that he deliberately chose to make it inconsistent. This conclusion is reinforced by the epilogue, which itself is a satire on all narrators who try to explain what they cannot. This is also directed at readers who in their quest for verisimilitude demand that all be explained.

Another reason for having so many different people in the novel involved in some way with Pontius Pilate is to strengthen the ties between the two narrative lines, which in turn strengthens the implication that the Pilate story has more than superficial relevance for the characters' lives. Motifs from the Pilate story are repeated in the Moscow narrative, suggesting parallels between people and events, through space and time. Most of the motifs that are repeated occur originally in the very first Pilate installment, which is particularly rich in sensual imagery. There are many such motifs – roses, dogs, yellow and black combinations,[15] New Testament reverberations,[16] the blood-red cloak,[17] the peculiar exclamation "Oh, gods, gods"[18] – that will not be treated in detail here. Instead, as evidence of Bulgakov's conscious use of repeated themes, two images will be traced through the novel – the sun and the moon.[19]

Sunlight is used to link Jerusalem and Moscow; both cities have buildings with golden roofs that reflect the sun – in Moscow it is the churches of the Kremlin and the domes of Novodevichi monastery. The glittering idols appear in Ivan's dream state: "He saw a city . . . with roofs that flashed in the sunlight . . . and above the garden bronze statues that glowed in the setting sun" (327). Margarita emphasizes the idols when she says:

> "Do you know . . . that just as you were going to sleep last night I was reading about the mist that came in from the Mediterranean . . . and those idols, ah, those golden idols! Somehow I couldn't get them out of my mind." (352)

The mist from the Mediterranean is mentioned in the first line of chapter 25, and the reference to the idols occurs a page later:

> Other shimmering flashes lit up the palace of Herod the Great facing the temple on the western hill; as they did so, the golden statues, eyeless and fearful, seemed to leap up into the black sky and stretch their arms toward it. Then the fire from heaven would be quenched again and a great thunderclap would banish the gilded idols into the mist. (292)

This repetition seems to be chiefly an exotic touch, but it could be argued that the allusion to "idols" has other implications for Soviet readers. It should also be noted that the black storm in Moscow when Woland leaves in the end echoes the storm in Jerusalem after the execution.

The sunlight itself has several other functions. It is a transitional time indicator, is used as a good omen (141, 371), and in the Pilate sections is a tormenting force. The author's numerous references to the sun underlines the important role the sun plays in the novel. These references occur both at the beginning of the novel and near the end, as the devil arrives in Moscow and as he is leaving: "His gaze halted on the upper stories, whose panes threw back a blinding, fragmented reflection of the sun which was setting on Mikhail Alexandrovich forever."[20] This passage is echoed near the end when Woland and his entourage are on Sparrow Hills: "Woland, Koroviev, and Behemoth sat mounted on black horses, looking at the city spread out beyond the river with fragments of sun glittering from the thousands of west-facing windows, and at the onion domes of Novodevichi monastery" (364). The symmetrical repetition of this imagery reinforces the other parallels between beginning and ending (Bezdomny and Pilate, the theme of immortality).

Many other references are made to the sun, and nearly all of them are connected directly to Pilate. The sun is clearly a symbol of torment for him, whereas the other characters, who have not compromised their consciences and failed in a moral dilemma, are not tortured by it. The quotation beginning "The Procurator glanced at the prisoner, then at the sun rising inexorably" (325) is especially revealing since it contains the direct juxtaposition of the inexorably rising sun with nausea and the thought of simply and unjustly condemning Yeshua to death without hearing further details.

The sunlight motif recurs most frequently in the first half of the novel, whereas the moonlight motifs increase in number and significance in the second half. Since both the Pilate narrative and the Moscow narrative take place at the same time of the month (another of the parallels between the two cities), they both have a full moon for much of their action, which takes place over three days (from sunset Wednesday to sunset Saturday in Moscow) – not counting flashbacks and the epilogue. Some of the references to moonlight (*pri lune*) are general, whereas others refer specifically to the full moon (*polnaia luna*) – always a time of the supernatural in mythology.

The moon, like the sun, appears very early in the novel as well as at the end. The first important reference to the moon is at the end of chapter 3, when, as Berlioz dies, "once more and for the last time the moon flashed before his eyes, but it split into fragments and then went black" (48).[21] This description is "doubled" near the end of the novel when Bezdomny is walking to the bench where he and Berlioz had sat that first evening, "that evening when Berlioz, now long forgotten by everybody, saw the moon shatter to fragments for the last time in his life" (380).

Although other characters (notably Ivan in the epilogue) are sometimes associated with images of the moon, a particularly large number of references to the moon in connection with Pilate and the Master are made in the main body of the novel. When Ivan meets the Master, who stares "at the moon floating past the grille" (137), the latter is called the "moonlight visitor" (142). At the end of chapter 15, the "nameless Master wrung his hands as he gazed at the moon" (168). The Master is returned on the night of the ball, and just after Margarita requests his return, the moon appears "not a setting moon, but the midnight moon" (279). Almost immediately the Master quotes from a section of his novel that we have not yet read: "The Master had suddenly lapsed into uneasy gloom, rose from his chair, wrung his hands and, turning toward the distant moon, he started to tremble, muttering, 'even by moonlight there's no peace for me at night . . . Why do they torment me? Oh, gods, gods'" (281).

Paralleling the Master's gazing at the moon in the asylum, Pilate does the same: "The naked moon hung far up in the clear sky, and for several hours the Procurator lay staring at it" (310). Pilate then dreams of the blue path of moonlight, a dream that foreshadows his eventual fate:

> The couch stood in half-darkness, shaded from the moon by a pillar, though a long ribbon of moonlight stretched from the staircase to the bed. As the Procurator drifted away from reality, he set off along that path of light straight up toward the moon . . . There had been no execution! This thought comforted him as he strode along the moonlight pathway. (310)

Echoing the Master's remark (281), Pilate says that even by moonlight there is no peace for him (311, 312). When the Master and Margarita eventually see Pilate, the moon motif is emphasized:

> The moon flooded the ground with a harsh green light, and soon Margarita noticed . . . the figure of a man . . . In the brilliant moonlight, brighter than an arc light, Margarita could see the seemingly blind man wringing his hands and staring at the moon with unseeing eyes . . . in the moonlight, there lay a huge, gray dog with pointed ears, gazing like his master at the moon. (369)

Woland explains that the full moon torments him, and Margarita, compassionate as usual, says, "Twenty-four thousand moons in penance for one moon long ago, isn't that too much?" (370).[22] This particular pattern is finished in the epilogue when Ivan dreams under sedation:

> After his injection the sleeper's vision changes. From the bed to the moon stretches a broad path of moonlight and up it is climbing a man in a white cloak with a blood-red lining.
>
> Then the moonbeam begins to shake, a river of moonlight floods out of it and pours in all directions. From the flood materializes a woman of incomparable beauty and leads toward Ivan a man with a stubble-grown face. (383)

The Master and Margarita tell Ivan how it ended and they walk away to the moon.

It should be noted that in the epilogue nearly everyone is tormented by the full moon. Bengalsky (master of ceremonies at the Variety) "developed a nasty, compulsive habit of falling into a depression every spring at the full moon" (37) and Nikanor Ivanovich "went out and, with the full moon for company, got blind drunk" (379). Those most tormented by their memories are Ivan Bezdomny and Nikolai Ivanovich (Natasha's cowardly lover).

In general the moonlight is associated with people who have been cowardly in some way or who have been men of little faith. Ivan is the only one who does not fit into either of these categories, but then he is the only person left who *knows* the story of Pilate – and knows that it is a true story. The passages quoted throughout this discussion of moonlight motifs show that in the main body of the novel the Master and Pilate are connected by being tormented by the moon. The Master and Pilate are both "burnt-out" cases, men who have little faith left in people. Yeshua tells Pilate that he has lost his faith in human beings, and that this is his trouble (27). Pilate's inability to overcome his cowardice, his refusal to step outside the rules of his office and react as a man rather than as a Procurator, eventually causes his grief.[23] The Master's case is different.

He says that the failure of his novel seemed to have withered his soul, that something began to happen to him – he was sunk in depression – and that a psychiatrist had probably figured it out a long time ago. Although it is difficult for the reader to determine precisely what happened, the total impression of all this is somewhat similar to the impression we get of the sick, hopeless Pilate. However, there is not a one-to-one correspondence – cowardice and fear are not identical. On the other hand, the Master obviously has few things in common with the hopeful, naive Yeshua, who believes all men are good. They share only persecution.

The sunlight and moonlight motifs have a larger significance for the novel as a whole. The key to the frequent repetitions of both motifs can perhaps be found in the words of Satan himself, when he chides Matthew for his monochromatic worldview:

> You spoke your words as though you denied the very existence of shadows or of evil. Think, now: where would your good be if there were no evil, and what would the world look like without shadow? Shadows are thrown by people and things. There's the shadow of my sword for instance. But shadows are also cast by trees and living beings. So you want to strip the whole globe by removing every tree and every creature to satisfy your fantasy of a bare world? (348)

Matthew's only answer to this is: "I won't argue with you, old sophist." On the basis of all the good the devil does in the novel, one is led to conclude that the devil's argument is one that explains the seemingly ambiguous attitude toward evil in the novel.[24] This is basically consistent with the meaning of the epigraph from Faust, since in Goethe's work the devil is seen as one who spurs men to action, who in testing and tempting man, forces him to find his salvation. This is also an application of Goethe's idea of polarities,[25] that at the heart of everything lies a contradiction – attraction and repulsion, creation and destruction – that men see as good and evil, heaven and hell. Goethe felt that moral concepts were really only one facet of the whole, a whole in which immorality and amorality are at least equally represented. The main thing is activity – this is all the surge of life, an everlasting repetition that never progresses;

good never really does triumph over evil, but the movement in itself is what is important. All these contradictions are inseparable from one another and from God himself. Goethe's influence on Bulgakov is also seen in that in *The Master and Margarita*, as in *Faust*, it is through the love and compassion of a woman that man is saved.

In conclusion, I wish to point out one more paradoxical feature of Bulgakov's novel. In chapter 13 the Master tells Ivan that he knew what the last words of his novel about Pilate would be: "The fifth Procurator of Judea, the knight Pontius Pilate" (139); in Russian, *piatyi prokurator iudei, vsadnik Pontii Pilat* (90). If the novel the Master wrote were the Pilate story, only the last installment of the Pilate story would end with this line. But the epilogue also ends with these same words: *piatyi prokurator iudei, vsadnik Pontii Pilat.* In this way we are told that the novel the Master wrote is the one we have read, that the Master's novel is really *The Master and Margarita.*[26]

NOTES

1. See Northrop Frye, *Anatomy of Criticism* (New York: 1968) and Gilbert Highet, *The Anatomy of Satire* (Princeton, N.J.: Princeton University Press, 1962). Other helpful discussions of satire can be found in David Worcester, *The Art of Satire* (New York: Russell and Russell, 1960) and John Russell, *Satire: A Critical Anthology* (Cleveland: World, 1967).

As I discovered only after preparing this paper for a seminar in early 1968, in the afterword to the original publication of *The Master and Margarita* (*Moskva*, no. 11 [1966]), A. Vulis devotes half a page to describing the novel as Menippean satire. However, the best Soviet Bulgakov critic more or less dismisses Vulis's suggestion (see V. Lakshin, "Roman M. Bulgakova *Master i Margarita*," *Novyi mir*, no. 6 [1968]: 284–311), and other important Soviet critics have largely ignored the problem. See, for example, L. Skorino, "Litsa bez karnaval'nykh masok," *Voprosy literatury*, no. 6 (1968): 24–43; I. Vinogradov, "Zaveshchanie mastera," *Voprosy literatury*, no. 6 (1968): 43–76; P. Palievskii, "Posledniaia kniga M. Bulgakova," *Nash sovremennik*, no. 3 (1969): 116–20. The more detailed treatment of genre here should help clarify that *The Master and Margarita* is indeed Menippean satire; it might be noted that Vulis reached this conclusion solely on the basis of Bakhtin, whereas I came to the same conclusion, originally, by reading only Frye and Highet.

2. "When he was asked whether he gave preference to dramatic or narrative form, Bulgakov answered that they were equally necessary to him, like the left and right hand to a pianist" (V. Lakshin, "O proze Mikhaila Bulgakova i o nem samom," in M. Bulgakov, *Izbrannaia proza* [Moscow: Khudozhestvennaia literatura, 1963]).

3. *The Master and Margarita* contains allusions to *Dead Souls*, *The Inspector General*, and *Don Quixote*. But the most important allusions are to another Menippaean work – *Faust*. In part 1, the Walpurgis Night scene, Woland is Satan's name (thus Vulis is quite wrong in saying that the name was chosen because it has "absolutely no literary associations" [Vulis, afterword, 125]). Margarita is Goethe's heroine too. Bulgakov's ball scene parallels Walpurgis Night. References are also made to the black poodle (Satan is one in Goethe), the witch on the Brocken, Gretchen's cellar, and the homunculus. Mikhail A. Berlioz (apart from sharing Bulgakov's first name and other two initials) has the name of the composer of "The Damnation of Faust." (Bulgakov scattered allusions to *Faust* in many other works. In *Belaia gvardiia* [The White Guard] the music to *Faust* is on the piano; in *Teatral'nyi roman* [Theatrical novel], at the end of chapter 3, the hero hears *Faust* playing on a record player, and in the next chapter a Mephistophelean figure enters the room; at the end of chapter 7 of *Sobach'e serdtse* [The heart of a dog], Bulgakov describes the doctor in "total solitude, green, looking like an aged Faust.")

Among other musical allusions in *The Master and Margarita* (Rimskii, Stravinsky, Strauss), again only one suggests witches and black magic. Bulgakov calls Golgotha "Lysaia gora," suggesting Mussorgskii's "Night on Bald Mountain."

Other writers Bulgakov alludes to include Griboedov, Lermontov, Pushkin ("Zimnii vecher," *Skupoi rytsar'*, *Mednyi vsadnik*), Panaev, Skabichevskii, Poplavskii, A. K. Tolstoi, Kuzmin, and La Fontaine.

4. M. Bakhtin, *Problemy poetiki Dostoevskogo* (Moscow: Sovetskii pisatel', 1963), 150–62.

5. Ibid., 152.

6. Zavalishin suggests that Bulgakov may be answering Nikolai Morozov, author of studies devoted to proving that Christ was a myth. The historical proof of Pilate's existence was one of Morozov's major problems.

In any case Vulis's account of the novel's genesis offers nothing to support this. See V. Zavalishin, "M. Bulgakov, *Master i Margarita*," *Novyi zhurnal*, Book 90 (March 1968): 296–99.

7. In Bulgakov's letter to Stalin (March 28, 1930), he refers to his satirical tales and their black and mystical coloration ("I am a mystical writer") (see *Grani*, no. 66 [1967]: 55–61).

8. Nikanor Ivanovich, Margarita, Ivan, and Pilate all have important dreams. They are a constant feature of Bulgakov's work; in *Beg* he even calls the acts "dreams."

9. The latter is Satan's standard-bearer in *Paradise Lost*:

> That proud honour claimed
> Azazel as his right, a Cherub tall:
> Who forthwith from the glittering staff unfurled
> The imperial ensign. (I, 533–36)

"Behemoth" is also mentioned in *Paradise Lost* (VII, 471).

10. Some of the differences between the style of the Pilate sections and that of the rest of the novel can be seen by analyzing the first five paragraphs of chapter 2: (1) the narrator is invisible; (2) the first four sentences are each a paragraph long, much longer than most sentences in the rest of the novel; (3) many sensual descriptions are used: sight (red cloak, palace, cypresses, and palms), smell (roses, leather, sweat, acrid smoke); (4) military terms, usually latinized, are repeated – *kogort*, *legion*; (5) the lexicon is exotic (foreign forms are used, such as *Yershalaim*, *Prokurator*, *Ha-Nozri*); (6) the word *Prokurator* is used four times in the first four paragraphs, and is repeated many, many times throughout the chapter. This device is called autonomasia – Pilate is not a man, but a position. There is an emphasis on the formulaic, ritualistic responses forced by the rigid code governing a man's behavior, which can lead him to misery if he blindly obeys it.

It should also be noted that the Pilate story is an example of *ostranenie*. The story of Christ is told from the point of view of his executioner, so we are forced to see it in an entirely new way. (One might compare the quite different approach to Pilate's character taken by Kazantzakis.)

11. Highet, *Anatomy of Satire*, 206.

12. Frye, *Anatomy of Criticism*, 310.

13. In "Ved'my i koty v sapogakh i bez sapog," *Vozrozhdenie*, no. 193 (January 1968), V. N. Il'in is unaware of the complex way the Pilate story is

told. He simply claims that the story does not match the version in the Gospels because the Master's story is identical to that of Satan, the father of falsehood.

14. M. Bulgakov, *The Master and Margarita*, trans. M. Glenny (New York: Harper and Row, 1967). Since at this writing the Glenny translation is the only complete text available, it has been used here (otherwise, the Ginzburg translation is far more faithful and accurate). Motif repetitions have all been checked against the abridged Russian edition (*Master i Margarita* [Paris: YMCA, 1967]) and against a microfilm copy of the complete part 2.

15. For example, Margarita, who is wearing a black dress and carrying yellow flowers the first time she meets the Master, makes the Master a black cap with a yellow *M* on it. Bulgakov himself wore such a cap, made for him by his wife Elena Sergeevna, as he was dictating the revisions of *The Master and Margarita*.

16. For example, *twelve* directors are on the board of the Griboedov (which does not seem unusual), and *twelve* detectives are on the Variety case (which does seem strange).

17. Pilate's white cloak with the blood-red (*krovavyi*) lining is mentioned in the first line of the opening Pilate section and referred to repeatedly thereafter – especially by Ivan (see pages 117, 135, 139, 327, 370, and 383). It quickly becomes a symbol of Pilate's "official" self and position. He wears it when he pronounces sentence on Yeshua, and the blood-red lining suggests cruelty and violence. Blood itself is a recurring motif, and red in general – as in the roses, wine, and poison – is one of the main colors in the novel.

18. In the opening Pilate section, Pilate exclaims, "O bogi, bogi," and he repeats it later, notably at the end (383). This is echoed by various characters from the Moscow narrative, including the Master (quoting his own novel, 281) and Ivan (who is looking at Natasha's cowardly boyfriend, 383). It is also used by the narrator in the unusual section on the "piratic" maître d'hôtel at the Griboedov. This is the only passage in which the narrator's comments seem to be a kind of indirect speech, conveying the thoughts of the maître d'hôtel. Pilate's exclamation and desire for poison is repeated verbatim here: "O bogi, bogi moi, iadu mne, iadu!" (cf. Glenny, *The Master and Margarita*, 62). The unusual word is the *mne* – does it refer to the maître d'hôtel or to the narrator himself?

19. Lakshin ("Roman M. Bulgakova," 288) correctly mentions the constant references to sunlight and moonlight and recognizes their role in the parallels between Moscow and Jerusalem. Note that this kind of repeated motif is a general feature of Bulgakov's work (see particularly *White Guard*) and that in his play *Don Quixote* important speeches are made on the symbolic meaning of the sun and the moon (Don Quixote himself is called "Knight of the White Moon").

20. The first reference to the sunset hour is in the opening sentence of the novel. Other references to the sun, sunlight, and high noon occur frequently throughout the novel.

21. Compare this to the sun-Berlioz reference (see note 20 above) (622).

22. The YMCA edition (which is a copy of the *Moskva* edition) has "twelve thousand" instead of "twenty-four thousand." The latter makes more sense; it occurs in the microfilm copy I have and presumably in the manuscript Glenny used in his translation.

23. Bulgakov's repeated references to cowardice emphasize its thematic importance. This is discussed briefly in two reviews: Zavalishin, "M. Bulgakov, *Master i Margarita*," and E. J. Simmons, "Out of the Drawer, into the Light," *Saturday Review*, November 11, 1967, 56. Soviet critics have dealt with it at more length, particularly Vinogradov.

24. The epigraph comes from the first scene with Mephistopheles, dressed as a traveling scholar, in Faust's study:

Faust. Nun gut, wer bist du denn?
Mephis. Ein Teil von jener Kraft,
Die stets das Böse will und stets das Gute schafft.
Faust. Was ist mit diesem Rätselwort gemeint!
Mephis. Ich bin der Geist, der stets verneint!
Und das mit Recht. (ll. 1336–41)

25. See Ronald Gray, *Goethe* (London: Cambridge University Press, 1967), 20. Of course, these observations should not be taken to suggest that Bulgakov was presenting a systematic philosophy.

The title to the long afterword to the East German translation of the novel promises information on *Faust* and Bulgakov, but its author gets tangled up in pointless discussions of everything from Thomas Mann to *The Life of Klim Samgin* (Rolf Schroder, "Bulgakows Roman 'Der Meister und Margarita' im Spiegel der Faustmodelle des 19 und 20 Jahrhunderts," *Der Meister und Margarita* [Berlin, 1968], 393–428).

26. Bulgakov's widow, Elena Sergeevna, told this writer that the epilogue was dictated after the novel was "finished" and the manuscript bound. Thus the epilogue is pasted into the original manuscript.

Beyond Parody: The Goethe Connection

ANDREW BARRATT

Overall Cosmology

The first (and deepest) level of similarity between *The Master and Margarita* and Goethe's *Faust* lies in their overall cosmology. Each work tells a tragic story of this world (the "kleine Welt," in Goethe's description), which finally becomes part of a larger universal scheme which permits that tragedy to be transcended. The sorrows and frustrations of earthly existence are annulled once they are perceived as the prologue to the extramundane mystery that will be experienced by the protagonists after the formal closure of the two works. Both works fit, therefore, within a conventional religious framework, according to which the "kleine Welt" is understood as a lesser, transitional state experienced as a test of worthiness for the higher realm. Yet the relationship between the events of "this" world and those of the higher realm is, in *The Master and Margarita*, no less than in *Faust*, a matter of no small difficulty, for both authors challenge what we might call a naive apocalyptic explanation of the divine scheme and its operation. The apocalyptic tradition, as represented by the myth of the Last Judgment, works with an uncompromising Old Testament notion of justice based on the ethical categories of vice and virtue – "and the dead were judged out of those things which were written in the books, according to their works" (Revelation 20:12). In its crudest form, this mentality finds expression in the idea of the New Jerusalem as a reward for good deeds performed on this earth, and of Hell as the place where the evil are punished for their sins.

Of the two works under consideration here, it is *Faust* that makes the greater assault on this conventional apocalyptic view. Much of Faust's behavior in the "kleine Welt" is bound to evoke a feeling of antipathy in the audience. No matter how much we admire or identify with his restless striving, this feeling will inevitably be counterbalanced by the moral abhorrence we must feel for the destruction of Gretchen and her family. Nor should it be forgotten that Faust's initial quest was predicated on his rebellion against God. The salvation of Faust was, as we know, Goethe's major innovation in his treatment of a legend which had hitherto reinforced the conventional apocalyptic mentality to which we have referred. To strive is to err, the Lord says in the "Prolog im Himmel," and, in the final reckoning, it is the striving, not the erring, that has to be taken into account. To accept this involves the abandonment of that "normal" moral perspective that would grant salvation only to those who lead a "virtuous" existence in the "kleine Welt."

The Master and Margarita does not challenge our everyday notions of right and wrong so radically. The Master is not implicated in any acts so heinous as those of Goethe's Faust; he is to a large extent more sinned against than sinning – hence the commonly held view that his ultimate fate is only a fair reward for the suffering he endured at the hands of the literary establishment. In the words of Leatherbarrow, "Bulgakov would seem to be suggesting that there exists an impartial, universal justice which eventually compensates for the injustices perpetrated by human law."[1] This judgment has its source in the feeling that most people, on reading *The Master and Margarita* for the first time, probably experience a sense of *rightness* about the Master's reward, which is certainly very different from the profound ambivalence generated by the fate of Goethe's hero. Nevertheless, Bulgakov's novel resists the reading offered above in two ways. First, it is made quite explicit in the text that the Master receives his "reward" not as a "compensation" for his unjust treatment by his contemporaries, but in recognition of *his achievement in writing the novel.* "He has read the Master's composition," Matthew tells Woland when he brings the news of Yeshua's decision, "and he asks you to take the Master with you and reward him with peace" (776). Much as we might sympathize with the Master's predicament in the philistine world of Moscow literary politics, this has no direct bearing on his "reward." There is nothing to suggest the working of any kind of "compensatory" ethic.

It is here that the second, and greater difficulty arises. If the ground for the Master's reward lies in the striving that produced the novel, it must be noted that this reward is granted even in the face of the Master's withdrawal from the struggle when he meets with adversity. Our admiration for his achievement has to be weighed, therefore, against his failure of will. It is here that the basic similarity with Goethe's *Faust* resides. Where Goethe tells us that to strive is to err, Bulgakov implies that to strive is to fail. In each case it is the striving that proves in the end to be the crucial thing. For both authors, therefore, even the most grave human failings do not automatically warrant the punishment demanded by the naive apocalyptic mind, for such failings are viewed as an inevitable consequence of life in an imperfect world. But the fact remains that Goethe's vision is the more profoundly disturbing of the two. This is not only because Faust's failings are more reprehensible than the Master's, but also because his final reward is (unlike that of Bulgakov's hero) unequivocally positive. At the end of Goethe's work there is no suggestion that Faust has been granted anything other than accession to the light. His sins, it seems, are of no account at all when it comes to the final reckoning. Bulgakov, however, shrinks from the boldness of the Goethean resolution. As we have just seen, he has his hero receive a "reward" that nevertheless appears to make an allowance for his failings: the Master has earned not light, but peace.

The Role of the Devil

Broadly speaking, the "devil" plays a similar role in the cosmological scheme of *The Master and Margarita* and *Faust.* Both authors adhere to an Old Testament conception neatly summed up in the words of Carus: "God needs the Devil for a servant and utilizes his malignity for the procreation of good."[2] In *Faust* the devil's part is spelled out in so many words in the "Prolog im Himmel" and is alluded to later in the famous words of Mephistopheles, which Bulgakov chose for the epigraph to his novel. Although Woland's place in the divine plan is never so explicitly stated in *The Master and Margarita*, it is made plain that his powers, like those of Mephistopheles, are limited and subservient to a higher authority. On each occasion, the limitation concerns an act of mercy (the release from suffering of Frieda and Pilate; the granting of "peace" to the Master), which Woland openly admits to lie outside his "jurisdiction."[3]

But the deep similarity between Woland and Mephistopheles should not blind us to some more important differences. Mephistopheles plays his part in the divine scheme unwillingly and unwittingly. Woland, by contrast, seems much more aware of the larger plan and participates in it with greater readiness.[4] The distinction is particularly marked in a passage (to which we will return in more detail below) where it is given to Woland to explain the operation of the universal order to Matthew. Equally different is the manner in which the devil-figure serves this order in his dealings with the hero. Where Mephistopheles uses every trick he knows to distract Faust from striving, Woland's task is the very opposite: to awaken the Master from the state of "unconditional repose" into which he has fallen after the destruction of his manuscript. And this is what leads to the feeling that Woland, for all his cynical posing with Margarita, is far less nihilistically inclined toward the mundane sphere than Goethe's devil. Mephistopheles, as M. W. Smeed describes him in a useful thumbnail sketch, is the "adversary of all faith and optimism, the personification of mockery."[5] The Woland who promises to drink to "being" from Berlioz's skull at the end of the ball (689) could hardly be further removed from the temperament that finds its most memorable expression in the lines: "Ich bin der Geist, der stets verneint!" (*Faust*, l. 1340). But this is only to say what we have already discovered, that Woland is far less "devilish" than Mephistopheles. In *The Master and Margarita* the "devil" is assigned the role of messenger; this is perhaps Bulgakov's most radical departure from the Goethean conception, the further implication of which will be considered in the conclusion of this chapter.

Man and Woman

Apart from the salvation of the hero, Goethe's principal innovation in his treatment of the Faust theme was to include a love story within the framework of the original legend. That Bulgakov follows both precedents in *The Master and Margarita* is what makes it so distinctly "Goethean" a work (compare the other great Faust novel of the twentieth century, Thomas Mann's *Doctor Faustus*, which adopts neither of Goethe's modifications). There are, of course, certain differences of scale and emphasis in Bulgakov's treatment of the love story. Most obviously, Margarita plays a much larger part in *The Master and Margarita* than Gretchen does in *Faust*. And, as we saw in chapter 7, Bulgakov excludes from the relationship between his hero and heroine the explicit sexual elements that feature so prominently in Goethe. Nevertheless, the Russian author adheres in his novel to the same broad mythopoeic conception of the sexes as that which informs Goethe's *Faust*. In both works the spirit of striving is invested in the hero, whereas it falls to the heroine to embody the merciful power of love. In each case, too, the potentially productive symbiosis of the "masculine" and "feminine" principles is rendered possible only beyond this world.

Good and Evil

The connection between Goethe and Bulgakov with regard to the problem of theodicy has already been touched on. The key to Bulgakov's view of the matter in *The Master and Margarita*, most critics have agreed, is to be found in Woland's words to Matthew in chapter 29: "You utter your words as if you don't acknowledge shadows, or evil either. But would you be so good as to consider this question: what would your goodness do if evil did not exist, and what would the world look like if all shadows disappeared from it?" (776).[6] This objection to Matthew's simplistic understanding of the working of a benevolent providence can be traced to the passage at the beginning of Goethe's "Prolog im Himmel," where Gabriel describes earthly life as the constant alternation of day and night, a condition that is explicitly contrasted to the pure light of heaven (*Faust*, ll. 251–54).[7] Commenting on this passage in Goethe, one critic has made an observation that holds equally for *The Master and Margarita*. The movement of night and day reminds us, she writes, that "the earth remains the unharmonious spot to which man is confined."[8]

Neither Bulgakov nor Goethe hold out any promise of reform for a world in this irretrievably fallen state. Their solution is the typically religious one of transcendence. Here is the same commentator on the conclusion of *Faust*: "What is suggested is a potential continuation of life in some sort of spiritualized essence, a life in which good and evil no longer exist, and past good and evil are accepted because they are part of the earthly lot."[9] Again, it could be *The Master and Margarita* that is being described here. Yet these comments cannot be applied to the novel without certain adjustments. The "continuation of life" promised to the hero and heroine at the end of Bulgakov's novel is much more concrete and physical than what is merely hinted at in *Faust*. Also, it is not so much the case that past good and evil are "accepted" in this new realm of existence, but rather that they are annulled. Nevertheless, there is no mistaking the similarity of the overall providential scheme.

No discussion of good and evil in Goethe and Bulgakov would be complete without some reference to what has remained one of the thorniest problems of all – Bulgakov's choice of epigraph. The issue here is once again the connection between Woland and Mephistopheles: can the latter's description of himself as a "part of that power which wills forever evil yet works forever good" be applied in any meaningful way to Bulgakov's character? Most critics have answered this question in the negative.[10] Although Woland does bring some evil into the world, this evil is largely incidental and inconsequential and, for the most part, does not result from his active participation in events. Even if one does hold Woland responsible for the behavior of his entourage, Matthew's later reference to him as the "spirit of evil" (775) must still appear the grossest oversimplification. Matthew seems unaware of motive or scale: it is one thing to frighten a doctor by having a sparrow dance on his desk, and another thing altogether to create the sort of mayhem that Mephistopheles does. What weighs even more heavily against Matthew's judgment, however, is Woland's behavior toward the hero and heroine. Where Mephistopheles works hard to break Faust's will and achieves the physical destruction of Gretchen, Woland does not even display the desire to thwart the Master and Margarita.

But if the majority of Bulgakov's commentators have been prepared to accept that the epigraph does not describe Woland, they have been much less willing to leave the matter there. Indeed, their determination to discern some other sort of relevance in this passage has resulted in some of the most inventive (although sometimes most confusing) interpretations. The most common line of argument has been to suggest that the epigraph should not be taken to refer to Woland at all. Thus one critic writes that it "alludes to other devils – agents of the Soviet system who are indeed shown as doing good when they will evil."[11] In other words, it is not Woland but such characters as Latunsky, Berlioz, and the rest who unwittingly serve an ultimate good that lies beyond their powers of understanding. Behind the obvious ideological appeal of such a reading lurks another, which is even more seductive; by transferring the Faustian reference from Woland to other characters in the novel, one is able to clear up what would otherwise have to remain the source of disturbing uncertainty.

My criticism of the above interpretation of the epigraph (and of others I have read) is that it does not so much explain its meaning as explain that meaning away. To shift the ostensible referent of Goethe's lines is an arbitrary act that deprives the epigraph of its rhetorical force and semantic density: a challenging paradox is converted into a harmless puzzle that permits an easy "solution." Boris Eykhenbaum puts his finger on the real problem in his well-known discussion of Tolstoy's epigraph to *Anna Karenina.* Taking issue with those critics who had attempted to translate the Tolstoyan epigraph into a condensed statement of the novel's meaning, he argued for a different approach, which would explore the rhetorical relationship between the epigraph and the novel it precedes.[12] Following Eykhenbaum's lead, the epigraph from *Faust* can be shown to serve several purposes. Its immediate function, as we have seen, is simply to trigger the all-important subtext, so that even as we embark on our reading of the novel we are set to wondering about its possible connection with Goethe. Subsequently, the epigraph takes on further significance. On the one hand, the question with which it begins may be seen as an allusion to the main theme of the novel (Who is Woland?). On the other hand, it complicates that crucial issue by inviting a simple identification of Woland with Mephistopheles which cannot finally be sustained. If we wish to make the epigraph "mean" anything more than this, it might be suggested that it captures a paradox that will set in train an interpretative exercise that leads to the very heart of the novel's philosophy. To say that *The Master and Margarita* is a "Faustian" novel does not necessarily mean that we need to make a final decision on the points of correspondence between the two works at all. What really matters is that the Goethean subtext is what brings the main issues of Bulgakov's novel into the sharpest focus.

NOTES

This excerpt is from the chapter "Beyond Parody: The Goethe Connection" in the author's *Between Two Worlds: A Critical Introduction to "The Master and Margarita"* (Oxford: Clarendon Press, 1987).

1. W. J. Leatherbarrow, "The Devil and the Creative Visionary in Bulgakov's *Master i Margarita*," *New Zealand Slavonic Journal*, no. 1 (1975): 39.

2. Paul Carus, *The History of the Devil and the Idea of Evil* (La Salle, Ill.: Open Court, 1974), 342.

3. The limits to Woland's powers were introduced at a relatively early stage in the novel's composition. Redaction 3 contained the following exchange between the Master and Woland: "Can you really be given orders?

"Oh, yes" (M. Chudakova, "Arkhiv M. Bulgakova. Materialy dlia tvorcheskoi biografii pisatelia," *Zapiski otdela rupkopisei Vsesoiuznoi biblioteki imeni V. I. Lenina* 36 [1976]: 3).

4. A. C. Wright, "Satan in Moscow: An Approach to Bulgakov's *The Master and Margarita*," *PMLA* 88 (1973): 1163.

5. J. W. Smeed, *Faust in Literature* (New York: Oxford, 1975), p. 45.

6. The reason this passage differs from the identical passage cited elsewhere in this volume is that Proffer is using the Glenny translation, which at the time was the only unabridged translation available, while Barratt used the Ginsburg translation and emended it slightly.

7. E. Proffer, "The Major Works of Mikhail Bulgakov," Ph.D. diss., University of Indiana, 1971, 387; Elena Mahlow, *Bulgakov's The Master and Margarita: The Text as Cipher* (New York: Vantage, 1975), 166.

8. L. Dieckmann, *Goethe's Faust: A Critical Introduction* (Englewood Cliffs, N.J.: Prentice-Hall, 1972), 40.

9. Ibid., 87.

10. An exception is V. Lakshin, "Roman M. Bulgakova *Master i Margarita*," *Novyi Mir*, no. 6 (1968): 295.

11. Val Bolen, "Theme and Coherence in Bulgakov's *The Master and Margarita*," *Slavic and East European Journal*, 16, no. 4 (1972), 430. See also E. Proffer, "*The Master and Margarita*," in *Major Soviet Writers*, ed. E. J. Brown (New York: Oxford University Press, 1973), 401; R. Pope, "Ambiguity and Meaning in *The Master and Margarita*: The Role of Afranius," *Slavic Review* 36 (1977): 21.

12. Boris Eykhenbaum, *Lev Tolstoy. Semidesiatye gody* (Leningrad: Khudozh lit, 1974), 168 f.

History as Hippodrome: The Apocalyptic Horse and Rider in *The Master and Margarita*

DAVID M. BETHEA

Although *The Master and Margarita* has been called "an apocalyptic fiction, one whose referential focus is, within its defined context, 'the end of all things,'"[1] little has been said beyond this.[2] Only Edward Ericson has ventured further than casual allusion to claim, in the closing of his article, that "the ending of the novel is an elaborate parody of the last book in the Bible, the Apocalypse of St. John."[3] We need have no doubt of Bulgakov's knowledge of the text of Revelation and of his willingness to use that text as an artistic point of departure: son of a professor of divinity at the Kiev Theological Academy, one schooled in both the sacred texts and the works of Russian religious philosophers (the writings of Father Pavel Florensky, in particular, as Chudakova and others have demonstrated,[4] had a profound impact on the conception of *The Master and Margarita*), Bulgakov was later to take a passage from Revelation as epigraph to his early novel *The White Guard*.[5] But even more intriguing, Bulgakov seems almost from the beginning of his writing career to have associated the horseman or knight (*vsadnik*)[6] with the ideas of eternal punishment, the burden of conscience, and the futility of atonement. One of his first feuilletons, "The Red Crown" (1922), involves a conscience-stricken hero who waits in vain for the return of his dead brother, described as "the familiar horseman with the unseeing eyes."[7] And by the time Bulgakov began work on *The Master and Margarita* in 1928 he had apparently discovered equine traits in his Satan, as several early variants of the title – "The Hoof of the Engineer," "The Consultant with a Hoof," "The Juggler with a Hoof," and "The Horseshoe of the Foreigner" – indicate, and a rich semantic field for further development.[8] What all this suggests is that Bulgakov probably had in mind the text of Revelation and the image of a retributive horseman as he worked on the novel. But what remains to be shown is how text and image are telescoped in the novel's form and composition. To this end we might best proceed from the explicit to the implicit, from the Yershalaim chapters, where horses and horsemen are an obvious and not unexpected feature of the setting, to the Moscow chapters, where horses and horsemen are much less obvious and more unexpected, to the concluding chapters, where the Yershalaim and Moscow subplots coalesce and the idea of the apocalyptic horse and rider is given its fullest treatment.

Bulgakov's picture of Jerusalem, or Yershalaim as it is called by its Aramaic name in the novel, is one dominated from the outset by implacable sunlight, the sharp blade of legality, and Roman military might. Everything in the Yershalaim chapters (2, 16, 25, 26) appears to have a realistic motivation, with the implication that Bulgakov intended to strip away any mythic coloration from his utterly verisimilar account of the trial and sentencing of Yeshua (the historical Jesus). Here Pilate is the cynosure; the exchange with Yeshua is seen through his eyes, for it is he who is standing in judgment over this earthly court. Thus it should come as no surprise that Pilate, as an extension of the Roman state and its temporal power, is given the attributes of a *cavalryman* – after all, by the time of Christ, horses had been an important element of strategic warfare for centuries. But Bulgakov's equine and equestrian allusions are even in this context so marked as to suggest the presence of some other code or subtext. Pilate walks with a cavalryman's gait; he is repeatedly referred to as a horseman (*vsadnik*; his most awesome title is "vsadnik Zolotoe Kop'e" – "Rider of the Golden Spear");[9] and he observes with pained interest a Syrian cavalry ala speeding to Bald Mountain (Golgotha) moments after he has read the death sentence. Thoughts of simply hanging Yeshua and being done with him are accompanied by distressed looks at the sun, "which (is) relentlessly rising over the equestrian statues of the hippodrome."[10] When Pilate vehemently denies Yeshua's claim that the kingdom of truth will come, he does so with a thunderous voice like the one in which he once commanded his horsemen to "Slash them (the Germans)! Slash them!"[11] during a battle in the Valley of Maidens. In his feelings of wrathful impotence before Caiaphas (here Bulgakov follows the Gospel of John by having Pilate, who wishes to save Yeshua, yield unwillingly to the legal pressure of the High Priest and the Sanhedrin), Pilate imagines his revenge in terms of a flood of Arab horsemen bringing "bitter weeping and moans"[12] to the streets of the Holy City. And as Pilate emerges from the Palace of Herod the Great to preside over the sentencing, he again notices the equine statues of the hippodrome, then hears, en route back to the palace, hoofbeats announcing the approach of the ala and shouts of children (from a street leading onto the Square of the Hippodrome) to "look out (for the horsemen)!"[13] The last image passing before Pilate's eyes as he leaves the Gabbatha is that of a lone cavalryman who, bringing up the rear, "gallop(s) past . . . with a trumpet on his back, flaming in the sun."[14]

The execution of Yeshua takes place in the next Yershalaim chapter (16) and is also pervaded – or perhaps more appropriate verbs for what ensues would be *encircled* or *surrounded* – by images of the horse and rider. The first sentence of this chapter, marked by being a separate paragraph as well, makes pointed reference to the double cordon (one made of cavalry) surrounding the place of execution: "The sun was already setting over Bald Mountain, and the mountain was encircled (*otseplena*) by a double cordon (*otseplenie*)."[15] There follows a detailed description of the ala and its route to Bald Mountain. Those charged with overseeing the execution, including the Centurian Mark, the chief of the palace guard, and Afranius,[16] the chief of the secret police, are distinguished by arriving at their destination on horseback (the century, on the other hand, which Mark commands arrives on foot). Scattered throughout the chapter are other references to the cavalrymen, the ala, the grooms, and their horses. Matthew the Levite understands the "joyful ending" (Yeshua's death) is near at hand by noticing the sudden activity of the grooms and horses preparing to depart. And when the cordon is broken after Yeshua's death and a massive storm breaks over Bald Mountain, we watch through a shroud of water as the cavalry (now the Russian *konnitsa* rather than the borrowed *kavaleriia*) rides back to Yershalaim.

The reader already alerted to the "magnetized" images of horse and rider cannot help but see the last two Yershalaim chapters, especially "Burial" (26), as straining the stays of Bulgakov's carefully wrought verisimilitude. This is not to say that the author's design is somehow flawed (for the careful reader feels from the start that something is afoot beneath the surface, laconic and muscular, of this realism), but that attempts to account for the tenacious presence of the imagery cannot be accounted for merely in terms of realistic motivation. Chapter 25 opens with still another sinister allusion (among others) to the hippodrome. By now we should be asking ourselves about the historical existence of this hippodrome. Why is it constantly in the background? What meaning can it have for Pilate and his story? That the execution is over and Afranius has arrived is signaled to Pilate (as the arrival of the "joyful ending" was earlier signaled to Matthew the Levite) by the movement of horses: "Now, breaking through the tapping of the thinning rain, the final sounds of trumpets and the clattering of several hundred hooves reached the Procurator's ears."[17] Pilate and Afranius then plot, in a bravura performance of Aesopian language, the murder of Yuda (Judas).[18] At this point Bulgakov's deviation from the Gospels is most significant: rather than have Yuda kill himself, he has him killed by Afranius and his henchmen. Pilate, the avenging horseman, and Afranius, his agent, seek out their quarry in a virtual flurry of equine and equestrian imagery. Afranius sends horsemen to see to the burial of Yeshua and the others; he then disguises himself by wearing an old chiton and riding a mule into the city (an ironic allusion to the Gospels' triumphant Christ?), where he meets Niza, his double agent and Yuda's lover, and sets the trap for Yuda; after that he disappears into a stream of pedestrians and riders. In his eagerness to get to his rendezvous with Niza, Yuda curses a mounted patrol that has momentarily blocked his passage. And after Yuda is murdered, Afranius changes back into his genuine costume in a passage full of magnetized imagery and allusive perhaps of Christ's legendary entry (thus the earlier mention of the mule) into Jerusalem. Retributive horseman, at least at this stage of the text, has totally superseded the Prince of Peace.

What should be clear by now is the symbolically charged role of Pilate: both as "Rider of the Golden Spear" responsible for the execution of Yeshua and as the mastermind who uses Afranius (the imposing "military rider" on the "spirited cavalry horse") to murder Yuda, he stands at the center of this punishing, deadly serious horseplay. He is the judge; his verdict in both cases is death; and his method of carrying out these executions is characterized by images of the horse and rider. But this is only half, the most obvious half, of Bulgakov's design. How does the text of Revelation and its notion of tragic secular history combine with Bulgakov's depiction of Pilate as the avenging horseman?

First, Bulgakov sets the stage for subtextual interplay by introducing into the Yershalaim chapters, usually in connection with Pilate's perception of the hateful city, motifs from the Book of Revelation. These include the repeated image of the catastrophic storm (to spill over into the Moscow chapters) promising to end history, that of the abyss over which the city, like the "Whore of Babylon," seems to hang, that of destruction by demonic fire, and that of the ominous Temple, with its roof covered by dragonlike scales and its pair of five-point candelabras recalling the dragon and the beast of ten horns (Revelation 13:1, 4; 17:3, 7, 12, 16).[19] As particularly noteworthy in this context we might cite the opening passage of chapter 15 ("How the Procurator Tried to Save Yuda of Kerioth"):

> The darkness which had come from the Mediterranean shrouded the city hated by the Procurator. The hanging bridges connecting the Temple with Anthony's dreaded tower disappeared. The abyss that had descended from the heavens engulfed the winged gods over the Hippodrome, the crenellated Hasmonaean Palace, the

> bazaars, the caravansaries, the alleys, ponds . . . The great city of Yershalaim had vanished as though it had never been. Everything was swallowed by darkness that threw fear into every living heart in Yershalaim . . .
>
> With its belly (the storm cloud) had already covered the Bald Skull, where the executioners were hastily piercing the hearts of the victims; its weight fell on the Temple in Yershalaim, it crept down the hill in smoking streams and flooded the Lower City. It poured into the windows and drove the people from the crooked streets into the houses . . . Whenever the black steamy mass was ripped by fire, the great bulk of the Temple with its glittering scaly roof would fly up from the solid murk. But the fire would go out in an instant, and the Temple would sink back into a dark abyss. Over and over, it rose and dropped again, and every disappearance was attended by the crashing of catastrophe.[20]

To anticipate a little, although everything here is given the expected realistic motivation (the storm), this cluster of apocalyptic motifs will be carried over into the Moscow chapters and given a largely fantastic (Woland-instigated) motivation.

It is not difficult to see that the wrath of the storm falls chiefly on the Temple, in Bulgakov's rendering the seat of Old Testament morality, retributive rather than redemptive justice, and satanic literalism. As critics have noted, Pilate is, for the most part, a sympathetic figure caught on the horns of a dilemma, trapped by the letter of the law. Neither the death of Yeshua nor Yuda brings him satisfaction, since he knows, all too painfully, that the law in the first case is driving an innocent (and to Pilate most appealing) man to his death and that his personal code of vengeance in the second case is poor compensation – it cannot bring Yeshua back to life. Thus Pilate is a tool of a system or intelligence (Roman and Jewish law) larger than himself, just as the Satan of Revelation is a deadly force whose acts, though apparently self-motivated, actually fulfill a larger divine dispensation. Perhaps it is in this respect that Pilate might be seen as Satan's deputy in a setting overlaid with the gathering presence of the Antichrist. Pilate, like Satan, is empowered to punish, but retribution alone cannot generate a genuine resolution, and so death in the Yershalaim chapters is relentlessly associated with endings that refuse to become beginnings. If the horsemen of Revelation bring destruction and judgment all according to divine plan, then some other agency (that of the Lamb) is needed to bring forgiveness and redemption.

It has been suggested by more than one critic that, by the final chapters of *The Master and Margarita*, the image of the closed circle develops into a significant element of the novel's structural integrity.[21] Yet the image of the circle is not for Bulgakov necessarily benign, and if the ending in fact does somehow return to the beginning, it is an ending that stresses *change through continuity*, not the tracks of futile, predictable motion. This becomes more obvious when we consider the negative images of circular confinement in the Yershalaim chapters. When Pilate rages at Caiaphas, "What are you saying, High Priest? Who can hear us now in this place (the palace garden)? . . . The garden is cordoned off (*otseplen*), the palace is cordoned off (*otseplen*), so that not even a mouse could slip through a crack,"[22] he uses the same verb form, the same image of a closed chain (*tsep'*), that will later appear several times to describe the execution of Yeshua and the setting of Bald Mountain, with its double ring of horsemen and cavalry.[23] Birds describe circles in the air over the dying Yeshua. And the cavalry ala, returning from the site of the execution, crosses the same square (of the Hippodrome?) as it did in the morning, thereby completing the circle of its deadly day's work.

Here it might be fitting to recall the hippodrome and the metaphor of the horserace, which, in the Moscow chapters, become central to the spirit of their dizzying play. There is no place, needless to say, for the pure entertainment of a horserace in the serious atmosphere of the Yershalaim chapters. Still, the urge to suggest an absurdly finite model for Pilate's view of history may be why Bulgakov moved the description of the Moscow hippodrome, which he certainly knew well, into Yershalaim, the sources – especially Brokgauz-Efron – for which make scant mention of such a hippodrome and offer no clues to its appearance.[24] Is not Bulgakov saying that the goals of the "realist," the "materialist," the one who denies the realm of the spirit and contemplates acts that will guarantee his success and security in this world, are nothing more than a race around the track of history's hippodrome? Inevitably they lead back to the reality of death. However clever and ruthless Pilate is as a horseman, he can never break the chain of his personal history. As Aristotle states in the *Metaphysics*, history at any given moment is an infinite series of possibilities, only one of which can be actual in terms of the next moment. And it is poetry's function, as he states further in the *Poetics*, to describe the possibilities that history in its inexorability has left out. Hovering with its equine statues at the edge of Pilate's thoughts, the hippodrome is Bulgakov's objective correlative for this idea of tragic inexorability: as the present unfolds, Pilate sees a future full of rich possibility (his walks with the wandering philosopher) retreating into a finite, guilt-ridden past that will, ironically, continue to haunt him forever.

To sum up, then, it has been demonstrated that Pilate's chief function as apocalyptic horseman is to bring judgment (both on others and, equally important, on himself) and death to Yershalaim. This function incorporates not only that of the Four Horsemen and the locustlike horses whose king is Abaddon (Revelation 9),[25] but also that of the avenging Lamb, described as a magnificent rider (Revelation 19) – dressed in a white robe dipped in blood[26] – on a white steed, before an army of heavenly cavalry amassed to inflict ultimate defeat on the troops of Satan. Bulgakov's view of Revelation does not, at this preliminary level, appear entirely canonical (after all, he deviates from, or "polemicizes"[27] with this subtext as he does elsewhere, reinterpreting it as he sees fit according to the philosophic and aesthetic requirements of his, the larger, text). His Christ figures, Yeshua and the Master, are much less the avengers than the forgivers. Therefore, one of Bulgakov's most puzzling apocryphal strokes becomes, in respect to the image of the apocalyptic horseman most significant: Yeshua, the historical Jesus, denies any basis for the legend that he entered Yershalaim astride an ass. "I have no ass,

Hegemon . . . It is true that I came to Yershalaim through the Susa Gate, *but I came on foot.*"[28] Apparently Bulgakov chose to transfer the role of retributive horseman away from the Lamb entirely, making Pilate, the fifth procurator (when he should traditionally be the sixth),[29] the fifth horseman as well.

The equine and equestrian imagery, quite explicit in the Yershalaim chapters, is not nearly so as we proceed to the outer text, and on first reading could easily be overlooked amid the background of farce and whimsy. Hence it should not seem curious that, of the many commentators who have traced the parallels between Yershalaim and Moscow,[30] none has sensed a link between Pilate the unwilling rider and a city of people *driven* by their satanic impulses. But as Gasparov points out, Moscow is a splintered, reduced version of Yershalaim.[31] What shall be argued, therefore, is that the tragic Pilate has become a mass of vulgarians (*poshliaki*), the ubiquitous horse a modern system of public conveyance, and the hippodrome of history, literally and figuratively, a circular, slapstick race around the streets of Moscow.

Leitmotifs provide the first clue to Bulgakov's shift in design from tragic to comic, from hippodrome as apocalyptic metaphor to horserace as pure entertainment. Korov'ev wears a jockey's cap that he raises while showing Berlioz the way to the tram (and to death);[32] Behemoth sports the whiskers of a cavalryman; as Woland and his helpers make their escape from Homeless, they are referred to as a "troika" (why, we might ask, has Bulgakov left out Azazello?); on the second floor of Griboedov House there hangs a poster depicting a rider, a balcony with palms (a motif borrowed from the Yershalaim chapters),[33] and an "inspired" young writer taking a seat with his pen (his *kop'e*?), and on the first floor the vaulted (i.e., probably circular) roof of the restaurant seems alive with Assyrian (as opposed to Syrian)[34] horses; Homeless is spirited off to Stravinskii's in a truck to the dismay of a coachman who yells, "You'd do better on a racehorse!";[35] the circus act of bicycle riders (also a "troika") that opens the performance at the Variety Theater is colored by equine imagery ("*na dyby*" – "on hind legs"; "*s sedlom naverkhu*" – "with the seat/saddle above")[36] and by fast motion in circles (here the metaphor of the circus and the horserace coalesce); the petrified Rimsky becomes in retreat from his haunted office a rider (*sedok* can be both a horseman and a passenger) who is jostled on his seat as he is borne by a speeding taxi along the "*Sadovoe kol'tso*" (ring road);[37] it is the mounted police along with those on foot (recall the combination of cavalry and foot soldiers that forms the ring around the site of Yeshua's execution)[38] that are sent to break up the line of ticket buyers gathered, on Sadovoe, outside the theater; and the unfortunate boss of the branch office of the Commission on Spectacles has an obsession with organizing clubs, including an equestrian circle ("*kruzhok verkhovoi ezdy*"). Moreover, and most convincing, Bulgakov has placed his centers of madcap activity (here, of course, Margarita's and the Master's apartments are important – and logical – exceptions) along the Sadovoe Ring Road; Berlioz's ill-starred apartment, the Variety Theater, and Griboedov House are all given precise locations on this street, and, indeed, Sadovoe is by far the most alluded to landmark in Moscow.[39] What emerges, as various Muscovites chase Woland or are chased by him, is an atmosphere of sheer "raciness."

Chapters 30 to 32 contain not only the most "elaborate"[40] but the most explicit parody of the Book of Revelation in Russian literature. What is in Dostoevsky's *The Idiot* an allusion to the imminent danger brought on by a godless stage of history becomes in Bulgakov a broad application of the text of Revelation involving themes, characters, and the very climax of the novel. This is the sort of elevating parody, as Nabokov has remarked, that pays a tribute to its source and "always goes along with (the spirit of) genuine poetry,"[41] and is not the sort, much in evidence in the Moscow chapters, that provides a "grotesque imitation" of the original.[42] We know at once that we are in the presence of something serious by Bulgakov's shift to an elegiac tone, best represented in the beautiful, ghostly opening of chapter 32:

> Gods, my gods, how sad the evening earth! How mysterious the mists over the bogs! Whoever has wandered in these mists, whoever has suffered deeply before death, whoever flew over this

> earth burdened beyond human strength knows it. The weary one knows it. And he leaves without regret the mists of the earth, its swamps and rivers, and yields himself with an easy heart into the arms of death, knowing that it alone can soothe him.[43]

Bulgakov has cleared the stage for this race beyond history by leaving Moscow behind in mock apocalyptic ruin. Like Yershalaim before it, Moscow is the city of the devil, a getting-and-spending world of petty Judases, the fallen Whore of Babylon with her "merchants . . . grown rich with the wealth of her wantonness" (Revelation 18:3). The "temples" of satanic impulse – Berlioz's apartment,[44] the Griboedov House, and *Torgsin* (a relative of the modern Berezka store[45]) – have been burned to the ground:[46]

> She (the Whore of Babylon) shall be burned with fire . . . (and) when they (the kings of the earth) see the smoke of her burning, they will stand far off in fear of her torment, and say, "Alas! Alas! thou great city, thou mighty city, Babylon! In one hour thy judgment has come." (Revelation 18:8–10)

And the cataclysmic storm[47] that first announced the appearance of the Master to Ivan – to be followed by the story of the Master's figurative crucifixion, and then the actual crucifixion of Yeshua – is given now, at the moment of the physical deaths of the lovers, its ultimate expression. With this apocalyptic manifold in place, the final destination of both Moscow and Yershalaim – the abyss that promises nonbeing and the utter insignificance of secular history – should come as no surprise.

The deaths in chapter 30 of the Master and Margarita, arranged by Woland at the behest of (the now divine) Yeshua,[48] provide the precise moment at which the "hidden" horses in the text, both those whose presence might be too easily justified by the realistic setting of Yershalaim and those whose presence has been ingeniously masked in the swirling backdrop of contemporary Moscow, emerge to take on their genuine mythic dimensions. The seriousness of the inner text seems to have penetrated into the fantastic atmosphere of the outer text to produce a new and urgent lyricism adequate for the coming scenes of flight and freedom. The intuitive Margarita, who has been reading the same apocalyptic opening to chapter 25, senses that a storm is on the way, but has no idea of its motivation. Torn by the past and the knowledge of his permanent psychic debility, the Master has an attack of anxiety. Suddenly, Azazello appears with greetings from Woland and an invitation to an "outing" (*progulka*). After regaling their guest with cognac ("*kon*iak"), the hosts drink Woland's present, the poison Falernian wine that is a favorite of Pilate. (Thus Pilate the horseman, it might be said, executes not only Yeshua and Yuda, but the Master and Margarita as well.) In the prestorm light the Master realizes immediately that his *end is approaching* ("nastaet *kon*ets").[49] "What does this new state mean?" asks the now dead Master.

> "It means," replied Azazello, "that it is time for us to start. The storm is thundering already, do you hear? It is growing dark. The *horses* paw the earth, the little *garden* shivers. Say farewell, farewell, to your little basement flat."[50]

As the group of riders leaves Moscow behind (in an earlier version Margarita's last gesture before departure is to save a child from the *balcony* of a burning house),[51] Woland, Behemoth, Korov'ev, and Azazello are transformed into Bulgakov's version of the Four Horsemen of the Apocalypse.[52] Each former jester is now distinct in his somber grandeur, but it is Woland, the ultimate horseman, who is grandest of all:

> And finally, Woland himself was also flying in his true shape now. Margarita would have found it difficult to say what his horse's reins were made of. She thought they might be chains of moonlight, and the horse itself only a hulk of darkness, his mane a cloud, and the rider's spurs white blurs of stars.[53]

The arrival of the horsemen at the site of Pilate's eternal torment brings us to the novel's mystifying climax. Chained Prometheuslike to the memory of his cowardice, Pilate has been reliving the immutable past for twelve thousand moons. It is time for the Master to finish his novel, to complete what he has left unresolved ("Your novel has been read . . . and the only comment on it is that, unfortunately, *it is not finished* ["on ne o*kon*chen"]).[54] The Master is given the same opportunity to release Pilate that Pilate once had to release Yeshua.[55] But the Master, motivated by Margarita's plea for Pilate, is able to make the right choice, to break the chain of history, and thus to end his masterpiece ("Well, now you can finish [*kon*chit'"] your novel with a single phrase!")[56] with a gesture that augurs new beginnings. The forever immobile Pilate is now free to *walk* with the wandering philosopher along the lunar path toward the New Jerusalem (Revelation 21).[57] Maybe, says Woland, they will finally come to an agreement on something. The novel about Pilate finished, the Master and Margarita are rewarded with the eternal refuge and peace (*pokoi*) that neither they nor their author had in life. It is interesting that Woland suggests it is not fitting that the lovers return to historical Moscow, on the one hand, or follow after the liberated Pilate, on the other ("Why follow in the steps of that which is already finished ["*kon* cheno"]?)[58] The reward they are to receive has somehow been specially earmarked for them. And so Woland and his horsemen disappear, the couple dismount,[59] proceed – like Pilate – on foot to their idyllic resting place, and, to complete yet another circle, their story closes with the Master being released from his hero, the horseman Pontius Pilate, by his author, just as he had released his hero from the burden of guilt.[60]

What is the meaning of this ending and how does it gear with the elaborate apocalyptic apparatus that Bulgakov has engineered? It would be a mistake, I think, to see this final moment as anything resembling an apocalypse of terrible judgment and retribution – that is, the Apocalypse of John. What Pilate deserves is punishment, and yet the Master frees him. The horses and horsemen symbolize physical death, to be sure, but that death is no ending (as it is, for example, in the case of Berlioz). Too much perhaps has been made of the Master's weakness, of the judgment that he deserves peace while Yeshua deserves light. Surely Pilate, who joins Yeshua on the lunar path, is no more worthy than the Master, his author? No, Bulgakov's unorthodox apocalyptic vision is finally benign and his horses and horsemen positive, at least inasmuch as death, the ultimate mystery, can be understood as a joyful opening into a state beyond history. The guiding intelligence here is not that, dominating Revelation, of the avenging Christ, but that of the merciful lamb, and it is for this reason that Margarita's voice ("Let him go!") emerges as especially resonant. Hers is the voice of the compassionate[61] Virgin, nowhere to be found in the last book of the Bible.

There are, we should not forget, three distinct settings to suggest the rewards earned by the various characters. Homeless is left in Moscow, fated to remain a captive of history and to experience each year the return (that is, the circle) of his nightmare about Pilate. Pilate, history's relentless horseman, and Yeshua, the peripatetic "good man" whose faith in others has little or no historical justification, mount the path toward the New Jerusalem, toward the point in the misty future when history is still infinite possibility, when they can at last "agree on something," and when all can be well. Yeshua's concern is ethical – man's perfectability – and that is why, comforting Pilate, he continues up the path. Thus if Homeless is a victim of the past and Yeshua and Pilate have their sights on a vision of the distant future, where does this leave the Master and Margarita? They are, I believe, left in a timeless present, one that is both free from the pain of the past and the promise of the future, but one from which, with the gift of imaginative empathy (a sort of Keatsian "Negative Capability"), the past can be recaptured and the future anticipated. Such a paradise cannot of course be imagined in this world, especially not in the Soviet Union, but were it to exist, it would look like the little home, with its Venetian window and climbing vine, given to the Master and Margarita. Until God, the final author hovering beyond the final text, brings history and religious mystery together in this world, we must rely on Bulgakov's version of a *poeta ex machina* to make things right. With the New Jerusalem still distant, only art can free Pilate, write history from actuality back into possibility.

Yet Bulgakov, even now, is not quite finished. In the epilogue he closes, and simultaneously opens, a final circle. Ivan Nikolaevich (Homeless) and Nikolai Ivanovich come each spring to Margarita's *garden* to relive what has been irretrievably lost. The latter, once turned into Natasha's porcine steed, is a parodic mirror of the former,[62] and chides himself for his faintheartedness – "What was I, an old ass [*osel*], afraid of?"[63] Homeless's predicament, however, is the more serious: he is haunted by a dream swarming with images of the noseless executioner, the dying Gestas, and the apocalyptic storm. Death is here in its tragic, inexorable character – Gestas is stabbed with the same spear that killed Yeshua. And, significantly, a merciful injection ("u*kol*") causes the nightmare to cease. The verb ("" *kol*ot' *kol*'nut' ") used to stab Gestas and Yeshua with Pilate's spear reappears in the noun whose prick releases Homeless and his lacerated ("is*kol*otaia") memory. What Bulgakov is suggesting in this ending that *continues* what has already ended, is that Homeless, the faithful disciple, must undergo his own spiritual death each Easter season in order to be released, if only for an oneiric moment, into that state beyond history where the Master and Margarita now reside. Only at this point in the text, and *not* in the preceding chapter, does Yeshua swear to Pilate that the execution never happened. Suddenly we have returned to the vicious circle of history to discover how, through Homeless's experience of periodic death-in-life, the circle is to be opened. Homeless perceives that endings can be happy after all. As he asks the Master:

> "So that's how it [the story of Pilate] *ended* ["*kon*chilos' "]?" "That's how it *ended* ["*kon*chilos' "], my disciple."

And as Margarita concludes:

> "Yes, of course ["*kon*echno"] that's how it did. Everything has *ended* ["*kon*chilos' "], and everything *ends* [*kon*chaetsia"] . . . And I shall kiss you on the forehead and all will be with you as it should."[64]

Little wonder, then, that Homeless wakes feeling calm and healthy after his dream. Together with the Master and Margarita, the author, the reader, and perhaps even Pilate himself, he can adjust to this ending, knowing he is free of "the cruel fifth Procurator of Judea, the horseman Pontius Pilate."

NOTES

This essay appears in expanded form in David Bethea, *The Shape of the Apocalypse in Modern Russian Fiction* (Princeton, N.J.: Princeton University Press, 1989). Readers are strongly urged to turn to that book for a fuller explication of the apocalyptic vision not only in Bulgakov but in Dostoevsky, Bely, Platonov, and Pasternak.

1. Bruce A. Beatie and Phyllis W. Powell, "Story and Symbol: Notes toward a Structural Analysis of Bulgakov's *The Master and Margarita*," *Russian Literature Triquarterly* 15 (1978): 237.

2. See Edward Ericson, Jr., "The Satanic Incarnation: Parody in Bulgakov's *The Master and Margarita*," *Russian Review* 33 (January 1974): 35–36; Boris Gasparov, "Iz nabliudenii nad motivnoi strukturoi romana M. A. Bulgakova, *Master i Margarita*," *Slavica Hierosolymitana* 3 (1978): 218–19; Georgii Krugovoi, "Gnosticheskii roman M. Bulgakova," *Novyi Zhurnal* 134 (1979): 60–61; W. J. Leatherbarrow, "The Devil and the Creative Visionary in Bulgakov's *Master i Margarita*," *New Zealand Slavonic Journal*, no. 1 (1975):42–43; and A. C. Wright, "Satan in Moscow: An Approach to Bulgakov's *The Master and Margarita*," *PMLA* 88 (October 1973): 1164; 1167–68.

3. Ericson, "The Satanic Incarnation," 35–36.

4. M. Chudakova, "A Vital Necessity: About Mikhail Bulgakov's Personal Library," *Soviet Literature*, no. 2 (1977), 143–44; Krugovoi, "Gnosticheskii roman," 49–50; Milne, "*Master and Margarita*," 9–12, 26.

5. See Sydney Schultze, "The Epigraphs in *White Guard*," *Russian Literature Triquarterly* 15 (1978): 213–18.

6. Piper sees the Master in chivalrous terms as "an important knight in an age-old battle, whose role . . . is to assert spiritual values in the teeth of and because of an evil whose existence he knows full well" (D.G.B. Piper, "An Approach to *The Master and Margarita*," *Forum for Modern Language Studies* 7 (1971): 157). Here the traits, such as idealism and love of beauty, of the romantic knight (*rytsar'*) should not be confused with those of the

rider(*vsadnik*). For Bulgakov, the rider is not a benign figure but one (such as Pilate) associated with the ideas of guilt and death.

7. See M. Chudakova, "Tvorcheskaia istoriia romana M. Bulgakova *Master i Margarita*," *Voprosy literatury*, no. 1 (1976): 243–44, 249.

8. Ibid., 219, 225, 233, 237. It might be argued, of course, that the "hoof" in these variant titles refers to the *cloven* hoof of Satan, and therefore an equine allusion should be ruled out. But the "horseshoe" in the fourth variant title suggests that indeed Bulgakov was linking, rather than trying to keep distinct, Satan and the image of the horse.

9. Mikhail Bulgakov, *Master i Margarita* (Frankfurt/Main, 1971), 64. This text is used throughout the essay. The translation, emended where necessary for precision, is Bulgakov, *The Master and Margarita*, trans. Mirra Ginsburg (New York: Grove, 1967). Hereafter cited as MM, with references to the Russian text separated from those of the translation by a slash; e.g., 64/37.

10. MM, 33/24.

11. MM, 42/31.

12. MM, 49/38.

13. Since the same verb is used in both cases, this warning anticipates the "Beware of the Tram!" sign that flashes before Berlioz moments before his death. See page 389 of this essay.

14. MM, 55/43.

15. MM, 217/182.

16. For a fine discussion of the problematical character of Afranius, see Richard W. F. Pope, "Ambiguity and Meaning in *The Master and Margarita*: The Role of Afranius," *Slavic Review* 36 (March 1977): 1–24.

17. MM, 380/314–15.

18. Pope ("Ambiguity and Meaning," 6–10) is especially good on this.

19. The English text of the Bible used throughout this essay is *The New Oxford Annotated Bible with the Apocrypha*, ed. Herbert G. May and Bruce M. Metzger (New York: 1977). It has been checked against the Russian text *Bibliia ili knigi sviashchennago pisaniia vetkhago i novago zaveta* (Valley Forge, Pa.: Judson, 1964).

20. MM, 378/312–13.

21. See Elizabeth Klosty Beaujour, "The Use of Witches in Fedin and Bulgakov," *Slavic Review* 33 (December 1974): 695, 706–7; J. Delaney, "*The*

Master and Margarita: The Reach Exceeds the Grasp," *Slavic Review* 31 (1972): 99.

22. MM, 48/37.

23. The double cordon is also mentioned earlier in the chapter "Pontius Pilate" (44/33). It is, of course, Pilate who gives the order to form the cordon around Bald Mountain.

24. The equine statues atop the hippodrome have no basis in any historical description of ancient Jerusalem and must have been added by Bulgakov from his knowledge of the Moscow hippodrome, which was indeed (and still is) adorned with such statues. Josephus, a primary source for anyone doing research on ancient Jerusalem, makes only passing reference to the hippodrome: In Josephus, *The Jewish Wars*, 20 vols. (New York: Putnam's, 1927), 2:339, he says that during an insurrection of the Jews in 4 B.C. one of their camps was located to the south of the city, near the hippodrome. The only other mention of the hippodrome, in Josephus, *The Jewish Antiquities*, 20 vols. (Cambridge, Mass.: Harvard University Press, 1963), 13:491, is likewise uninformative. Bulgakov's leading source, Brokgauz-Efron, *Entsiklopedicheskii slovar'*, vol. 13, 652–58, tells us merely that "during the reign of Herod the Great, Jerusalem again entered a period of flowering and became adorned with magnificent buildings (a theater, amphitheater, and *perhaps even a hippodrome*)" (657; emphasis added).

25. There is an Abaddon who also shows up in the chapter "By Candlelight" (329/274–75).

26. Pilate's cloak has a blood-red lining as well. See Gasparov, "Iz nabliudenii," 204 n. 3.

27. Ibid., 198, 228.

28. MM, 37/26; emphasis added.

29. Ibid., 213; and Krugovoi, "Gnosticheskii roman," 56–57.

30. For the parallels between Ershalaim and Moscow, see Beatie and Powell, "Story and Symbol," 220–23; Ericson, "The Satanic Incarnation," 25; Gasparov, "Iz nabliudenii," 215–21; Leatherbarrow, "The Devil," 31–33; Mahlow, *The Text as Cipher*; Proffer, "On *The Master and Margarita*," 548–59; and Wright, "Satan in Moscow," 1170–71.

31. Gasparov, "Iz nabliudenii," 215–21.

32. Other references to the jockey's cap appear on pages 12/4 and 121/106.

33. The balcony and the palms resurface in other Moscow chapters: "Schizophrenia, as Said Before" (90/77) and "Ivan Splits in Two" (148–49/132).

34. Noted by Gasparov, "Iz nabliudenii," 215.

35. MM, 85/72.

36. MM, 150/133.

37. In this same chapter a mustachioed (like Behemoth) coachman drives up on the Sadovoe to one of the victims of the magic show, reigns in his nag, and grins diabolically (192/170).

38. Noted by Gasparov, "Iz nabliudenii," 219.

39. Gasparov ("Iz nabliudenii," 222) places the Griboedov House on Tverskoi Boulevard. Yet the opening description of the house sets it convincingly on a ring road (and my assumption is that this ring road is Sadovoe): "Starinnyi dvukhetazhnyi dom kremovogo tsveta pomeshchalsia na bul'varnom *kol'tse* v glubine chakhlogo *sada*, otdelennogo ot tratuara *kol'tsa* reznoiu chugunnoiu reshetkoi" ("The old, two-story, cream-colored mansion was situated on a boulevard circle [and was set] deep within a rundown garden, divided from the sidewalk of the circle by a wrought-iron fence") (71/59). Whether this boulevard is Sadovoe really makes no difference, however, as Bulgakov deliberately links the image of the circle and the garden (thus *Sad*ovoe *kol'tso*) from the start. Both Berlioz's apartment (97/84) and the Variety Theater (131/116) are explicitly placed by Bulgakov on Sadovoe Ring Road. As mentioned, Sadovoe is by far the most alluded to geographical landmark in Moscow: of the sixteen Moscow chapters in book 1, eleven make precise reference to Sadovoe (often several times); in chapter 1, for example, the sun (presumably of Berlioz's life) is setting beyond Sadovoe (11/3); in chapters 3 and 4, it is Annushka "from Sadovoe" who is responsible for Berlioz's death (65/51); in chapter 10, Varenukha is attacked by satanic forces in the garden of the Variety Theater and then spirited along Sadovoe to Likhodeev's apartment (142–44/126–28); and in chapter 14, Rimskii escapes the same forces by catching a taxi and rushing away from the theater, again along Sadovoe (201/178).

40. Ericson, "The Satanic Incarnation," 36.

41. Vladimir Nabokov, *The Gift* (New York: Putnam's, 1963), 24.

42. Vladimir Nabokov, *Strong Opinions* (New York: McGraw-Hill, 1973), 76.

43. This passage, argues Chudakova ("Tvorcheskaia istoriia," 252), is strongly autobiographical.

44. The title of chapter 27 is "*Kon*ets kvartiry no. 50" ("The End of Apartment 50").

45. A Berezka store is a store predominantly for tourists which accepts only foreign hard currency as payment.

46. On the motif of fire, see Gasparov, "Iz nabliudenii," 222–29.

47. Cf. Revelation 16:17–19: "The seventh angel poured his bowl into the air and a loud voice came out of the temple, from the throne, saying, 'It is done!' And there were flashes of lightning, voices, peals of thunder, and a great earthquake."

48. An earlier version has Matthew the Levite visit Woland as a "violet horseman" (*fioletovyi vsadnik*) (Chudakova, "Tvorcheskaia istoriia," 238).

49. MM, 464/375.

50. MM, 466/376.

51. Ibid.

52. This, of course, makes the absence of Hella logical. Beaujour ("The Use of Witches," 704 n. 22) suggests, I think erroneously, that the witch's absence is carelessness on Bulgakov's part.

53. MM, 478/384–85.

54. MM, 479/385.

55. Cf. 53/42.

56. MM, 480/387.

57. Bulgakov considered the possibility of having Ieshua come to Pilate on the *balcony* (Chudakova, "Tvorcheskaia istoriia," 239).

58. MM, 481/387.

59. The couple was originally to gallop to their eternal refuge on horseback (Chudakova, "Tvorcheskaia istoriia," 247).

60. Bulgakov here clearly links Pilate, Ieshua, the Master, and himself as ultimate author: Pilate had the chance to release Ieshua, but released Var-Ravvan (Barabas) instead ("Imia togo, kogo seichas pri vas *otpustiat na svobodu*" ["The name of him who shall now, in your presence, be released"] [53/42]); the Master, urged on by Margarita, is now able to release the captive Pilate ("*Otpustitie* ego!" vdrug kriknula Margarita . . . Master . . . slozhil ruki ruporom i kriknul . . . '*Svoboden! Svoboden*!'" ["Release him!" suddenly cried Margarita . . . The Master cupped his hands like a megaphone and

shouted: 'You are free! You are free!'"] [480/386–87]); and finally Bulgakov releases the Master from the past and obsessive thoughts of his hero Pontius Pilate with the same phrase ("Kto-to *otpuskal na svobodu* mastera, kak sam on tol'ko chto *otpustil* im sozdannogo geroia" ("Someone released the Master as the Master had just released his hero") (482–83)/omitted from the Ginsburg translation; emphasis added).

61. "'What is he (Pilate) saying?' asked Margarita, and her utterly calm face was clouded by compassion (*sostradanie*)" (479/386). For Margarita's link with the Virgin Mary, see Ericson, "The Satanic Incarnation," 31–35.

62. Noted by Gasparov, "Iz nabliudenii," 227.

63. MM, 496/400.

64. MM, 498/402.

Houses, Homes, and the Rhetoric of Inner Space in Mikhail Bulgakov

LAURA D. WEEKS

In her recently published diaries, Elena Sergeevna Bulgakov makes the following observation not once, but twice: "For Mikhail Afanas'evich, *apartment* is a magical word. He doesn't envy anything on earth, only a nice apartment. It's a kind of fetish with him."[1] Readers have long noted the importance of apartments and other dwelling spaces in Bulgakov's prose – both their symbolic significance, and that they are, in Haber's words, "one of the key organizing images,"[2] both early and late. As a structural principle, Bulgakov's dwellings organize the text spatially, providing continuity when temporal and causal connections have been suppressed or eliminated (this is especially true of *The Master and Margarita*). Symbolically they represent a hierarchy of moral values, a "moral and metaphysical topography," again borrowing Haber's words. In short, they constitute a mental landscape every bit as detailed as Dostoevsky's, with his 730 paces from sin to redemption.[3]

In this essay I will take a closer look at the houses in Bulgakov's first and last novels, using a hybrid of the archetypal, the phenomenological, and the semiotic approaches. All three approaches have a common denominator in the thematics of the house. For a psychologist, the house or dwelling is an archetype symbolizing the structure of the psyche. For a phenomenologist, the house, with its attributes of verticality, centrality, and stability, is "our corner of the world, our first universe, truly a cosmos."[4] For a semiotician, it is the quintessential boundary breaking up the continuity of cultural and personal space into internal and external space.

> Man's canonical mode of habitation is the source of some very common value oppositions associated with the difference between an inner and an outer space, or sphere. Its most typical, if not primary, manifestation is the opposition between the interior of a house, representing the positive values of domestic life, like security, warmth and nourishment, and of cultural continuity, and on the other hand, the world outdoors.[5]

It is precisely this conflict between the enclosed inner space and the unbounded outer space that is critical to an understanding of Bulgakov's universe.

For the phenomenologist Bachelard, the house where one is born is the most important of all dwellings. It is, as he says, "physically inscribed in us."

> Even beyond memories, the natal house is physically inscribed in us. It is a group of organic customs. After an interval of twenty years, despite all the anonymous staircases, we will recapture the reflexes of the "first staircase," we will not stumble over that one step that's a little too high. The entire being of the house will deploy itself, faithful to our being.[6]

Accordingly, I will begin with the house of Bulgakov's childhood, the legendary house at No. 13 Alekseevsky Spusk where the Turbin brothers and their sister, the golden-haired Elena, preside over a motley crew of White officers during the terrible year of our Lord, 1918.

The first thing we notice about the house is the incredible clutter of realia – tables with their starched white tablecloths, vases with or without roses, couches, rugs, lampshades; everything is catalogued down to the least feather duster, and, moreover, most of these will become rather transparent symbols of the Turbins' cultural codes. The next attribute we notice is how alive it is. With its talking clocks, its attentive lampshades, and its cream colored blinds, this is a house with eyes, ears, and a voice. Even the column of mercury in a thermometer can achieve the status of an animate being. So great is the harmony that reigns within the inner space that objects and inhabitants become interchangeable. Clocks become people; people's faces become clocks.

Finally we notice how absolute is the barrier between the inner and outer spaces. Outside the space defined by the house are darkness, cold, violence, hunger, and death. Inside are light, warmth, order, food, and comfort. There is an appealing, almost childlike quality in Bulgakov's insistence on the insularity of the space behind the closed cream-colored blinds. Like a proverbial three-year-old child ("If I shut my eyes you can't see me") the Turbins shut their blinds to the world at large. This attitude arises every time the outer space threatens to erupt into the inner space as, for example, when the two brothers lounge by the stove listening to the first volleys as Petliura approaches the city.

> The patterned tiles were luxuriously hot, the black clock going tonk-tank, tonk-tank, as it had done for thirty years. The elder Turbin, clean-shaven and fair-haired, grown older and more somber since October 25, 1917, wearing an army officer's tunic with huge bellows pockets, blue breeches, and soft new slippers, in his favorite attitude – in an upright armchair. At his feet on a stool Nikolka with his forelock, his legs stretched out almost as far as the sideboard – the dining room was not big – and shod in his buckled boots. Gently and softly Nikolka strummed at his beloved guitar, vaguely . . . everything was still so confused. The city was full of unease, of vague foreboding . . .
>
> On his shoulders Nikolka wore sergeant's shoulder straps to which were sewn the white stripes of an officer cadet, and on his left sleeve a sharp-pointed tricolor chevron (Infantry, No. 1 Detachment, 3d Squad, formed four days ago in view of impending events).
>
> Yet despite these events, all was well inside the Turbins' home: it was warm and comfortable and the cream-colored blinds were

> drawn – so warm that the two brothers felt pleasantly languorous.[7]

Or again, after the fall of the city, as Lariosik, the only alien element to be admitted to the inner sanctum, prepares to sit down to whist:

> Lariosik blushed, looked embarrassed, and said hastily that he did play, but very, very badly . . . that he hoped they wouldn't swear at him in the way his partner, the tax inspector, used to swear at him in Zhitomir . . . that he had been through a terrible crisis, but that here in Elena Vasilievna's house he was regaining his spirits, that Elena Vasilievna was quite an exceptional person and that it was so warm and cozy here, especially the cream-colored blinds on all the windows that made you feel insulated from the outside world . . . and as for that outside world, you had to agree it was filthy, bloody, and senseless.[8]

Bulgakov's rigid division of the inner and outer spaces into a representation of chaos and cosmos is remarkably like that of Gogol's *Old World Landowners*, as described by Lotman.

> In the *Old World Landowners*, the structure of space is one of the principle means of expression. The entire artistic space is divided into two unequal parts. The first of these . . . is "the entire rest of the world." It is distinguished by its vastness, its vagueness. The second is the world of the Old World landowners. The principle distinguishing feature of this world is its insularity. An understanding of the boundary separating this space from the other is of the utmost importance; moreover, the entire complex of notions belonging to Afansy Ivanovich and Pulkheria Ivanovna is organized by this division, subservient to it.
>
> The estate of the Tostogubovs has one other feature: it is "one's own," whereas that which lies beyond its borders is "alien." Moreover, this feature is not relative: it characterizes the space of the Old World landowners as such, and not only in relation to its direct owners. It is no coincidence that when the author dropped by at the Old World landowners, "the horses gaily pulled up

> under the porch, the coachman peacefully slid off the box and lit his pipe as if he had arrived at his own home." This is no coincidence: the estate of the Old World landowners is a HOME in capital letters.
>
> Cordiality, hospitality, and goodwill are likewise the constant features of this "homely" space. The law of the inner world is comfort.[9]

The house at No. 13 Alekseevsky Spusk is a similarly insular inner space with rigidly demarcated boundaries where the same laws of cordiality, hospitality, and comfort apply. Small wonder that for Myshlaevsky, Karas', and Shervinsky the Turbins' apartment is more of a home than their own apartments.

The inner space is also cultural continuum. As described by Lotman, the division of space into finite and infinite sets commonly involves identifying the enclosed inner space with one's own nation, with notions of culture, of the intelligentsia, of cosmos versus the unbounded external space, which is identified with foreign nations, barbarism, the masses, and chaos.[10] The Turbins' inner space is defined by the "chocolate smelling books, with their Natasha Rostovas and their Captain's Daughters." It is a space devoted to the Russian language and to Great Russian culture, which in turn belongs to the larger set of Western European culture, symbolized by the score to Gounod's *Faust* left open on the piano. As Lesley Milne has recently pointed out, the Turbins' highly cultured existence is deliberately intended as a blow in defense of prerevolutionary bourgeois culture:

> *The White Guard* is very aware of itself as a cultural artifact inspired by cultural traditions. It is full of literary echoes and theatrical devices, but also displays a particular fondness for the opera, which is, within the city, a further concentration of culture: an urban, social art, convention-laden and synaesthetic.[11]

The outer space in *The White Guard* is characterized by Ukrainian language, invariably portrayed as a hostile, alien element – witness the intrusion of the perfidious Captain Talberg's Ukrainian grammar and the butchered half-Russian, half-Ukrainian speech of the robbers who will invade the bottom floor of the house.

The mention of the bottom floor brings up another aspect of the house. The house, as Bachelard tells us, is a vertical being: it appeals to our sense of verticality.[12] Moreover, verticality, when contrasted with horizontality, is the universal axis for modeling hierarchies and hierarchical values.[13] In this regard, the Turbin household is literally at the apex of the cultural and moral hierarchy, situated as it is at the top of the house near the top of a hill near the center of a city itself situated on hills overlooking the Dniepr. Predictably, ascent spells safety whereas descent spells danger and death.

With its insularity and its cultural continuity, the Turbin household is a classic example of radial space. Radial space, which Toporov calls "*espace rayonnant*," is "concentric," and "is typical of agricultural and urban cultures whose center is the house."[14] Its antithesis is dynamic space, or "*espace itinerant*" – a migratory vision of space whose symbol is the road or journey. Returning again to Lotman's analysis of the *Old World Landowners*, we find that an exact analogy can be made between the "circular" topography of their estate and the topography of Bulgakov's novel. The Old World landowners' estate is surrounded first by a ring of outlying peasant huts, themselves ringed by trees, then by a garden hedge, followed by the garden itself, and finally the covered porch that circles the entire house. The final barrier between inner and outer space is formed by the singing doors, the barrier between the "external cold and the inner warmth."[15] According to Lotman, each of these concentric rings denotes "a particular boundary which, the closer it comes to the center, the less accessible it becomes for the outside world."[16] The Turbins' apartment is likewise the center of a universe that is ringed by the circumference of the hill, itself ringed by the city of Kiev, which is described in a series of concentric rings formed by terraced hillsides that expand infinitely until they reach the sea.

> The beautiful hills rising above the Dnieper were made even lovelier by gardens that rose terracewise, spreading, at times flam-

ing into color like a million sunspots, at others basking in the perpetual gentle twilight of the Imperial Gardens, the terrifying drop over the escarpment quite unprotected by the ancient, rotting black beams of the parapet. The sheer hillsides, lashed by snowstorms, fell away to the distant terraces below which in turn spread further and wider, merging into the tree-lined embankments that curved along the bank of the great river. Away and away wound the dark river like a ribbon of forged steel, into the haze, further than the eye could see even from the city's highest eminence, on to the Dnieper rapids, to the Zaporozhian Sech, to the Chersonese, to the far-distant sea.[17]

What is striking is the extent to which Bulgakov identifies with the inner space, which Lotman defines as archetypally female.

> The house with its attributes: bed, stove, and warmth, in general a *closed* and *habitable* space, is conceived of as the "female world" in chivalrous and epic tales. The "field" is contrasted to it as the "manly space." Thus from the female's point of view, E [external, unbounded space] is the field, but from the man's point of view it is the house. Compare the biblical . . . plot of the departure of the hero from the closed (nonheroic, nonprincely, woman's) space to "freedom": into the steppe and into the desert.[18]

Although today we might question Lotman's distinction, or at least the absolute assignment of male and female spaces, we might agree that it has historical validity, and it is certainly valid for Bulgakov's universe, Bulgakov being an unabashed romantic who would in his sunset novel produce a stunning example of the *ewige weibliche* (eternal feminine). It is also true that within the Turbin apartment the characters engage in the archetypally female activities of eating and drinking, whereas outside they engage in the archetypally male activity of fighting. More than that, the identification of the female nature of the enclosed inner space reveals the female principle that governs the Bulgakovian universe.

It is commonly acknowledged that Bulgakov wrote *The White Guard* for his mother, and the mother image is omnipresent. As the novel opens the mother has died and Elena has taken her place. Elena occupies the mother's former room, which is inhabited by a wonder-working icon of the Mother of God. Just as the apartment is the heart of the novel's topographical space, Elena is the heart of its cultural space. Only Elena can provide the starched white tablecloths, the roses, the cultural continuity without which the male characters are lost. The brothers are so dependent on her that they resent the intrusion of her husband Talberg into their inner sanctum, and not only because of his foreign blood.

> The wedge-shaped badges of rank of the Hetman's War Ministry had a depressing effect on the Turbin brothers. Indeed, dating from long before those badges, practically since the day Elena had married Talberg, it was as if some kind of crack had opened up in the bowl of the Turbins' life and imperceptibly the good water had drained away through it. The vessel was dry.[19]

It is no coincidence that the novel takes place in the Mother of Russian Cities. The analogy between Elena and the city is transparently obvious from the beginning. The city is restless, ill-at-ease, full of foreboding as it awaits Petlyura; similarly, Elena is restless, ill-at-ease, full of foreboding as she awaits Talberg. Bulgakov cements the analogy by repeating the same adjective: "Trevozhno v gorode" (The city was full of anxiety), "Trevozhnyi vzgliad" (A glance full of anxiety). Symptomatic emblem that life in the city has gone awry is the invasion of the definitive female space, Madame Anjou's, significantly located in the heart of the city, by the male element:

> The colonel was seated at a little desk in a low, green, very feminine armchair on a kind of raised platform in the front of the shop. Pieces of blue cardboard hatboxes labeled "Madame Anjou, Ladies' Milinery" rose behind him, shutting out some of the light from the dusty window hung with lacy tulle.
>
> Innumerable people with gold artillery badges milled around the colonel. To one side stood a large deal box full of wire and field telephones, beside it cardboard cases of hand grenades looking like cans of jam with wooden handles; nearby were heaps of

> coiled machine-gun belts. On the colonel's left was a treadle sewing machine, while the snout of a machine gun protruded beside his right leg.[20]

Through Elena we realize that the sacred inner space in the Bulgakovian universe can be violated. The first "movement" of the plot, if the novel can be said to have a plot, involves the arrival of the long-overdue Talberg and the first indications that he will abandon Elena. He does leave, ostensibly for a brief period until he can rejoin the family with the advancing White Army. However, after he leaves it becomes clear that the rift threatens to be permanent. His departure causes the violation of one of the cardinal rules of the inner space: never remove the shade from a lamp. More important, there has been a breach in the innermost wall, and this breach is conveyed by clothing, perhaps the single most important artifact in Bulgakov's universe, second only to food.[21]

> "Oh my God, what am I saying? Sergei, what am I saying about you? Suddenly we're cut off . . . He's gone and here am I . . .
>
> "My husband," she said with a sigh, and began to unbutton her neglige, "My husband . . . "[22]

Immediately after this passage, Alexei begins dreaming of the city, once again equating the threat to Elena with the threat to the city, which is in imminent danger of being abandoned by the Germans. The close identification of Elena with the city of Kiev allows Bulgakov to digress for a moment from the poetics of the hearth to invoke the poetics of the elements and of invasion.[23] As Lesley Milne observes, the city and the history and culture it represents are all equally vulnerable:

> The city in *The White Guard* is both a specific place and a universal symbol: it is a progenitor of culture and a concentration of cultural life, but like its predecessor, the proud Kievan state of the twelfth century, it is vulnerable to invasion from what in *The White Guard* is described as "the poverty, delusion, hopelessness, and irredeemable savagery of the steppes."[24]

The symbolic breach in Elena's defenses becomes final when the threat of death actually invades the sacred inner space. The severely wounded Alexei is helped into the Turbins' apartment by the mysterious Julia Reiss and is laid on the couch.

> Wearing another man's black overcoat with a torn lining and a pair of strange black trousers Alexei Turbin lay motionless on the divan below the clock. His face was pale, with a bluish pallor, and his teeth were clenched. Elena was fussing around him, her dressing gown untied and showing her black stockings and the lace of her underwear . . .
>
> . . . "Undress him completely and straight into bed," said the pointed beard in his bass voice. Anyuta poured water from a jug onto his hands, and blobs of lather fell into the bowl as he washed. The stranger stood aside from the confusion and bustle, at one moment gazing unhappily at the broken plates, at the next blushing as he looked at the dishevelled Elena, who had ceased to care that her dressing gown was completely undone.[25]

The resolution of the nonplot occurs after the miraculously resurrected Alexei is sitting down (what else?) to table with his friends and the fateful letter for Elena arrives, announcing the full level of Talberg's perfidy. He has not only abandoned her but is already planning to enter into another marriage without the benefit of divorce. Once again the laws of the inner space are violated:

> Although the bedroom lamp was shaded, Elena had the unpleasant impression as if someone had ripped off the colored silk shade, and the unshaded light had struck her eyes. The expression on Elena's face changed until it looked like the ancient face of the Virgin in the fretted silver icon cover. Her lips trembled, then her mouth twitched and set into folds of contempt.[26]

As Elena struggles with her emotions, the others, gathered in the dining room, are laughing and eating. Thus the outer rings of radial space have been breached. Talberg has gone and the city has fallen, but by her sacrifice she has preserved the sanctity of the inner space.

With the help of our Freudian imaginations, we can stretch the definition of Bulgakov's inner space (Elena = the Mother of all Cities = the Mother = the vessel that holds their life) to see that it is a kind of womb. This would explain its peculiar insular quality, as well as the fact that it is small (constant references are made to the size of the rooms: "Nikolka stretched his legs out almost to the sideboard – the dining room was not large"; Alexei's little study – "it was sparse, cramped but comfortable") and yet so full of life.

If *The White Guard* was written for Bulgakov's mother, *The Master and Margarita* was heavily influenced by his father. Truly, in his father's house there are many mansions. In setting them before us, Bulgakov resorts to that same Gogolian radial space: the concentric circles that defined the universe of the *Old World Landowners*. The notorious Griboedov House, for example, is located on a ringed boulevard, in the depths of a run-down garden, circled by a wrought-iron fence. Moreover, two of the novel's most significant spots, the Variety Theater and Apartment Building No. 302, are located on the "ring road" – the Sadovoe Koltso. Since the ring road is near the center of the city, and the city itself is partially ringed by the Moscow River, we get the same impression of infinitely expanding circles.

A great deal has been written about the spatial, temporal, and narrative circularity in *The Master and Margarita*.[27] What is important for our purposes are the moral and ideological values attached to the inner spaces defined by the circles. These have been succinctly set forth by Lotman, who identifies the symbolism of "houses and anti-houses" as the defining feature of Bulgakov's entire opus.[28] In Lotman's analysis, "houses" represent "a concentration of spirituality which is expressed in a richness of inner culture, creativity, and love."[29] "Anti-houses," of which there are any number of examples in *The Master and Margarita* (Lotman specifically lists the Griboedov House, the insane asylum, and the log hut of the concentration camp) are a source of evil and falsehood, whose "chief characteristic is that in them people do not live – they disappear from them (they run, fly, or walk away, only to disappear without a trace)."[30]

Lotman then goes on to explain the complex hierarchical structure of homes and houses in *The Master and Margarita*. The lowest rung is occupied by liars and philistines, who need not so much a home as "living quarters" or an "apartment," a word that is itself fraught with evil connotations in the novel. The highest rung is occupied by "pure spirituality" which has no need of a home.[31] In establishing this hierarchy Bulgakov also illustrates Lotman's theory of cultural definition through opposition ("our own" versus "alien"; "initiates" versus "laymen"), which ascribes positive values to the group that lies *outside* the "chosen" or closed set.

> The opposition "initiated" – "lay" may be connected with the fact that the cultural text is oriented from the point of view of an initiated person, and initiation is appraised very positively . . . However, in the opposition "plebian" (as simply a man) – "aristocrat" (a man of estate) in democratic texts of the eighteenth century, or "poor of spirit" (standing outside) – "pharisee" of biblical texts, it is the "not entering," the "not being initiated," "not belonging" that will be evaluated positively.[32]

Thus, although it is obvious from what Booth called "the rhetoric of titles"[33] that homes and especially apartments are going to play a large part in the novel (cf. the chapter headings "A Sinister Apartment," "Unfortunate Visitors," "The End of Apartment No. 50," "Absolution and Eternal Refuge"), it is those who *have* apartments – the Berliozes and Latunskys – who are the philistines, whereas the have-nots, the homeless – the Master, the poet Homeless, and the vagrant Yeshua Ha-Nozri – are the heroes. This is in stark contrast to *The White Guard*, where the preservation of the inner space was a sacred duty, "the only reason for which a man ought to go to war."

Bulgakov performs another volte-face in the ordering of the hierarchies along the vertical axis. Suddenly descent has become positive, whereas ascent can be positive, negative, or even ambivalent. The Master lives in a basement flat. Margarita must descend from her ivory tower in order to find him; moreover, much is made of the three steps she descends in order to enter his retreat. Her descent along the fifth-dimensional staircase in Apartment No. 50 has the ultimate effect of resurrecting the Master, whereas his ascent from his retreat with his novel in his hands causes his destruction.[34]

It is time to concentrate on the Master's inner space, the heart of radial space in *The Master and Margarita.* Once again we notice the familiar concentric rings: the Master's basement apartment is surrounded by a garden, surrounded in turn by a fence. The state of the garden is worth mentioning, as the state of the moral health of the inner space is reflected by the surrounding garden: thus the Turbins had a small but vigorous garden on the steep hillside at the back of the house; the Master's garden is full of blooming lilac bushes, maples, and lime trees; and the garden outside Margarita's Gothic townhouse is described as *pyshnyi* (luxuriant), whereas the garden at the Griboedov is described as *chakhlyi* (run-down or faded).

The same loving detail that characterized the descriptions in *The White Guard* is devoted to the furnishings of the inner space, which is in effect a re-creation of "paradise lost." Note the reappearance of the key items that symbolized the Turbins' cultural codes: the books, the lamp, the stove:

> "There was a couch and across from it, another couch, and between them a small table with a beautiful night lamp on it, and closer to the window, books. Here, a small desk, and in the first room – an enormous room, fourteen square meters – books, more books, and a stove. Ah, what a great place I had!"[35]

Under Margarita's influence even the roses in the crystal vase will reappear. However the size of the inner space has shrunk considerably, from seven rooms to two. In another feature of Bulgakov's rhetoric of inner space the diminutive size is mentioned repeatedly. Everything about the flat is described in diminutives. Even Woland refers to it as the "*podvalchik*."[36] There is something disturbing in this contraction of the inner space, especially in light of Von Franz's observation that the size of the chambers in a dwelling are often a good indication of the dimensions of the psyche.[37] It is as if Bulgakov, writing his sunset novel in the face of his ragged treatment in the world of Soviet letters, felt his physical capacity for resisting the outside world shrinking. The diminished size of the Master's "psychic space" also serves as a reminder that the womblike insularity of the hero's inner space is not entirely healthy. This is as true of the Turbins in their magical apartment as it is of the Master in his basement flat. In his brilliant analysis, Barratt produces a "plot" for *The White Guard* that is the obverse of ours above: not the elements' invasion of the inner sanctum, but rather the two brothers' journey outside its confines.

> In Chapters 6 and 7, we follow Aleksey and Nikolka as they venture outside the confines of their apartment. For the reader, no less than for the characters themselves, this is a symbolic journey, a release from an environment, both physical and psychological, that is restricted and restrictive.[38]

Barratt concludes that for all its obvious virtues, the Turbins' worldview is limited, and that they are largely unaware of its limitations:

> The poverty of Aleksey's vision stands exposed: just as he cannot accept a Kiev overrun by "outsiders" or admit the possibility of a Russia governed by a political party of which he disapproves, so he cannot conceive of a heaven from which all "godless" Bolsheviks are not automatically excluded. His version of the Apocalypse is one which allows for all his beliefs to go unchallenged.[39]

Returning to the Master's apartment, we find that the insular, womblike quality of the inner space is, if anything, more pronounced than it was at the Turbins'. Notice how the Master describes his "emergence" from the womb:

> It [the novel] was finished in August and given to some obscure typist, who typed up five copies. At last the moment came when I had to quit my secret refuge and emerge into life.
>
> "And I emerged into life, holding it in my hands, and at that moment my life ended."[40]

In Bulgakov's universe, to emerge from the womb is to die.

As if in compensation for the shrinking inner life, we are given

Margarita's rooms, which are a nearly perfect mirror image of the Master's, so much so that it is almost as if they occupied different floors in the same house. He lives in a house on a side street near the Arbat; so does she. He occupies the basement; she occupies the top floor. He has two rooms; she has five. Put them together and we get the magic number seven, the number of rooms occupied by the Turbins, as well as the number of rooms in another very important apartment for Bulgakov's spatial topography, that of Professor Preobrazhensky in *The Heart of a Dog*. Thus only the presence of Margarita turns the inner sanctum into a complete spatio-cultural continuum.

After the Master's disastrous attempt to have the novel published, the enclosed, inviolable inner space becomes less of a repository of culture and creativity and more a transparent analog of his psyche. Under the onslaught of critical censure, the Master's health fails, and the same "virus" attacks his sacred inner space. The laws that governed it no longer hold, and no longer is it a haven of light, comfort, food, and repose. In the Master's description of the night before his arrest, the hostile forces have been transformed into the elements that breach the windows and doors protecting his inner sanctum. The poetics of invasion have been brought closer to home.

> That was at dusk, in mid-October. And she left. I lay down on the couch and fell asleep without turning on the lamp. I woke up with the sensation that the octopus was nearby. Fumbling around in the dark, I barely managed to turn on the lamp. My pocket watch showed 2:00 A.M. I had lain down a man beginning to fall ill and awoke a sick man. It suddenly seemed to me that the autumn darkness would break the window panes, would pour into the room and that I would gasp about in it like drinking ink.[41]

After his arrest, interrogation, and detention, the Master returns. The following passage is central to his relationship to the inner space. Notice the state of the garden and the relationship of the speaker to the boundaries demarcating inner and outer space.

> Yes, so there I was in my little yard in the middle of January, at night, wearing the same coat, but with the buttons torn off, shivering from the cold. Behind me were snowdrifts, covering the lilac bushes, and in front of me and down below – my feebly lit, blind-covered windows. I drew up to the first of them and listened – in my rooms a phonograph was playing. That was all I could hear, but I couldn't see anything. After standing there for awhile, I went out through the gate into the lane. The snow was falling heavily.[42]

As Lotman indicates, "the walls of a house . . . the curtain, a night window differentiate space into 'internal' (home) and external space, but belong to the internal."[43] The windows with the (cream-colored?) blinds belong to the inner space from which the Master is now totally excluded. He is now an exile and must begin the painful transition from radial to dynamic, itinerant space.

The first stop on the Master's journey is a kind of limbo, a no-man's-land, a wasteland that is the antithesis of the Bulgakovian inner sanctum, a true "anti-house."

> Margarita dreamed of an unfamiliar place – hopeless, mournful, under the overcast sky of early spring. She dreamed ragged scraps fleeing across a grey sky, and under it a soundless flock of rooks. Some kind of crooked little bridge, and beneath it a murky spring rivulet. Dismal, scrubby, half-bare trees. A solitary aspen, and beyond it, among the trees, beyond some kind of garden, a log hut – maybe an outside kitchen, maybe a bathhouse, maybe a – the devil knows what! The entire surroundings were somehow so lifeless that it made you want to hang yourself on the aspen by the bridge. Not a breath of wind, not a cloud moving, not a living soul. What a hellish place for a living human being.[44]

The end point of the journey is no better. It is indicative of Bulgakov's discomfort with itinerant space that he compresses the entire journey into a single phrase: "I knew this clinic had already opened, and crossing the entire city on foot, I went to it." (In this connection it is also of interest that in one of his many drafts of the novel Bulgakov intended to have the resurrected Master take a trip around the world in the company of Woland, but this idea was abandoned.[45]) This is the final contraction of the inner life. Once in the asylum, the Master tells Ivan, "And, you know, I find it's not so bad here. One doesn't have to trouble oneself with grandiose plans."

As readers of the novel know, it takes an extratextual authority and, equally important, a steep vertical ascent (positive in nature this time) to free the Master from his internal exile. The ultimate end point in his journey through itinerant space brings up the question that has occasioned more critical commentary than any other single question with the exception of Woland's identity. This is the question of the Master's final reward, or why doesn't he join Pilate in the final ascent into the light? Using the paradigms established above (houses versus homes, radial versus itinerant space) allows us to see that final resting place in a more positive light. Earlier we defined the two extremes of philistinism, which requires a "living space," and absolute spirituality, which requires no home. Between them lies the realm of art.

> It has a purely human nature and does not rise to the absolute (the Master has not earned the light). But it is hierarchically higher than the physically more powerful servants of Woland or figures of the type of Afranius, who are similarly not lacking in creativity. This greater spirituality manifests itself spatially. Woland's suite, having arrived in Moscow, establishes itself in an apartment. Afranius and Pilate meet in the courtyard. The Master needs a home. The search for a home is one of the points of view from which we can describe the Master's journey.[46]

This hierarchical ordering of space, with homelessness as the summit of virtue and art housed somewhere between heaven and earth, seems especially appropriate because it echoes the Gnostic worldview with which Bulgakov's theology has increasingly come to be identified. "It should be noted that the conception of 'this' world as a 'dwelling' or 'house' is fundamental to Gnostic ideas; it is those who feel alien to this dwelling – in a word, *homeless* – who bear the mark of their higher calling," says Barratt, who similarly locates the Master "between two worlds."[47] Homelessness was also a virtue for the early Christian. One recalls Augustine's definition of a Christian as "a wanderer seeking a country that is always distant."

In terms of radial versus itinerant space, the Master, who is permanently oriented toward radial space, does not participate in Yeshua's universe, which is constantly in motion: shimmering, shifting, re-creating itself (cf. the final exchange between Pilate and Yeshua: "What a vulgar and banal execution! . . . tell me it didn't happen, did it?" "Of course, it didn't happen"). It is also a classic example of itinerant space, with its lack of closure and its paen to the open road:

> "I need nothing else!" cries out the man in the cloak in a broken voice, as he ascends higher and higher toward the moon, taking his companion with him. Walking behind them, calm and majestic, is a huge dog with pointed ears.[48]

What the Master earns as his reward is a place where the laws of the inner space are in force and comfort reigns. Most important, in this new inner space, the active female principle once again dominates. It is Margarita who leads the Master to his new home, and it is she who will guard his sleep. In yet another of the many parallels between *The Master and Margarita* and Goethe's *Faust*, the stability of the universe is dependent on the presence of the active female principle.

At this point it occurs to us that the entire panoply of dwellings in the Moscow chapters were not just "anti-houses" but a series of false paradises, be it the Latunskys' apartment, the Griboedov, or any of the "paradises" attached to it (the writers' colony of Perelygino, the posters advertising exotic dwellings in exotic places). What is real paradise like? It's a lot like home.

> Look, there up ahead is your eternal home, which they have given you as a reward. I can already see the Venetian windows and the grapevines curling all the way up to the roof. There is your home, your eternal home.[49]

NOTES

1. Elena Bulgakova, *Dnevnik Eleny Bulgakovoi* (Moscow: "Knizhnaia palata," 1990), 220. A slightly modified variant of this same observation occurs on page 220 of the diaries under the entry for November 13, 1938.

2. Edythe C. Haber, "Dwellings and Devils in Early Bulgakov," *Slavic and East European Journal* 37, no. 3 (Fall 1993): 326.

3. I have in mind, of course, the 730 paces that separate Raskolnikov's garret room (his "coffin") from the pawnbroker's, as well as the precision of the spatial organization of *Crime and Punishment* as a whole.

4. Gaston Bachelard, *La Poetique de l'espace*, 4th ed. (Paris: Presses Universitaires de France, 1964), 24.

5. J. J. Van Baak, *The Place of Space in Narration: Studies in Slavic Literature and Poetics*, vol. 3 (Amsterdam: Rodalpi, 1983), 61.

6. Bachelard, *La Poetique*, 32.

7. Mikhail Bulgakov, *The White Guard*, trans. Michael Glenny (Chicago: Academy Chicago, 1987), 15 (translations sometimes emended).

8. Bulgakov, *The White Guard*, 216.

9. Iurii M. Lotman, "Problema khudozhestvennogo prostranstva v proze Gogolia," *Trudy po russkoi i slavianskoi filologii*, vol. 11: Literaturovedenie (Tartu, 1968), 22.

10. Iurii M. Lotman, "On the Metalanguage of a Typological Description of Culture," *Semiotica* 14, no. 2 (1975): 105.

11. Lesley Milne, *Mikhail Bulgakov: A Critical Biography* (Cambridge: Cambridge University Press, 1990), 75. Milne's inventory of characters as opera heroes and landscapes resembling stage backdrops is wonderful.

12. Bachelard, *La Poetique*, 34–35.

13. Van Baak, *Place of Space in Narration*, 55.

14. Quoted in ibid., 77.

15. Lotman, "Problema khudozhestvennogo," 23.

16. Ibid., 22–23.

17. Bulgakov, *The White Guard*, 55.

18. Lotman, "On Metalanguage," 122.

19. Bulgakov, *The White Guard*, 27.

20. Ibid., 79.

21. For the significance of food in Bulgakov, see Ronald D. LeBlanc's contribution in this volume, and his earlier "Feeding a Poor Dog a Bone:

The Quest for Nourishment in Bulgakov's *Sobach'e Serdtse*," *Russian Review* 52 (1993): 58–78.

22. Bulgakov, *The White Guard*, 53.

23. Lotman, "On Metalanguage," 112.

24. Milne, *Mikhail Bulgakov*, 77.

25. Bulgakov, *The White Guard*, 177–78.

26. Ibid., 287.

27. See, for example, Elizabeth Klosty Beaujour, "The Use of Witches in Fedin and Bulgakov," *Slavic Review* 33 (1974): 706–7; Joan Delaney Grossman, "*The Master and Margarita*: The Reach Exceeds the Grasp," *Slavic Review* 31 (December 1972): 99; and David Bethea, "History as Hippodrome: The Apocalyptic Horse and Rider in *The Master and Margarita*," *Russian Review* 41 (October 1982): 373–99.

28. Iurii M. Lotman, "Zametki o khudozhestvennom prostranstve," *Uchenye Zapiski Tartuskogo Universiteta* 720 (1986): 36.

29. Lotman, "Zametki," 40.

30. Ibid., 38.

31. Ibid., 40.

32. Lotman, "On Metalanguage," 106.

33. Wayne C. Booth, *The Rhetoric of Fiction*, 2d ed. (Chicago: University of Chicago Press, 1983).

34. These three steps are analogous to the three steps Pilate takes to ascend the Gabbatha where he will pronounce the words that lead to his own destruction.

35. Mikhail Bulgakov, *The Master and Margarita*, trans. Burgin and O'Connor (Ann Arbor, Mich.: Ardis, 1994), 115.

36. Although there is no English equivalent, "basement flatlet" might convey some of the quasi-derogatory, diminutive connotations associated with the Russian.

37. Marie Louise Von Franz, "The Process of Individuation," in C. G. Jung, *Man and His Symbols* (New York: Doubleday, 1964).

38. Andrew Barratt, "Apocalypse or Revelation? Man and History in Bulgakov's *Belaya gvardiya*," *New Zealand Slavonic Journal* (1985): 118.

39. Barratt, "Apocalypse or Revelation?" 117–18.

40. Bulgakov, *The Master and Margarita*, 118 (emended).

41. Ibid., 121–22 (emended).

42. Ibid., 124 (emended).

43. Lotman, "On Metalanguage," 110. In this scene the sound symbolism also plays a very significant role. As Lotman defines it, the sound of the phonograph characterizes the "anti-house." The "house" is characterized by the presence of a piano (Lotman, "Zametki," 40).

44. Bulgakov, *The Master and Margarita*, 187 (emended).

45. The third version or the first complete version; see the introduction to this volume. The thought of never being allowed to leave the confines of the Soviet Union weighed heavily on Bulgakov. In her diary entry for February 12, 1937, his wife notes, "This [the subject of travel] is a sore point with M. A. 'I'm a prisoner . . . They will never let me out of here . . . I will never see the world'" (Elena Bulgakova, *Dnevnik*, 129). In this barely concealed frustration he echoes his master Pushkin, as he does in the theme of home itself: "In Pushkin's poetry of the second half of the 1820s to 1830s, the theme of the home becomes a focal point, incorporating concepts of cultural tradition, history, humanity, and the "independent man" (Lotman, "Zametki," 36).

46. Lotman, "Zametki," 41.

47. Andrew Barratt, *Between Two Worlds: A Critical Introduction to The Master and Margarita* (Oxford: Clarendon, 1987), 310.

48. Bulgakov, *The Master and Margarita*, 335 (emended).

49. Ibid., 325 (emended).

The Mythic Structure of Bulgakov's *The Master and Margarita*

EDYTHE C. HABER

Yeshua and the Devil: The Moonlit Realm

It has already been suggested that Woland is not evil in the usual sense; he and Yeshua are not so much inimical as complementary forces. Woland himself develops this idea, using the images of light and shadow to explain the relationship of the divine and diabolical:

> "What would your good be doing, if there were no evil, and what would the earth look like if shadows disappeared from it? After all, shadows are cast by objects and people. There is the shadow of my sword. But there are also shadows of trees and living creatures. Would you like to denude the earth of all the trees and all the living beings in order to satisfy your fantasy of rejoicing in the naked light?"

In Margarita there seems to exist that very blend of light and shadow which, according to Satan, is necessary for life itself.

If one looks beyond Margarita, one finds that, in general, Bulgakov's Satan and Christ, although they use opposite means, serve the same ends. For although Yeshua works through light and love and Woland through darkness and violence, the aim of both is the destruction of the deadening and coercive status quo in the name of life and freedom. Thus, while Woland's cohorts destroy the hellish Griboedov and Apartment No. 50, Yeshua advocates, at least figuratively, the destruction of the temple and the overthrow of Caesar.

The high priest Caiaphas, echoing Jesus' words in the Gospels, recognizes that this mild-mannered visionary is not a prince of peace but a disruptive, anarchic force: "It is not peace, not peace, which the seducer of the people brought to us in Yershalaim." (*Romany*, 454).

The close relationship between Yeshua and Woland is further supported by an examination of the symbolism of sun and moon in the novel. It has been claimed that Bulgakov here adopts traditional symbolism, associating Yeshua with the sun and Woland with darkness and the moon.[1] Athough the second half of the statement is indisputable, Yeshua's tie with sun imagery does not hold up to close scrutiny. Instead, the sun and the oppressive heat associated with it seem to be allied to the harshness of absolute authority against which both Christ and Satan struggle.

An examination of references to the sun in the chapter entitled "Pontius Pilate" makes this clear. We see Yeshua "with a face maimed and bruised by blows . . . standing before (Pilate) under the *pitiless morning sun* of Yershalaim" (23; emphasis added). Later Pilate sees that a ray of sun "was creeping up to Yeshua's worn sandals, and that he was trying to *step out of the sun*" (24; emphasis added). When the high priest Caiaphas arrives at the palace the sun "was scorching Yershalaim . . . with extraordinary fury" (33). Pilate, who wants to save Yeshua, invites Caiaphas "out of the merciless heat," but the high priest, who wants the prisoner executed, refuses. When Pilate realizes he has been defeated in his power play with Caiaphas, "the fiery sphere was almost overhead" (38). Finally, when Pilate announces to the Jerusalem crowd that it is Barrabas and not Jesus who is to be released, "it seemed to him that the sun rang out and burst over his head and filled his ears with fire" (42).

In the later chapter that describes the crucifixion, the sun plays the same merciless role, dispersing onlookers and tormenting the condemned. It is only the centurion Rat-killer, that servant of tyranny, who is unbothered by the blazing sun. He has not even removed his breastplate, decorated with silver lion heads (also emblematic of autocracy): "The sun beat down on the centurion without effect, and the lion heads were intolerable to look at – the eye was blinded by the blaze of silver boiling in the sun" (185). It is impossible to link this merciless, oppressive sun with the gentle and forgiving Yeshua. Rather, it reminds one of the "naked light" which "denude[s] the earth of all the trees and living things" mentioned by Woland. This image may well be meant to symbolize all authoritarian states or sets of dogma (including Matthu Levi's Christianity, but not Yeshua's) where the Wolandian "evil" is not allowed and people must live in an enforced state of "goodness."

The sun and stifling heat are associated with such coerciveness in the main plot as well. Thus the oppressive heat described in chapter 1 is a fitting background for the scene of social command we are to witness. And in the last view the devils have of Moscow, "innumerable suns were melting the glass across the river under the pall of mist, smoke, and steam hanging over the city, scorched to white heat during the day" (381).

Both Christ and the devil are opposed to stifling earthly authority, and we find that both of them are associated with the moon, not the sun.[2] In general, the moon is linked in the novel with an entire order of existence unacknowledged or suppressed by the sunlit "real" world: with madness, dreams, the spirit realm, rather than the material. Its association with the devil, as I have said, needs no demonstration. Its symbolic tie with Yeshua becomes clear when Bulgakov describes how, on the night after the crucifixion, the moon of the new faith rises above the candelabra of the established religion:

> Passing the tower, Yuda turned and saw two giant five-point candelabra light up at a tremendous height above the Temple. . . . It seemed to him that ten enormous lamps were lit over Yershalaim, vying with the light of the single lamp which rose higher and higher over the city – the moon. (330)

Later, after Yuda's murder, Aphranius, who has arranged this revenge against Yeshua's false disciple, glances "at the five-pointed candelabra . . . or at the moon which hung still higher than the lights" (333).

The link of the moon with Yeshua is reinforced in Pilate's dream in which the Procurator imagines himself walking up a moonbeam with the ragged philosopher. The same imagery reappears at the end of the novel, when Yeshua and Pilate, followed by the Master and Margarita, are engulfed in a river of moonlight. Thus both these unearthly beings, Satan and Christ, whose existence is denied by the sunlit world, are tied to the moon. Indeed, the ambiguous moon, both chaste Diana and dark, demonic Hecate, is a singularly fitting symbol for the seemingly opposed, yet united forces of Jesus and Satan.

The death of Yuda illustrates the convergence of the forces of Christ and Satan. In contrast to the gospel account, Yuda does not hang himself but is murdered in the moonlight by order of Pilate. Here murder, a Satanic act, is performed in the service of Christ. That the murder is to be looked upon as a devilish deed is indicated by an analogous event that occurs at Satan's Ball: the murder of Baron Meigel. The baron, an informer and a spy like Yuda, is murdered by the devils on what is apparently the anniversary of that murder long ago.

The life-giving nature of such murders is suggested by the strange words Woland murmurs to Margarita as he orders her to drink Meigel's blood: "'Don't be afraid, Queen . . . Don't be afraid, Queen, the blood has long run down into the earth. And on the spot where it was spilled, grapevines are growing today'" (289). And Margarita indeed discovers that Meigel's blood has been transformed to wine, making this ritual a sort of eucharist in reverse. The blood that "has long run down into the earth" refers, perhaps, to that of the biblical prototype of Baron Meigel, Yuda, whose destruction, paradoxically, brought new life, the life-giving grape.

All of this is not to say, of course, that the forces of Christ and Satan are entirely coequal, that the means of violence and love are put on the same moral level. This is made particularly clear in the story of Pilate, whose act of retribution against Yuda does not at all wipe out his earlier failure in love and courage:

> It was clear to [Pilate] that during that day he had let something slip away irrevocably, and now he wanted to correct the slip by

> some petty and insignificant and, most important, belated acts. His self-delusion consisted in the fact that the Procurator tried to convince himself that these acts, the present, evening ones, were no less important than the morning sentencing. But in this the Procurator succeeded very badly. (*Romany*, 725)

The end of the novel also indicates that in the divine hierarchy Satan occupies a lesser position than Jesus. For Matthu Levi brings an order from Yeshua, which the devil is to obey.

One must hasten to repeat, however, that the intentions of Yeshua do not at all conflict with the devil's. The latter is certainly not opposed to the rescue of the Master and Margarita, and even the occasional victories of the Christian spirit of mercy over his Queen Margot only call forth a few sardonic utterances from this not at all vile Prince of Darkness.

Everything Ended and Everything Ends

And so the Master and Margarita leave behind the sun-scorched capital to receive their final reward in the higher realm of justice and mercy. Because of his failure of courage, the Master is not granted the highest reward, the light. Instead, his will be a life of idyllic rest. Woland compares the Master in his new life to Faust: "Don't you want to sit, like Faust, over a retort, hoping to create a new homunculus?" (388). As Stenbock-Fermor rightly points out, in Goethe's work it was not Faust but his rather mediocre assistant, Wagner, who created the homunculus.[3] And in general Faust never led, and never would have been content with, the serene and drowsy life of the Master's eternal home. Such a life could satisfy only a Faust who is lacking the fearless, restless spirit of the Goethean hero. Indeed, as earlier demonstrated, such a description fits the Master very well.

In his epilogue Bulgakov returns to earth. In this world little permanent and significant change has been wrought by the devil's visitation. Indeed, the Yuda-like Aloisy is now prospering as financial manager of the Variety Theater, a sinister comment on the state of affairs. And everyone, in spite of his or her experiences, continues to deny doggedly the existence of the devils and all supernatural forces.

Only Ivan Nikolaevich Homeless, who was so affected by the devils, the Master, and the moon, has changed profoundly. On the surface it appears that the former poet, now professor of history and philosophy, Ponyrev, has been cured of his earlier schizophrenia. In other words, he has become an acceptable member of Soviet society. Although he has rejected his former excesses as MASSOLIT poet, he still supports the rationalistic bases of his society and does not accept the notion of diabolical intercession in his life: "Ivan Nikolaevich knows everything and understands everything. He knows that in his younger days he had been a victim of criminal hypnotists, had undergone treatment, and had been cured" (398).

But his normalcy is more apparent than real. For during the spring full moon Ivan Nikolaevich's reason loses its power; he grows restless and dreams strange dreams. In other words, the schizophrenia is still in force. Indeed, it seems that such an illness is inevitable in one who has vision of higher truth and yet is striving to survive in the earthly sunlit world. This split in the life of the Master's secret disciple bears more than a passing resemblance to that in Pilate's, a secret disciple of Christ who is also disturbed by the full moon. (Could hemicrania and schizophrenia be related phenomena?) In the person of Ivan Homeless, Bulgakov seems to be suggesting that this Pilatelike double life is bound to appear in the Soviet artist or intellectual who tries to live both in the world of his imagination and in the atheistic and oppressive everyday world. In this sense Bulgakov's novel, no less than his hero's, is about Pontius Pilate.[4]

It is fitting that Ivan, a current victim of Pilatism, should be granted Bulgakov's final vision in the form of a dream under the full moon. The dream is suffused by moonlight. Pilate and Yeshua are walking, arguing, and trying to reach some agreement. They engage in a puzzling dialogue:

> "Gods, gods!" says the man in the cloak, turning his haughty face to his companion. "What a vulgar execution! But tell me, please

> tell me," and his face is no longer haughty, but pleading, "it never happened! I beg you, tell me, it never happened?"
>
> "Of course, it never happened," his companion answers in a hoarse voice. "You imagined it." . . .
>
> "That is all I need!" the man in the cloak cries out in a broken voice and rises higher and higher toward the moon, drawing his companion with him. (401)

An odd reversal has taken place here. In this moonlit realm, associated throughout the novel with fantasy, madness, and the imagination, we are told that an occurrence in the "real" world was imagined. Bulgakov seems to be saying that in this spiritual land a different level of reality is in force. The factual event as such is irrelevant; only movements of the spirit are important. And once Pilate's soul, after long centuries of suffering and repentance and aided by Yeshua's love and mercy, has renounced his terrible deed, it is as if it had never taken place.

Earlier in the novel there is another such occurrence, contrary to all earthly logic: the devil, reversing the Master's Pilatelike act of burning his manuscript, restores it whole with the declaration, "Manuscripts don't burn" (300). And indeed, as a spiritual phenomenon, the manuscript, the work of art, is indestructible, whatever its material fate might be. It is fitting, therefore, that the Master, whose path in the novel has, in many respects, been parallel to Pilate's, should at the end follow the Procurator up the moonbeam, led by his beloved Margarita. It is also significant that this vision of reconciliation and love that ends the novel should provide comfort to yet another victim of Pilatism, Ivan Homeless. Margarita's words to the historian, "Everything ended and everything ends" (402), promise a final release to him as well.

Furthermore, it might be said that with these words Bulgakov is offering solace to all the followers of Pilate in Stalinist Russia, to the artists and thinkers who have had a glimpse of the truth but have retreated from it. In their world few are courageous enough to fully emulate Faust or Christ. Many have succumbed in some measure to

Gretchen's crime and Pilate's vice. But even to those it is promised that, because of their higher vision, the spiritual realm will ultimately redeem them. Then all the sinister Yershalaims and Moscows will disappear, and the marvelous moonlit realm, imagined but the highest form of reality, will be triumphant.

NOTES

This essay is a condensed version of "The Mythic Structure of Bulgakov's *The Master and Margarita*," *Russian Review* 34 (October 1975): 382–409.

1. V. Lakshin, "Roman M. Bulgakova *Master i Margarita*," *Novyi Mir* 6 (1968): 288; Ellendea Proffer, "On *The Master and Margarita*," *Russian Literature Triquarterly* 6 (1973): 551–55. For a detailed and more general discussion of leitmotifs than mine, see Proffer's articles.

2. Rzhevsky sees the connection of the moon with Jesus, but not with Woland (L. Rzhevsky, "Pilatov grekh: o tainopisi v romane M. Bulgakova *Master i Margarita*," *Novyi Zhurnal* 40 (1968): 60–80).

3. Elizabeth Stenbock-Fermor, "Bulgakov's *Master and Margarita* and Goethe's *Faust*," *Slavonic and East European Journal* 13 (1969): 314.

4. Rzhevsky ("Pilatov grekh," 79–80) suggests this pervasive *Pilatism* in Stalinist Moscow but applies the term only to the minor satiric characters. These share with Pilate his bondage to material well-being and to this degree are victims of Pilatism. They do not have an inkling, however, of the other, spiritual world and therefore do not experience his inner conflict. Only such higher natures as that of the Master and Ivan Homeless are capable of doing so.

Stomaching Philistinism: Griboedov House and the Symbolism of Eating in *The Master and Margarita*

RONALD D. LEBLANC

Much has already been written about the tremendous influence exerted on Bulgakov by the life and works of Nikolai Gogol, the famous nineteenth-century writer whom he openly acknowledged to be his favorite Russian author and whose oeuvre he often attempted to adapt and recast in his own literary works.[1] One aspect of this Gogol-Bulgakov connection, however, has been as yet largely unexplored, and I would like to look into it a bit further in my essay, that is, their shared interest in gastrology. Gogol's obsessive concern with food and eating is well documented. From the testimony of family and friends, we know, for instance, that Gogol was a person endowed with an immoderate appetite, a prodigious stomach, and a notorious sweet tooth.[2] Moreover, he seems to have had some serious culinary skills and ambitions, for he frequently regaled his St. Petersburg acquaintances with exotic Ukrainian dishes from his homeland. After visiting Rome, where he first discovered the joys of pasta, he insisted on serving up enormous portions of Italian macaroni to his Moscow friends. Sergei Aksakov even went so far as to assert that had Gogol not become a great poet, he most certainly would have been a talented chef-artiste.[3] The gastronomic interests that occupied Gogol in his personal life are, of course, amply reflected in his art. From *Evenings on a Farm Near Dikanka* (1831), where Rudy Panko raves about the delicious homemade pies that his wife prepares for him, to

Dead Souls (1842), where provincial landowners such as Sobakievich and Petukh celebrate the joys of the Russian table, as well as the capacity of the Russian stomach, Gogol's prose works abound with a colorful array of gourmands, gluttons, and gastronomes. Eating plays a large role, moreover, in the construction of Gogol's plots: several critics have noted that food – rather than love or romance – provides the primary motivation for the action in his stories.[4] As Nabokov so memorably put it, "The belly is the belle of his stories, the nose is their beau."[5]

When we turn from Gogol to Bulgakov, we see that gastronomic motifs play a similarly significant role in his works. The theme of food and eating is especially prominent in *The Heart of a Dog* (*Sobach'e serdtse*, 1925), for instance, where Professor Preobrazhensky's dinner table serves, in one critic's words, as "a gastronomic celebration of NEP."[6] Lesley Milne observes that in his satiric novella "Bulgakov reaches out over the hungry years of War Communism to shake hands with Gogol, that nineteenth-century Russian Homer of the dinner table."[7] Indeed, one finds in *The Heart of a Dog* ample evidence of what Milne elsewhere refers to as a "gastronomic expansiveness" inherited from Gogol.[8] Dr. Preobrazhensky's lucrative private practice as a surgeon for an economically elite clientele allows him, among other things, to indulge an expensive taste for fine food and drink. "Thin slices of salmon and pickled eel were piled on plates adorned with paradisiac flowers and wide black borders," the narrator notes as he describes the professor's opulent dining room.

> A piece of fine, moist Swiss cheese lay on a heavy board, and near it stood a silver bucket with caviar, set in a bowl of snow. Among the plates stood several slender liqueur glasses and three crystal carafes with liqueurs of different colors. All these objects were arranged on a small marble table cosily set against a huge sideboard of carved oak filled with glass and silver, which threw off sheaves of light. In the center of the room a table, heavy as a sepulcher, was covered with a white cloth, and on it were two settings, with napkins rolled like papal tiaras, and three dark bottles.[9] (2:140)

Throughout the remainder of the text the narrator continues to draw the reader's attention to the elements of haute cuisine that are a central feature of Preobrazhensky's home: the main dishes of rare roast beef, sturgeon, caviar, lobster, turkey, and veal cutlets; the desserts of rum cake with coffee; the after-dinner cordials of cognac or brandy.

Despite the Homeric quality of Bulgakov's description, which is highly reminiscent of Gogol, the gastronomic abundance represented by Preobrazhensky's household is not without its negative aspects. In an article that explores the demonic imagery surrounding Philipp Philippovich as a "mad" scientist, Diana Burgin points out that "hellish forces are fomenting just beneath the surface of the Professor's well-ordered home existence."[10] In a similar vein, Susanne Fusso argues quite cogently that *Heart of a Dog* ought to be read as part of a genre she calls the "literature of hunger" – "the literature that investigates what happens when bodily needs and desires corrupt the spirit."[11] Lured to his fate by the "imperatives of the belly," the dog Sharik may be considered to have sold his spiritual and moral freedom rather cheaply for the enticing bourgeois comforts found in Preobrazhensky's affluent home.[12] The theme of bodily needs and material desires corrupting the spirit undergoes even further satiric treatment in *The Master and Margarita*, where Bulgakov portrays the members of the official literary establishment as venal, nouveaux riches philistines who are more concerned with filling their bellies with food than with nourishing their intellects with ideas or their souls with art. Through food imagery, Bulgakov seeks to depict the greed, avarice, and egoism characteristic of Russia's new privileged class.

The Soviet literati portrayed in Bulgakov's final novel are, of course, closely associated with Griboedov House, where the headquarters of MASSOLIT[13] is located. If RAPP served as the inspiration for this fictional literary organization, the real-life prototype for the "House of Griboedov" (*Dom Griboedova*) was provided by the "House of Writers" (known as the "House of Herzen," *Dom Gertsena*) that was set up in Moscow during the 1920s as a center for writers and journalists. Interesting speculations have been advanced as to why Bulgakov should have chosen to rename this writers' club in honor of the author of *Woe from Wit* (*Gore ot Uma*, 1826).[14] In addition to the possible literary and cultural significance one might attach to its name, however, Dom Griboedova continues to resonate meaningfully at a basic etymological level, since this literary club proves to be a veritable house of "mushroom eaters" (*griboedov*) or at least of "eaters" in general.[15] Indeed, the importance of Griboedov House resides less in its administrative offices, which are located upstairs on the second floor, than in its highly exclusive restaurant – "rightly considered the best in Moscow" (5:57) – which takes up the entire ground floor of the building.[16] The spatial topography of the building thus supports quite nicely the vertical hierarchy of values that Mikhail Bakhtin claims has long been dominant within Western culture, where an "upper" spiritual realm of the sacred, serious, and sublime is juxtaposed to a "lower" physical realm of baser human impulses dominated by what he calls the "material bodily principle."[17]

To underscore the gastronomic significance that attaches to Griboedov House, the narrator reports a conversation he once overheard between two club members as they stood talking at the front gate to the establishment. In this dialogue, the strapping poet and "gastronome" Ambrose describes for his colleague Foka what is available on the menu at the Griboedov House restaurant. He lavishes praise on the superior quality of its food and its eminently reasonable prices, especially when compared to those at the popular Colosseum Restaurant (5:57). Speaking on behalf of the "old inhabitants" (*starozhily*) of Moscow,[18] the narrator then jumps in and shares his own fond memories of the fine food available there, delivering a veritable ode on the culinary wonders served up at Griboedov House.

> But boiled fillets of perch was nothing, my dear Ambrose! What about the sturgeon, sturgeon in a silver-plated pan, sturgeon filleted and served between lobsters' tails and fresh caviar? And

> oeufs en cocotte with mushroom puree in little bowls? And didn't you like the thrushes' breasts? With truffles? The quails a la Genovese? . . . Do you remember, Ambrose? But of course you do – I can see from your lips you remember. Not just your salmon or your perch either – what about the snipe, the woodcock in season, the quail, the grouse? And the sparkling wines! But I digress, reader. (5:58)

For readers familiar with Bulgakov's earlier fiction, this lyrical outburst calls to mind the "gastronomic expansiveness" in *The Heart of a Dog*. But the context here, it should be noted, has changed considerably. In Bulgakov's satiric novella, which thematizes the physical and spiritual malnutrition that plagued Soviet Russia under communist rule, the urbane professor had served to epitomize the good taste, genteel breeding, and cultural refinement characteristic of upper-class life in prerevolutionary Russia – features of a civilized existence that the new ruling class woefully lacks. Through Preobrazhensky, Bulgakov intended the act of eating to serve as a parallel for the lost art of gracious living.[19]

In *The Master and Margarita*, on the other hand, elegant dining is being enjoyed not by the urbane and gentlemanly Philipp Philippovich, whom Andrei Sinyavsky characterizes as a "typical representative of the old Russian intelligentsia,"[20] but by a band of mediocre Soviet writers who have prostituted their art for the sake of socioeconomic privilege. These "artists in uniform" are portrayed as nothing more than wanton gluttons who are less interested in the calling of a true artist than in the material benefits that accrue to an obedient and loyal writer in Soviet Russia. As T.R.N. Edwards puts it, "The Griboedov is a place for indulgence in the medieval deadly sins, rather than for literary activity."[21] Bulgakov's Griboedovites, as a result, bear an uncanny resemblance to the damned souls Dante depicts in his *Divine Comedy*: sinful gluttons who, in the words of one critic, care "more for stuffing their mouths with food than for opening them with words."[22]

Although one might reasonably expect that Griboedov House, as home to a writers' club, would provide the principal setting for the development of the novel's literary themes, those *topoi* in *The Master and Margarita* are invariably played out elsewhere. The conversation between the editor Berlioz and the writer Bezdomnyi over the latter's antireligious poem about Jesus Christ, for instance, takes place at Patriarchs' Ponds; Riukhin's moment of epiphany, when he recognizes that he is indeed a second-rate hack writer, occurs in the shadow of the Pushkin monument; and the tragic fate of the Master, the author of a politically dangerous novel about Pontius Pilate, unfolds within the basement apartment he shares with Margarita and in the mental clinic run by Dr. Stravinsky. Indeed, with the notable exception of the narrator's initial account of the petty squabbles that take place among jealous club members (over such mundane matters as the issuance of vacation travel warrants and the assignment of dachas at writers' colonies), those narrative events in the novel that do take place at Griboedov House involve this building less as the home to a writers' organization than as the location of a famous restaurant.[23] In terms of Lotman's analysis of the spatial semiotics at work in Bulgakov's novel, one could say that Dom Griboedova apotheosizes not a *dom* but an anti-*dom*: rather than culture, security, and life, this "anti-house" instead represents the alien, the demonic, and the material.[24]

The two most important events that transpire at Griboedov House are the dinner taking place on the evening of Berlioz's death in part 1 (chapter 5) and the fire that burns down the establishment as a result of the final escapades of Koroviev and Behemoth in part 2 (chapter 28). The first of these two scenes is fraught with obvious parallels to the biblical account of the Christ story: twelve MASSOLIT writers have gathered upstairs at Griboedov House to await the arrival of their leader, Berlioz, the chairman of the management committee (5:58). Unlike Christ's disciples, however, Berlioz's followers do not proceed to celebrate a eucharistic "last supper" (*tainaia vecheria*), marked by a commensal spirit of unity, fellowship, and kinship.[25] Instead, at the stroke of midnight, these twelve writers abandon the building's upper level and descend to the restaurant in the nether world below, where they proceed to indulge their baser corporeal instincts. In an orgiastic scene replete with the kind of infernal imagery that anticipates Satan's Ball in part 2, the club members – some of whom possess speaking names (e.g., *Sladkii*, "sweet") that support what one critic has called the text's "gastronomic semantics"[26] – are portrayed eating, drinking, and dancing wildly to the strains of the famous Griboedov jazz band. "In a word – hell," the narrator intones on concluding his description of the wild revelry taking place at the writers' club (5:61).[27] Even the terrible news of their leader's sudden death does not seem to quell the Griboedovites' voracious appetite for the pleasure provided by food and drink. "Yes, he died, died," the narrator exclaims, mimicking the sentiments of the club members. "But we are still alive!" (5:62). As one of the club members returns to his table and resumes eating and drinking, the narrator asks double-voicedly: "What's the sense, after all, of wasting the chicken cutlets de volaille? How are we going to help Mikhail Aleksandrovich? By going hungry? But we are still alive!" (5:62). This passage suggests that the revellers at Griboedov House, as Riitta Pittman rightly observes, "are physically alive, but morally bankrupt and spiritually dead."[28] There is a delicious irony to be enjoyed, therefore, when a barefoot Bezdomny – clad only in undershorts and a dirty Russian blouse, wearing a paper icon, and carrying a lighted candle in his hand – suddenly appears amid this hellish scene at Griboedov House and interrupts the hedonistic diners with the nearly biblical exhortation, "Brothers in literature! Listen to me, all of you! He has come!" (5:63).

Archibald Archibaldovich, the imperious maitre d'hotel who is the devil-in-charge at this gathering, severely reprimands the restaurant doorman for having admitted the modern-day John the Baptist (and pseudoexorcist) into Griboedov House. "How was I not to admit him, since he is a member of MASSOLIT?" the doorman replies by way of explanation (5:65). As this brief exchange indicates, one of the principal attractions of the Griboedov House restaurant is its very exclusivity. The narrator himself had pointed out earlier that "not just anyone off the street can get in there" (5:57),[29] and in his initial description of Griboedov House he observes that every visitor to this establishment immediately becomes aware of the high quality of life enjoyed by those who were fortunate enough to have become a member of MASSOLIT and thus to have acquired a membership card that allows them admittance into the club:

> A black envy would at once begin to torment him. And at once he would bitterly reproach the heavens for having failed to reward him at birth with literary talent, without which, naturally, one could not so much as dream of acquiring a MASSOLIT membership card – the brown card, smelling of expensive leather and embellished with a wide gold border, that was known to all Moscow. (5:56)

We recall that one of Bezdomny's two immediate concerns after his fruitless search for Woland in the Moscow River is that his MASSOLIT membership card, "with which he never parted" (5:54), has disappeared. And it is precisely the lack of this highly coveted card, of course, that will make it difficult for Koroviev and Behemoth to gain entry to Griboedov House in part 2, in the second of the two scenes in the novel where the writers' club figures prominently as a setting for the action.

In terms of plot chronology, the visit to Griboedov House by these two members of Woland's retinue follows directly on the heels of their trip to yet another mainstay of the Soviet system of elitism and official privilege: the Torgsin store.[30] The mischievous duo headed straight for the junction of the "food" sections within this special shop – the delicatessen and confectionery departments (5:338), where the ravenously hungry Behemoth, referred to throughout the episode as a "fatso" (*tolstiak*), gorges himself on tangerines, chocolate bars (gold wrappers and all), and kerch herring, much to the displeasure of the sales staff, who demand that these luxury food items be paid for in foreign currency. This leads to the inspired speech, filled with mock pathos, that Koroviev delivers on behalf of Behemoth:

> Citizens! What is going on here? Eh? . . . This poor fellow, this poor fellow has been repairing his kerosene burner all day long;

> he's starving . . . and where is he to get any foreign currency? Where? – I ask you all this question! He's racked with hunger and thirst! He's hot. So the poor fellow tried a tangerine. (5:340)

Playfully donning the mask of an advocate for economic democracy and social egalitarianism, Koroviev asks why it is that his poor suffering comrade should be denied the culinary treats that are readily available in Moscow to foreigners (or foreign-looking Russians), such as the "fatso" in the lilac-colored coat who is "all bloated with salmon, all stuffed with foreign currency" (5:340). Although Koroviev's speech may strike the reader as merely a ridiculous jest, his brilliant rhetorical performance manages nonetheless to arouse some of the customers in the store, who turn angrily on the foreign-looking man in the lilac coat. Amid the wild melee that ensues, Behemoth pours some kerosene from his primus burner onto the counter of the confectionery shop and sets the store on fire.

Koroviev and the "glutton" (*obzhora*) Behemoth are next seen standing on the sidewalk in front of the entrance to Griboedov House.[31] There they engage in a heavily ironic conversation that provides a nice parallel to the earlier conversation between Ambrose and Foka. The conversation between Koroviev and Behemoth, however, centers instead on the literary activity that supposedly goes on there. "Look, there's the writers' house (*pisatel'skii dom*)," Koroviev says. "You know, Behemoth, I have heard many good and complimentary things about this house. Pay attention, my friend, to this house. How pleasant it is to think about how a whole multitude of talents lies hidden there, ripening under that roof" (5:342). "Like pineapples in a hothouse," Behemoth adds.[32] Koroviev then launches into another of his impassioned (yet mocking) speeches, this time about the cultivation of artistic talent.

> Quite right. And what a delicious thrill touches your heart when you consider that in that house is now ripening the future author of a *Don Quixote* or a *Faust* or – who knows? – *Dead Souls*! Eh? . . . Yes, what astonishing things await us from the seedbeds of that house, which has gathered together under its roof several

> thousand zealots who have chosen to devote their lives selflessly to the service of Melpomene, Polyhymnia, and Thalia. You can just imagine the furor that will arise when one of them, to start with, presents the reading public with an *Inspector General*, or at the very least a *Eugene Onegin*! Yes, but! But, I say and I repeat this – but! Provided these tender hothouse plants are not attacked by some microorganism, provided they are not nipped in the bud, provided they do not rot! And this does happen with pineapples, you know! Oh yes, it does happen! (5:342)

Koroviev's soliloquy, which suddenly and ironically switches the text's gastronomic discourse over to a horticultural trope, reminds the reader that Griboedov House was not meant to serve as a fancy eatery marked by the excessive consumption of food and drink.[33] This writers' club should instead be functioning as an artistic "hothouse" – a shelter or cloister that nurtures young literary talent and produces future writers who will, in turn, nourish the reading public spiritually and intellectually through their creative output. In alimentary terms, Koroviev's speech tells us that the Griboedovites should be artistically feeding others rather than corporeally feeding themselves; these club members should be selflessly producing (for others) food for the spirit, rather than selfishly consuming (for themselves) food for the body.

Yet no sooner does Koroviev deliver his oration on what ought to be the true purpose of a writers' club then we are reminded once again of what Griboedov House has actually become, namely, a gastronomic pleasure palace reserved for the benefit of the literary nouveaux riches. "By the way," Behemoth inquires upon the conclusion of Koroviev's monologue, "What is it that they're doing out there on the veranda?" "Eating," replies Koroviev. "I should add, my dear fellow, that this place has a quite decent and inexpensive restaurant" (5:342). The ensuing scene, where Koroviev and Behemoth are initially denied entry to Griboedov House because they lack MASSOLIT membership cards, is best remembered for the memorable exchange that occurs over Dostoevsky's credentials. "Look here,"

Koroviev implores Sofiia Pavlovna,[34] the woman who is checking names at the entrance to the veranda,

> If you wanted to be convinced that Dostoevsky is a writer, would you really have to ask him for his credentials? Why, you only have to take any five pages from any of his novels and, without any membership card, you'll be convinced that you're dealing with a writer. Why, I don't suppose that he even had a membership card! . . . Forgive me, but this is ridiculous – a writer isn't considered a writer because of a membership card, but because of what he writes. (5:343)

Koroviev's defense of Dostoevsky – and, by extension, the Master and every true writer – provides a scathing critique of the contemporary literary establishment in Soviet Russia which, as we know, had caused the author considerable anguish in his own life. As J.A.E. Curtis correctly noted, "this exchange suggests in a mortal dimension Bulgakov's resistance to the idea of the bureaucratization of literature and the imposition upon it of exclusive constraints."[35]

We should not overlook the fact, however, that in this episode Koroviev and Behemoth are seeking not the right to be recognized as writers, but merely entry to the outdoor restaurant set up on the veranda at Griboedov House. Hungry and thirsty, these two adventurers are searching mainly for a snack and a frosty mug of cold beer. What is at issue here, just as was true at the Torgsin store, is the exclusivity of the Griboedov House restaurant – its elitist status as a gastronomic paradise for the few set amid a wilderness of severe food shortages and chronic hunger for the many. "Alas," Koroviev notes sadly to Behemoth when another customer is allowed to pass by them and proceed onto the veranda, "we won't, we won't, but he will have that icy cold mug of beer that you and I, poor wanderers, were so longing for" (5:344). Upon the intervention of Archibald Archibaldovich, who is wise to the identity of this duo, Woland's two hungry cohorts are eventually granted admittance to the restaurant and seated at a table "under the awning of the unforgettable Griboedov veranda" (5:345).[36] Shortly afterward, they will create a melee not unlike the one they had started earlier at the Torgsin store: a shoot-out with the police will be followed by a fire that spreads to engulf all of Griboedov House. As Curtis notes, "The devil's campaign against the literary establishment, which began with the murder of Berlioz, now ends in the destruction of the building in which it is housed."[37] Divine retribution in *The Master and Margarita* is thus visited on two gastronomical establishments – a special food store and an elite restaurant – that cater to the rich, the privileged, and the gluttonous.

In summary, the main function of Griboedov House as a motif in Bulgakov's novel is to satirize the vulgar philistinism of the Soviet literati: their utterly bourgeois values and special economic privileges are implicitly condemned as they have transformed this writers' club into a gastronomic temple. In addition to providing some of the funniest scenes in *The Master and Margarita*, the two episodes involving the Griboedovites allow the author to vent his anger against the literary establishment as he satirizes those "official" writers who are motivated primarily, if not exclusively, by aspirations of material gain. By employing gastronomic motifs to advance these satiric aims, Bulgakov shows himself to be a true heir of Gogol, who likewise exploited food imagery not just positively – as a means of joyfully celebrating nature's fertility and abundance – but also negatively, as a way to reveal the triviality, venality, and banality (*poshlost'*) of his characters. By depicting human beings in "the physiology of their existence,"[38] Gogol was able to suggest the spiritual vacuity of those "dead souls" who populate his fictional universe. Indeed, as Gogol the humorist evolved into Gogol the moralist, the festive celebration of the positive aspects of food gave way increasingly to a negative valorization of the act of eating, which was reduced to the degrading sin of gluttony. During the final years of his life, as he lapsed further into religious mysticism, Gogol came to associate food more and more with the devil.[39]

At the same time, Gogol came to associate art closely with God. Living in a society that was growing highly modernized, secularized, and materialistic, Gogol viewed the artistic profession in quasi-religious terms as a sacred calling. Like a medieval monk, Gogol's artist must first purify himself through rigid ascetic discipline in order to make himself spiritually worthy to bear the divine Word. Thus in part 1 of "The Portrait" (*Portret*, 1842), the struggling young artist Chartkov is initially described in terms suggesting a hermit monk: he dresses in shabby old clothes, survives on a meager diet, and devotes himself with self-denying zeal to his work. Despite repeated admonitions by his mentors that he not become a "fashionable artist" (*modnyi zhivopisets*), who sacrifices the purity of his art for commercial gain and worldly fame, Chartkov succumbs to the temptations presented to him by his newly found wealth: after having starved for so long, he cannot resist the attraction of eating well at last.[40] Seduced by the evil allure of money, Chartkov begins to prostitute his art, painting in accord with social demand rather than personal inspiration; as a result, he suffers a painful personal as well as professional demise.[41] In part 2 of "The Portrait," Gogol presents us with a second artist, this one self-taught, who succeeds in freeing his art from demonic influences only when he quits the secular world and joins a remote monastery. There he takes monastic vows and leads an austere life of fasting, celibacy, poverty, and spiritual contemplation. It is only after he has passed through the "purifying fire" (*chistilishche*) of God's spirit at the monastery and rid himself of the passion born of earthly lust that this painter is able to produce lofty and sublime artistic creations.

Like Gogol, Bulgakov attached profound significance to art as a repository of his nation's abiding spiritual values. Indeed, the fate of the artist – whether it be Moliere, Pushkin, or the Master – comes to dominate thematically those works that Bulgakov wrote during the last decade of his life. His depiction of the Griboedovites in *The Master and Margarita* as gluttons and venal philistines would seem to support this theme as well, "the grotesque behavior of the official literary world only highlighting the significance of the Master's achievement by suggesting how certain writers have opted for the 'false' choice of compromise and conformism."[42] The satiric portrait of the Soviet literary establishment that Bulgakov paints in *The Mas-*

ter and Margarita, Julie Curtis notes, puts into sharper relief "that false approach to art to which the Master's own dedication is opposed."[43] I would merely add that this contrast between the true artist and the false one is reinforced in Bulgakov's novel at the gastronomical level as well: whereas the Griboedovites (the "false" writers) gluttonously indulge their selfish appetites for the sins of the flesh, the Master (the "true" artist) develops an inner spirituality by renouncing such gastronomic pleasures. "The Master," T.R.N. Edwards writes, "in many ways suggests a monk, with his conscious withdrawal from society, his lack of concern for material things, his introspection, and the singleness of his purpose."[44] The Griboedovites, in this respect, could be said to fulfill an important function as contrastive foils for the Manichaeistic ideals that are advanced in Bulgakov's novel, since these literary sybarites set into such bold relief the author's disdain for those who covet worldly things as well as his attempt to liberate the spirit of the artist from the contaminating influence of base matter.[45] As a result, the memorable portrayal of the Griboedov House restaurant in *The Master and Margarita*, paradoxically enough, may ultimately reveal Bulgakov's close gastrological kinship not so much with the "feasting" Gogol, the Russian Homer who celebrated in epic fashion the joys of the bountiful table, as with the "fasting" Gogol – with the "hunger artist" whose quest for spiritual grace, moral purity, and religious salvation eventually led him to starve himself to death.[46]

NOTES

1. Several studies examine this Gogol-Bulgakov connection. See, among others, Lesley Milne, "Gogol and Mikhail Bulgakov," in *Nikolay Gogol: Text and Context*, ed. Jane Grayson and Faith Wigzell (New York: St. Martin's, 1989), 109–26; M. O. Chudakova, "Gogol i Bulgakov," in *Gogol': Istoriia i sovremennost'*, ed. V. V. Kozhinov et al. (Moscow: Sovetskaia Rossiia, 1985), 360–88; Claude de Grève, "Un grand héritier de Gogol: Boulgakov," *Slavica Gandensia* 12 (1985): 61–67; Nadezhda Natova, "Mikhail Bulgakov i Gogol': Opyt sopostavitel'nogo analiza," *Zapiski russkoi akademicheskoi gruppy v SShA* 17 (1984): 83–114; and V. A. Chebotareva,

"O gogolevskikh traditsiiakh v proze M. Bulgakova," *Russkaia literatura*, no. 1 (1984): 166–76.

2. V. Veresaev, *Gogol v zhizni* (Moscow-Leningrad: Academiia, 1933; rpt. Ann Arbor, Mich.: Ardis, 1983), 185–86.

3. S. T. Aksakov, *Istoriia moego znakomstva s Gogolem* (Moscow: Akademiia nauk, 1960), 35.

4. For studies of food imagery in Gogol's works, see Alexander Obolensky, *Food-Notes on Gogol* (Winnipeg: Trident, 1972); Natalia M. Kolb-Seletski, "Gastronomy, Gogol, and His Fiction," *Slavic Review* 29, no. 1 (1970): 35–57; Ronald D. LeBlanc, "Dinner with Chichikov: The Fictional Meal as Narrative Device in Gogol's Dead Souls," *Modern Fiction Studies* 18, no. 4 (1988): 68–80; and Ronald D. LeBlanc, "Satisfying Khlestakov's Appetite: The Semiotics of Eating in *The Inspector General*," *Slavic Review* 47, no. 2 (1988): 483–98. For psychoanalytic studies that examine how Gogol's characters (owing to their creator's own fear of sexual intimacy) are made to regress to the oral pleasures provided by eating, see Hugh McLean, "Gogol's Retreat from Love: Toward an Interpretation of Mirgorod," *American Contributions to the Fourth International Congress of Slavicists* (The Hague: Mouton, 1958), 225–44; Daniel Rancour-Laferriere, *Out from Under Gogol's Overcoat: A Psychoanalytic Study* (Ann Arbor, Mich.: Ardis, 1982); and Simon Karlinsky, *The Sexual Labyrinth of Nikolai Gogol* (Cambridge, Mass.: Harvard University Press, 1976).

5. Vladimir Nabokov, *Nikolai Gogol* (New York: New Directions, 1944), 3.

6. Lesley Milne, *Mikhail Bulgakov: A Critical Biography* (Cambridge: Cambridge University Press, 1990), 65.

7. Ibid.

8. Milne, "Gogol and Mikhail Bulgakov," 116.

9. Mikhail Bulgakov, *Sobranie sochinenii v piati tomakh* (Moscow: Khudozhestvennaia literatura, 1992). All quotations from Bulgakov used in this essay come from this five-volume collection of his works; the references are indicated parenthetically in the text by volume and page number. I am quoting here from the Mirra Ginsburg translation, *Heart of a Dog* (New York: Grove, 1968), 31.

10. Diana L. Burgin, "Bulgakov's Early Tragedy of the Scientist-Creator: An Interpretation of *The Heart of a Dog*," *Slavic and East European Journal* 22, no. 4 (1978): 498.

11. Susanne Fusso, "Failures of Transformation in *Sobach'e serdtse*," *Slavic and East European Journal* 33, no. 3 (1989): 395.

12. Ibid., 396.

13. MASSOLIT is Bulgakov's parody of the Russian Association of Proletarian Writers (RAPP) which set itself the task of dictating the course of literature in Russia in the late twenties and early thirties. See the introduction to this volume and also J.A.E. Curtis's essay in this volume.

14. T.R.N. Edwards, for example, argues that Bulgakov uses the name of the author of *Woe from Wit* for the club to underscore the irony of writers "who in his view are excessively concerned with the intellect at the expense of the spirit." See *Three Russian Writers and the Irrational: Zamyatin, Pil'nyak, and Bulgakov* (Cambridge: Cambridge University Press, 1982), 155. In a recent study that he characterizes as belonging to the genre of "literary topography," Boris Miagkov chronicles the real-life prototyes for the various sites and characters in Bulgakov's novel (see *Bulgakovskaia Moskva* [Moscow: Moskovskii rabochii, 1993]). For a brief survey of the architectural and social history of *Dom Gertsena* itself, see B. P. Kraevskii, *Tverskoi bul'var' 25* (Moscow: Moskovskii rabochii, 1982).

15. Witness how the novel's most notorious overeater, the glutton Behemoth, is pictured precisely as a "mushroom eater" the first time Stepa Likhodeev lays eyes on him. The manager of the Variety Theater awakes to see before him "a black cat of terrifying proportions with a glass of vodka in one paw and a fork, on which he had succeeded in spearing a marinated mushroom, in the other" (5:82).

16. Boris Miagkov reports that a large writers' restaurant was installed on the ground floor of *Dom Gertsena* when it was converted for use by various literary organizations during the 1920s. The restaurant was closed in 1931, however, when it was replaced by an auditorium for the Literary Institute, which began to hold classes there in 1933 (see *Bulgakovskaia Moskva*, 125–26). According to Evgenii Zamiatin, Bulgakov himself was not averse to frequenting the fine restaurant at the House of Writers. In a letter to his wife, dated November 10, 1930, Zamiatin writes: "Yesterday and the day before I dined at Hertzen House with Mikhail Afanasevich and Olesha" (see *Neizdannyi Bulgakov: Teksty i materialy*, ed. Ellendea Proffer [Ann Arbor, Mich.: Ardis, 1977], 27).

17. See Mikhail Bakhtin, *Rabelais and His World*, trans. Helene Iswolsky (Cambridge, Mass.: MIT Press, 1984).

18. Bulgakov's use of the term *old inhabitants* (*starozhily*) in connection with the gastronomic splendor of Griboedov House may well constitute an oblique reference to Gogol's "Old World" (*starosvetskie*) landowners in Mirgorod, Afanasy Ivanovich and Pulkheriia Ivanovna, both of whom are said to be "very fond of good food, as was the old-fashioned tradition of Old World landowners" (see Gogol, *Polnoe sobranie sochinenii* [Moscow: Akademiia nauk, 1937–38], vol. 2, 21).

19. As I argue elsewhere, one of the important gastronomic themes developed in *The Heart of a Dog* concerns the woeful lack of discriminating taste among the new ruling elite in Soviet Russia (see my article, "Feeding a Poor Dog a Bone: The Quest for Nourishment in Bulgakov's *Sobach'e serdtse*," *The Russian Review* 52 [1993]: 58–78).

20. Andrei Sinyavsky, *Soviet Civilization: A Cultural History*, trans. Joanne Turnbull (New York: Little, Brown, 1990), 147.

21. Edwards, *Three Russian Writers and the Irrational*, 155. Svetlana le Fleming considers Bulgakov's depiction of the writers' club to be a typical example of his use of the grotesque in the novel. "Written in the best tradition of satirical literature," she notes, "it is focused mainly on the restaurant, and the conversations of the venerable writers are no more than eulogies on the food. Bulgakov reduces the world of Moscow poets to the baser aspects of life usually ignored by poetic inspiration" (see "Bulgakov's Use of the Fantastic and Grotesque," *New Zealand Slavonic Journal*, no. 2 [1977]: 30).

22. Maggie Kilgour, *From Communion to Cannibalism: An Anatomy of Metaphors of Incorporation* (Princeton, N.J.: Princeton University Press, 1990), 72. For a study that explores the possibility that Dante's *Divine Comedy* served as a source for Bulgakov's novel, see Bruce A. Beatie and Phyllis W. Powell, "Bulgakov, Dante, and Relativity," *Canadian-American Slavic Studies* 15 (1981): 250–69.

23. Edwards makes a similar observation: "Bulgakov's satire of this writers' collective is made particularly telling by his selection of material, by what he does not say: the reader learns almost nothing of the actual work which the Massolit members produce, but much of the pleasant life enjoyed in what is in effect an exclusive Moscow club" (*Three Russian Writers and the Irrational*, 154).

24. Lotman describes this binary opposition between *dom* and anti-*dom* in *The Master and Margarita* in "Zametki o khudozhestvennom pros-

transtve," *Trudy po znakovym sistemam* 19, no. 720 (1986): 25–43. See especially section 2, "Dom v *Mastere i Margarite*," 36–43.

25. Several critics have argued that this scene parodies the Last Supper. See, for example, Val Bolen, "Theme and Coherence in Bulgakov's *The Master and Margarita*," *Slavic and East European Journal* 16, no. 4 (1972): 428–30, and Edward E. Ericson, Jr., "The Satanic Incarnation: Parody in Bulgakov's *The Master and Margarita*," *The Russian Review* 33, no. 1 (1974): 29–32. Bakhtin discusses how during medieval times Cyprian's Supper regularly served as a parodia sacra that travestied the scriptural account of Christ's Last Supper (see *Rabelais and His World*, 13, 286). For an anthropological study that examines the significance of the Last Supper in terms of the language of food and meals, see Gillian Feeley-Harnik, *The Lord's Table: The Meaning of Food in Early Judaism and Christianity* (Washington: Smithsonian Institution, 1994).

26. O. A. Podgaets, "Bezdomnyi, Latunskii, Riukhin i drugie," *Russkaia rech'*, 3 (1991): 15.

27. Critics have noted a number of parallels between the Griboedov dinner and Satan's Ball. See especially the useful discussion in the section entitled "Transgressors at Revelry" in Riitta H. Pittman's *The Writer's Divided Self in Bulgakov's The Master and Margarita* (New York: St. Martin's, 1991), 118–24. Parallels have also been recently established between Bulgakov's depiction of Satan's Ball and a party the author attended during the spring of 1935 at Spaso House, hosted by William K. Bullitt, the U. S. ambassador. See, for example, Leonid Parshin, *Chertovshchina v Amerikanskom posol'stve v Moskve, ili 13 zagadok Mikhaila Bulgakova* (Moscow: Knizhnaia Palata, 1991), especially 114–27, as well as chapter 9, "Posol i satana: Uil'iam Bullitt v bulgakovskoi Moskve," or Aleksandr Etkind's book *Eros nevozmozhnogo: Istoriia psikhoanaliza v Rossii* (St. Petersburg: Meduza, 1993), 342–76. A detailed description of the ball, as well as Bulgakov's relationship with Bullitt and his staff, is the subject of J.A.E. Curtis's contribution to this volume.

28. Pittman, *The Writer's Divided Self*, 119.

29. The "gastronome" Ambrose says much the same thing when he compares the Griboedov restaurant to the Colosseum, where "there is no guarantee that you won't get a bunch of grapes thrown in your face from the first fellow to burst in on his way back from the theater district" (473).

30. In a book that describes the system of privilege that flourished in the Soviet Union, David K. Willis devotes an entire chapter ("Food as Klass") to

the issue of elite restaurants, special food shops, and luxury food deliveries. "The privilege of superior food," Willis writes, "certainly extends to Soviet writers and their guests, who dine excellently in a comfortable restaurant in the Tsentralnyi Dom Literatorov, the Central Writers' Union building, which serves some of the nation's best French cuisine in its main dining room. Under vaulted ceilings, lit by table lamps shaded with lace, Soviet writers, their families, and friends leisurely enjoy fresh perch, *oeufs en cocotte* with mushroom puree, sturgeon served with lobster tails, quails *alla Genovese*, *potage printaniere*, snipe and grouse" (see *Klass: How Russians Really Live* [New York: St. Martin's, 1985], 27–28).

31. Nadine Natov points out that in ancient mythology Behemoth represented the demon of gluttony (see *Mikhail Bulgakov* [Boston: Twayne, 1985], 98).

32. It should be noted that after Satan's Ball, when Woland invites Margarita to dine with him and his retinue, Behemoth is shown munching on pineapple slices (5:268). For a study of the use of the pineapple as a culinary motif in Russian literature, see Reinhard Lauer, "Ananas – ein kulinarischer Topos in der russischen Literatur," in "*Primi sobranie pestrykh glav*": *Slavistische und slavenkundiiche Beitrage für Peter Brang zum 65 Geburtstag*, ed. Carsten Goehrke et al. (Bern: Peter Lang, 1989), 169–87.

33. In his 1928 poem, "Dom Gertsena (tol'ko v polnochnom osveshchenii)," Vladimir Maiakovsky likewise satirizes the sybaritic pleasure palace that this home for the official literary establishment had become by the end of the first decade of Soviet rule. "Gertsen, Gertsen," the poet writes, "of an evening beyond the grave, tell us, please, do you ever dream of how wonderfully they have immortalized you – by means of beer, the foxtrot, and Viennese schnitzel?" (185) (see V. Maiakovsky, *Polnoe sobranie sochinenii v 13 tomakh*, vol. 9 [Moscow: Khudozhestvennaia literatura, 1958], 183–86).

34. Andrew Barratt points out that this woman's name suggests a further Griboedov connection, since Sophia Pavlovna is also the name of the heroine in *Woe from Wit* (see *Between Two Worlds: A Critical Introduction to The Master and Margarita* [Oxford: Clarendon, 1987], 120).

35. J.A.E. Curtis, *Bulgakov's Last Decade: The Writer as Hero* (Cambridge: Cambridge University Press, 1987), 166.

36. Archibald Archibaldovich's "strange" activity during this scene (before he checks on the grouse being cooked in the kitchen, he sneaks down to

the restaurant larder, where he wraps up two frozen fillets of smoked sturgeon) would seem to provide an early example of the practice of having so-called special food rations (*paeki*) set aside for the Soviet elite. For a brief discussion of this practice, see Willis, *Klass*, 3.

37. Curtis, *Bulgakov's Last Decade*, 167.

38. Kolb-Seletski, "Gastronomy, Gogol, and His Fiction," 48.

39. In his correspondence Gogol often associated food and eating with Satan. "There seems to be some kind of devil sitting in my belly," he writes, for instance, to A. S. Danilevsky on December 31, 1838, "a devil who positively ruins everything, at times drawing some tempting picture of a meal that is difficult to digest" (see Gogol, *Polnoe sobranie sochinenii*, vol. 11, 192). This association between food and the devil became even stronger, of course, during the late 1840s when Gogol fell under the influence of Father Matvei Konstantinovsky, the religious fanatic who encouraged him, among other things, to practice extreme abstinence and fasting.

40. "Everything which he had before looked at with envious eyes was now within his reach. That which he had from afar looked at longingly could now be his. His heart beat when he merely thought of it! To be able to wear a stylish coat, to be able to eat well after so long a fast, to be able to rent a fine apartment, to be able, at any time, to go to the theater, to the confectioners, or to other places" (Gogol, *Polnoe sobranie sochinenii*, vol. 3, 97).

41. Appropriately enough, Gogol describes the enticing allure of earthly temptation for Chartkov in gastronomical terms. The young artist is said to be unable to tear his thoughts away from visions of wordly success and fame, "like a child who sits in front of a plate of candy and, with watering mouth, watches other people eating it" (Gogol, *Polnoe sobranie sochinenii*, vol 3, 93).

42. Curtis, *Bulgakov's Last Decade*, 159.

43. Ibid., 133.

44. T.R.N. Edwards, *Three Russian Writers and the Irrational*, 156.

45. See Gareth Williams, "Some Difficulties in the Interpretation of Bulgakov's *The Master and Margarita* and the Advantages of a Manichaean Approach, with Some Notes on Tolstoi's Influences on the Novel," *The Slavonic and East European Review* 68, no. 2 (1990): 234–56.

46. I am using the term *hunger artist* here in much the same way that Maude Ellmann does in her recent book about the social and political aspects of anorexia nervosa, *The Hunger Artists: Starving, Writing, and Imprisonment* (Cambridge, Mass.: Harvard University Press, 1993). For two

of the more recent accounts of Gogol's death by starvation, see Vladimir Adamovic, "Gogolj: Depresija i smrt," *Savremenik* 5 (1984): 432–37, and V. Mil'don, "Otchego umer Gogol'?" *Voprosy literatury*, no. 3 (1988): 119–30. The details surrounding Gogol's death remind one of the self-starvation behavior patterns – analogous in many ways to modern cases of anorexia nervosa – prevalent among medieval female saints in Italy that Rudolph Bell examines in his book, *Holy Anorexia* (Chicago: University of Chicago Press, 1985).

III PRIMARY SOURCES

Chapter 5 from the First Version of *The Master and Margarita*: "An Interlude at Griboedov's Hut"

Reconstructed by MARIETTA CHUDAKOVA

Translated from the Russian by Thomas Epstein

Moscow, my dear comrades, is an unusual city. Many wonders can be seen on its streets. One of them, among other astonishing monuments to our century, . . . Across from Pushkin [?], on the boulevard, a statue in honor of our . . . [famed] poet has been erected.

In Moscow, directly across the street from the statue of the famous poet Alexander Ivanovich Zhitomirsky, who died in 1933, stands a restaurant for writers known by the preposterous name of "Griboedov's Hut."

The name "hut" was given it by Kozoboev, the famous liar and theater reviewer. He named it the day the restaurant opened, after having drunk himself silly. All the writers found "The Hut" a delightful designation.

If not for Kozoboev, the building in which the restaurant was located would have been known by its official name, that is, "Griboedov's House," since – if we are to believe Kozoboev himself – it had once belonged either to Griboedov's aunt or had been lived in by a niece of the author of *Woe from Wit*. However, it appears that Griboedov had neither such an aunt nor niece. But no matter. Here, where in the past were held . . . dinners, there was now housed all manner of offices serving the needs of writers while the basement had for some reason been converted into a restaurant.

From the day of its opening the restaurant was full. . . . On this evening dinner guests were being seated outside, on an asphalt patio under a canopy. Soon, however, when these places were filled, the customers . . . were forced to proceed indoors, where the rooms were furnished with spartan simplicity . . . In the lower . . . rooms, whose walls were painted with . . . and with stone harlequins, there was nothing except wooden tables covered with paper that was stained yellow by borscht served at lunch and . . . jars of conserves with golden . . . while in the room that adjoined the basement, which was shaped like a ship, were stored bottles and . . .

By [midnight] 11:00 P.M. the restaurant was completely full. Little did these Muscovites suspect the event that would befall them several days later . . . , they laughed and shouted. The waiters, with an expression of strange, indomitable hatred in their [ashen] grey . . . faces, scurried among the streaming crowd, either wheezing, "Sorry. Please excuse me," or simply elbowing one of the happy few out of their way . . . A blue-grey cloud of tobacco smoke rose over the tables. Wine glasses clinked. Plates chimed in the hands of busboys, and from the kitchen wafted a smell of rancid oil and overcooked cabbage.

Suddenly, from the corner of the restaurant where the piano was located, there was a sound, as if someone had struck its cover. A child, or rather a young man, in . . . a tightly knotted tie . . . rolling his vodka-inflamed eyes around his head, sat down at the stool and banged the piano top with the palms of both hands.

"Dum-tuh-rum-dum dum!" the piano answered back . . . delicate fingers . . . pulling open the lid . . . and drawing them across the bass strings like a branch . . . a victorious military accompaniment roared. . . . the nail-bitten, delicate fingers touched the keys, while the second player echoed him. . . . Then the bass strings again . . . quivered. Through the smoke . . . in black masks . . . the chords swept . . . to the powerful peals of a regimental march. Small hands ran along the treble keys, giving off a mournful sound that was like the cock's crow . . . It was as if . . . a gang of sounds, torn from the instrument, was whirling out of control . . . Suddenly, from a table near the piano, a man stood up. His hair was cut short and slicked back in the American manner, and the individually combed locks made his pig-skin pate visible. He was wearing a brown suit. . . . Gazing around the room with brazenly bright eyes, he grabbed around the waist a woman in a child's dress, who had jumped up just behind him. The dress was immediately pulled up in back by her partner's strong hand. A stripe of pale female skin was visible . . .

The veins, blue as a little stream . . . began to produce broken movements. The lady [obediently] followed the movements of her Knight in pink socks . . . and brightly colored dancing shoes . . . She alternately kicked out . . . her legs, or bent them at the knees, . . . turning out the soles of her feet. From another table leaped someone else, wearing horn-rimmed glasses and hair so greasy it seemed to have been smeared with oil. He was wearing the kind of suit that foreign golfers wear: plus-fours with a slit-knee, and high-quality [?] woolen checkered socks and tan shoes. He turned his back and began to stamp his feet, clicking his heels, while at the same time using his legs to spin around the lady . . . in the dress.

A third person briefly joined in: a short, bow-legged man who wore pants with holes at the knee, a Tolstoy shirt, and who sported a dirty, unruly beard that smelled of anchovies.

"Nope, I can't do it!" he shouted, momentarily joining the crowd of dancers as if someone had asked him to dance.

A scrawny, dirty man . . . the teenage girl, finding herself in his gnarled little claws, could smell the anchovies and the sharp odor of alcohol that emanated from around his shaggy mouth. She began to use her thin, shapely legs to dance in step to her partner's bearlike movements.

"Now let's squat!" he shouted with shrill gaiety.

His back banged into a waiter's tray and he stepped on the woman's foot with his own left one . . . and with an unhappy face and wide-open mouth, she then began to move, trying to force the man into the beat of the thundering music.

The woman took giant steps. She leaned her head to the side as if she were exhausted . . .

Dancing was virtually impossible. Through the roar and shouting one couple after another whirled . . . someone . . . was singing in English, that he loved someone . . . shouted:

"Comrades! Listen! We now have pickled herring in sour cream!"

The waiters, carrying full tankards, . . . dived through the dancing pairs. Their faces seemed terrified.

Suddenly, tossing aside herring-filled forks and unfinished glasses of wine, everyone made for the adjoining room. And from there into the third . . . even though the music only reached there in snatches.

They shuffled and stamped. The latecomers tried to reach the crowded room, looking for a place to dance [?]. In the kitchen, fires burned in the stove, water ran noisily from the taps.

Wheezy voices, . . . as at the baths, shouted imperiously:

"An order of cutlets!"

"Polish pike! One!"

The essayist [Bobchenko?] was dancing . . . Everyone was dancing, their cognac eyes opened wide . . . their hair falling forward . . . The poet Vodogreinikov danced through, . . . Fabulists and their wives, as well as several suspicious personages – not writers, but well-dressed folk, with mistrustful faces, pitiless eyes and jaws – were also dancing.

As the evening progressed the air became more comfortable: as midnight approached the cool penetrated the stone crevices of the weary city. Occasionally the wind blew . . . There was noise on the boulevard. A groan . . . A squeal was carried along it. Knives sounded and a quiet conversation . . . could be heard, the delicate sound of a glass tinkling when a fork banged lightly against it.

Immobile, a rather strange man stood on a lighted portion of the verandah. He was wearing tails. His person exuded a sultry Spanish night. Memories of jaunty French . . . musketeers, the sound of guitars, hand-clapping . . . the sharp thrusts of sabers . . . He was clean-shaven. His black eyelashes cast spiny shadows on his dark cheeks and black eyebrows . . . they pointed upward like arrows, the black beard sharp as a blade, his left arm resting deftly and comfortably at his side. A diamond shone on his finger. His eyes, from underneath his lowered eyelashes, skipped over the crowd before turning to the stars above Moscow.

The appearance of such a handsome man in Moscow, on this boulevard, among these drunken people, seemed strange, almost incomprehensible.

Anyone unacquainted with this handsome man would have shuddered and stood motionless, paralyzed at the sight of him. However, the patrons of this restaurant saw him daily and had, alas, grown used to him, not at all surprised by anything . . .

The liar and wit Kozoboev, with whom the reader is already acquainted, had spread the rumor that the handsome man, before his sudden appearance at "The Hut," was a pirate in the Pacific Ocean and had sailed in a black brig along the Tuscarora Basin.

This, of course, was pure rubbish, and indeed it has not even been established that the Tuscarora Basin itself exists in reality . . . Nevertheless inevitably, at first sight of the handsome man in the restaurant on the boulevard, one's first thought is that the handsome man ought to remove his tails, and wrap a red silken kerchief around his . . . silken head, pistols drawn to his side as a wind blows through the restaurant on the boulevard. But, alas, for ages pirates have not sailed on fast-moving brigs in the direction of . . . the Tuscarora Basin, and no English ships chase after them.

At that very moment the handsome man was listening intently to a whispered conversation between one of the writers and a woman who was seated with him at a nearby table. Hard as it may be to believe, they were discussing Berlioz's death, the news of which had mysteriously [?] made its way to "The Hut" . . . he fell . . . a horrible accident . . . of the Writers' Association . . . in despair he listened and from . . . and from the apartment of the late Berlioz, at house number 210, housing various offices and organizations, with which the deceased was most intimately connected. The curious forced their way through his little doorway and began to ask . . . the rumor had already begun to spread up and down the stairs . . . then crawled . . . to the table. There . . . it was deemed to be a rumor that fell under the rubric of "Kozoboev's Fantasies." There the rumor was silenced but not killed. It scampered off . . . behind the buffet table, crept past the fourth [?] . . . and then crawled away like a well-fed snake. Meanwhile, in the main hall, the fox-trot was reaching its peak, and in the first room . . . it had already gone dark and . . . They sailed along . . . in pairs, as the demonic waiters . . . moved dexterously between the dancers . . . "Please stop," he [the handsome man] said in earnest to the virtuoso.

The offended pianist turned his head toward the pirate.

"Archibald Palych, on what grounds?" he asked, cognizant of his dignity. "Can you at least explain that to me?"

"I ask you to stop," the handsome man softly said. "Comrade, it's about Berlioz . . . "

"What's going on? What? What?" voices could be heard from all sides.

Within a minute . . . The piano had been shut and the key that locked it had disappeared inside the wide pocket of the pirate's pants. At their tables . . . people stood up all around . . . called to each other . . . discussing the event. How . . . , what was obvious was that death was as far from the minds of the visitors to "The Hut" as it was from the deceased himself. . . .

"What in the world is that?" someone suddenly exclaimed in surprise.

From the gates that gave onto the boulevard an apparition seemed to be approaching the restaurant. Shouts were heard from the flock of waiting cabdrivers . . . in a second they were dispersed.

"Huh?" someone shouted . . . and then was silent.

The apparition made straight for the verandah. The watchman, in white livery, shouted in fear and rushed away. . . . The blue . . . of the beard completely . . . The apparition was . . . Candlelight flickered in front of his chest. The light wavered, at times threatening to go out, at other times blazing up with a warm, comforting flame . . .

"What the devil is that?" someone on the verandah wondered.

The wavering light approached . . . and the petrified public saw that this apparition was no apparition at all but rather a walking man whose head was bloodied. The public was not able to make out anything more than that because the candle suddenly went out and the man disappeared behind a trellis, over there, where . . . the winter entrance to the restaurant was located. No more than a minute had passed when . . . from "The Hut" a howling . . . could be heard, . . . and then after that . . . amid the general fright Ivanushka Bezdomny [Bezrodny][1] was again visible in the revived candlelight glowing in his hands.

An unbuttoned undershirt, secured by a giant safety pin, . . . was draped across his chest. Affixed to the pin, God knows how, was a paper reproduction of an icon of Jesus. That part of his body was covered with blood, flies buzzing around it. His legs were wrapped by a pair of striped, white long underwear. He wore nothing else.

Barefoot, Ivanushka shuffled lightly to the center of the asphalt verandah and, after making a threatening gesture at a deranged body in glasses, gazed suspiciously under the table, using his candle for light.

"Not there, no," Ivanushka told himself as he searched, sighing plaintively. At this very moment the crowd from inside the restaurant surged forward like a wave but just as quickly fell silent, walking on tiptoe. The waiters' jaws dropped. Suddenly, from out of the crowd, the pirate emerged and approached Ivanushka. His eyes, expressionless but shining, stared attentively at him.

"Comrade, more quietly," Ivanushka mysteriously whispered. "I would have liked dark wax."[2]

After these words . . . a more silent silence couldn't have been desired. It was broken only by the occasional, feline step of the pirate's white shoes. As he wasn't in the least interested in the important announcement Ivanushka was about to make, the pirate headed off . . . back inside the restaurant.

Now for the first time everyone stared at Ivanushka and saw that . . . his eyes were pearl-colored and at the bottoms there gleamed the quiet . . . flame of madness. The silence became . . . more silent.

"Comrades, I need wax," Ivanushka repeated.

"No need for explanations. It's delirium tremens," a voice softly spoke but the speaker was immediately shushed.

"He has come!"[3] Ivanushka declared, raising his now obviously insane eyes. "Citizens," he continued, pointing with his hands . . . toward the heights where fires burn in high-rise apartments. "Catch him now, before it's too late! Citizens!" Ivanushka shouted. "There are signs . . . His last name begins with the letter *V*." [?] Ivanushka wondered to himself, rubbing his forehead and staring with insane eyes. "No! That's not it!" he called out bitterly and began to mutter: "Vlasov . . . Vorozh . . . Oh, help me! What station was it? Where is it? On what line?"

"Kiev? Moscow?" It was a woman's hurried and frightened voice, herself touched by Ivanushka's frenzy.

"Fool!" Ivanushka shouted.

"Go pray, go home and pray! Citizens! Someone go now, straight to the Ministry, to Alexei Ivanych's house. Tell him that I said he ought to see to it that the *Streltsy*[4] are sent! . . . and catch the engineer[5] who's riding a motorcycle. Otherwise they won't ever be able to catch him. I was just over there but they wouldn't listen, the fools: Man of God, they told me, awake and go, otherwise you'll end up in jail! Why do I have to wake up? I haven't had a bite to eat all day!"

"Ssss!" someone distinctly and significantly whistled.

"I don't understand how the police let him get by dressed that way."

"I came by the back alleys, good people, all the way by back alleys!" Ivanushka yelled. "He's killed Berlioz!" The crowd shuddered, a hum ran through it.

A man of unknown profession pushed his way through the crowd, clamoring . . . and emerged by Ivanushka's side. He stared closely at him.

"Guilty in the murder of Comrade Berlioz?" he asked. "Tell us frankly, Comrade Bezdomny, you're saying someone pushed him in front of the train?"

"Pushed!" Ivanushka ironically repeated. "Oh, you dear little fool! If he'd only pushed, then the militia could simply have held him for questioning. But him? Him! Him!" Ivanushka suddenly shrieked, and shuddered. "He knew about the accident a minute before Berlioz's death! Do you understand? He knew about Pelageia[6] beforehand . . . I tell you, go to Alexei Ivanych's! Just say that icons – icons I say! – must be worn across the chest, and if there aren't enough icons then a cross will have to do . . . thus . . . and so . . . " Histrionically the madman began to make signs of the cross over the physiognomy of the man in the plus-fours and comical yellow jacket. The young man shrugged and disappeared, as if swallowed up by the asphalt.

"I attached the icon to my chest with this safety pin . . . Serves me right . . . Serves me right!" Ivanushka screamed. "This bloodletting. With my boots I trampled on our savior, the Lord Jesus Christ! . . . Repent, Orthodox Christians!" he adjured. "Repent! . . . . He is in Moscow! . . . with false teachings . . . and with a demonic beard."

The windows of the houses that girded the courtyard of the Writers' Ass. began to open. From out of them peered the physiognomies of the locals.

" . . . ," shouted a hysterical female voice. "There's never any peace and quiet around here! With all the screaming our children can't sleep! Once again . . . some scandalous happening at 'The Hut.' When will the Soviet authorities," and now the voice was made shrill for effect, "finally close down this den . . . , where thieves, calling themselves writers . . . "

Suddenly a window frame came crashing down and the sentence was cut off as if by a knife.

"Comrade Bez . . . domny," a snout in very short pants affectionately said, "you're all worn out."

"You . . . ," Ivanushka began, turning, and in his eyes once more that fanatical [sacred] fire burned. "You," he repeated with hatred, "crucified our Lord, Jesus Christ. That's what you did!" The crowd was listening.

"Yes," Ivanushka said earnestly and . . . his eyes flashed. "I recognized you. The secretary to the Igumen.[7] You're the one who tricked the Igumen into accepting the Limfostatmonic protocols! You're the [Jew] secretary of the Sanhedrin, that's who you are!" In the course of Ivanushka's brief monologue the physiognomy of the golf enthusiast changed like a chameleon. He stood, wishing the earth would swallow him up.

"Citizens, slay the [Jew] Aramean!" Ivanushka suddenly wailed. With his left hand he lifted up his candle while with the right he decked the golf enthusiast who was innocent of the monstrous crucifixion. . . .

. . . pale, he lay on the asphalt . . .

Only now did they think of rushing at Ivanushka . . . Bellicose Ivanushka . . . began to pound his hands.

"Anti-Semite!" someone hysterically shouted.

"What are you saying?" another objected. "Can't you see the condition the man's in? How can he be an anti-Semite? He's out of his mind."

"Call in the psychiatrists!" was shouted from everywhere.

The handsome man was standing by the cloakroom in the vestibule of "The Hut." The shaking doorman, who was reaching across . . . stood in front of him.

"Did you see that he was dressed only in underwear?!" the pirate [coldly] queried the doorman.

"Yes, sir, Archibald Palych . . . ," the doorman answered servilely, but at the same time he stared brazenly.

"Did you see that he was dressed in underwear?" the pirate coldly repeated.

"Yes, but you see, Archibald Palych," the doorman answered, but no longer so brazenly. "What can I do? This is the members' entrance – and they're all members. The other day Vodogreinikov and his crew walked by me with the birch twigs from the bath still in their hands. I saw them I did, and I didn't want to let them in – but they walked right by me, and stuck the twigs in my face. Mr. Bezdomny is a man whose conduct is well known but . . . I'm a man who puts fear in nobody, Archibald Palych . . . "

Uninterested in Vodogreinikov, the pirate's only, pitiless question was, "Did you see that he was dressed in underwear?" A cold reflection of the distant, pale clouds of Tuscarora was visible in his eyeballs.

The doorman . . . dissolved. He could already see the tarred hemp noose hovering above him, could hear the rumble of the sea's waves.

"Call the Chairman of the Writers' Ass." The pirate spoke the last words enunciating each word separately: "Tell him that Mr. Bezdomny has had an attack of delirium tremens. On . . . at our restaurant."

A few minutes later a procession headed for the gates of "The Hut" . . . An overcoat – not his own – was wrapped around Ivanushka. Several distraught poets carefully led him by the hand. He did not resist but, gazing scornfully at the sympathetic glances cast on him, muttered about . . . falling stars, and the woe awaiting all Orthodox Christians.

Beyond the gates flocks of cabdrivers brawled, tearing at each other and fighting over . . . Wheezy, savage shouts carried over the boulevard:

"I'm driving!"

"I'm driving to the hospital!"

"I'm driving to the hospital!"

One of the dancers, completely white-faced, who had received a slap in the face for no reason whatsoever, took a seat . . . and the woman he was with, slightly less pale, sat down next to him. In his hands the man held a broken . . .

A half hour later Ivanushka was seated in the waiting room of the newly renovated wing of the famed Semashko psychiatric clinic. A receptionist sat there too, under a blinding light and surrounded by harshly lacquered walls. The windows, blocked up by a narrow gauge but solid metal grating, were as if hermetically sealed by stiff white curtains.

The chairman of the Writers' Ass. and two attendants . . . seated Ivanushka on a couch. The poet . . . was now calm but he did complain about their having taken away his candle.

A glass door opened and through it entered the doctor who was on duty, wearing a white smock.

"Doctor," the chairman whispered. "We have brought in the

famous poet Bezdomny. He's apparently suffering from delirium tremens."

At the words *delirium tremens* the doctor turned to Ivanushka . . . and, extremely suspicious, leaned over politely and said to him:

"Hello there."

"Hello [good sir], idiot," the madman gloomily answered him.

"Why 'delirium tremens'?" the doctor half-whispered.

"Well, you see . . . "

"Did he drink a lot?"

"No, he drank moderately."

"Was he trying to catch any cockroaches or rats as you were driving him over here?"

"No, doctor . . . "

"He doesn't have 'delirium tremens,'" the doctor mumbled through his teeth.

The chairman was silent.

"Let me have a look at your eyes," the doctor softly addressed Ivanushka.

"I won't allow you to," Ivanushka answered.

"If you don't want me to, then I won't," the obliging doctor said, studying him through his eyeglasses. "Tell me, please, why are you wearing underwear? Were you taken from bed? At a restaurant? Why did they bring you here? Oh, he had a fight! With whom?"

A sudden change came over Ivanushka: he seemed revived, his eyes sparkled.

"Listen please, comrade," Ivanushka unexpectedly spoke, rising calmly, "let me use the telephone."

"You have something to tell someone?" the doctor politely asked.

"Yes," Ivanushka replied.

" . . . " the doctor ordered the attendants.

Ivanushka tossed off his jacket and removed his galoshes . . . he headed for the telephone that hung from the wall.

"Please, comrade, give me the office of Alexei Ivanovich . . . "

"Please call his highness to the telephone." The chairman of the Writers' Ass. made a signal in the direction of the on-duty doctor that meant, "You see. I told you." There was a pause.

"You fool!" Ivanushka suddenly shouted threateningly into the receiver. "Fool!" he repeated. "Scum bag!"

The attendant cautiously removed the receiver from Ivanushka's hand.

"Why the cursing?" the doctor observed. "Tell me what you want to say and I'll make the call."

"Fine!" Ivanushka shouted. "Now listen," he said to the doctor. "Call and say that an engineer who kills people has appeared at Patriarchs' Pond."

"Okay," . . . "I'll say it," and he turned questioningly to the chairman.

"He was a witness," the other whispered, "to the death of Comrade Berlioz, today at Patriarchs' Ponds. He was run over by a trolley."

"Oh, so that's it," the doctor spoke in a low voice. He turned to Ivanushka and asked loudly, "So you believe that he threw Berlioz under the wheels of the trolley?"

Ivanushka shook indignantly.

"Do you speak Russian, doc?" he asked, himself hissing. "Then who have you been listening to?" He prodded the chairman with his finger. "Couldn't you tell by his face that he's . . . ?"

The chairman . . . his lips trembled.

"He has," . . . "I just don't know where they were looking," the madman continued. "The Chairman of the Writers' Ass. went there – he appeared from somewhere." Ivanushka spoke loudly and clearly, his eyes full of . . . "The mysterious engineer, his last name begins with a *W*."

"*W*?" the doctor asked.

"Not *W* alone," Ivanushka screamed. "The name begins with a *W* . . . I didn't get his last name clearly, the demons would have had me . . . Don't you see, he knew everything before it happened. He knew about Pelageia, about the jar being dropped – knew about it before it happened!"

"Under the trolley?" you said. "How did he do it?"

"Oh, you idiots!" Ivanushka shrieked." You all want to hear how he pushed him! That he kicked him in the back or something! He was a hundred feet away from him, knew about it beforehand. In a word, . . . " The orb high in the sky shined with a mysterious light.

"Good gracious," Ivanushka whispered. "Listen, I've got to talk with you right now. Call and say . . . "

"I'll call later," the doctor said.

"You're lying," Ivanushka shrieked, stamping his feet. "Lying! You won't call! You won't . . . so go to hell! Sons of bitches! Just let me out. Let me out!"

The attendants, as was their habit, calmly blocked the exits.

"Let me out," he shouted, trying to pull the attendant's arm away – but the attendant didn't budge.

" . . . ," Ivanushka shouted, staring around like a caged animal. "You have no right to hold against their will citizens who are loyal to the Soviet state. Let me out!!"

"Ivan, Ivanushka," the chairman murmured softly, rubbing his hands together.

"Excuse me for saying it, but you're not wearing pants," the doctor said kindly. "How can you go? Why don't you stay with us, spend the night and . . . "

"Ward 16, a private room," the doctor whispered through his teeth, half-turning to the receptionist.

With one hand the receptionist noisily scribbled on the admittance form, with the other she lifted up the false top on the side of her desk. A white, sleeveless shirt was pulled from a case.

"What union do you belong to?" the receptionist asked automatically.

The chairman had not time even to nod in answer to the question before Ivanushka, with a shout of "God have mercy," dove like a fish, headfirst into the drapery . . . with a soft snapping sound the drapery completely encircled Ivanushka, lifting him up . . . he found himself in the arms of the attendants who restrained him without the least effort. Red spots . . . broke out on his face.

"Do you know who killed Berlioz?" Ivanushka asked pensively.

The receptionist, the attendants, and the chairman were all ears.

Ivanushka began again but a milky curtain was suddenly drawn over his eyes. Unable to say what he wanted he fell lifelessly into the arms of the attendants and . . . "With signs . . . false teachings . . . Sleeveless . . . flying through the air." The attendants began to remove Ivanushka's dirty underclothes.

In a sudden frenzy Ivanushka nearly tore a muscle as he pulled himself from the arms of the attendants and roared: " . . . I was among the Sanhedrin . . . Pontius Pilate . . . Comrades," he intoned, "Repulse . . . the Arameans, let us stand and defend Holy Russia, our Tsar! . . . "

[After the exhortation]

Having shouted himself out, Ivanushka suddenly gave in. He had given it his all. Now, unresisting, he lay down on a bed that had been pulled from the wall. It was made up and had rubber wheels . . . and he was rolled away by the attendants.

Shaken . . . the chairman asked in fright:

"So what kind of illness is it, comrade doctor?"

"*Mania furibunda*," answered the doctor, yawning [lighting up].

The chairman shuddered.

"What, is it incurable?"

"Don't be so gloomy! On the contrary. It is my opinion that Comrade Bezdomny will leave this hospital in perfect health. But perhaps . . . "

The chairman shook his head mournfully. He . . . took leave of the doctor . . . he turned back at the door, wracked by a vague thought.

"Tell me, doctor, . . . what was all that telephone business . . . what did he say about the engineer? . . . wasn't he talking about some engineer at 'The Hut' as well?"

"Listen, my friend, I myself was not witness to Berlioz's death.

Perhaps something real fired his imagination. Or maybe there was no such thing: perhaps he simply got scared."

"So that's how he got this terrible illness?! Just from seeing Berlioz die? Is it possible?"

"Yes, it's quite possible," the doctor replied.

The chairman left.

By one o'clock the insane asylum had fallen silent. The patients began to drift off to sleep. Strange lights, white and green, shone in the garden that surrounded the vast yellow building. In all the hallways green, hooded nightlights glowed. Dream . . . visions began to descend on the sufferers. Snores and moans occasionally rose skyward . . . in the circular rooms where agitated people lay, whose consciousness refused to serve them.

It was about a quarter to one. Dawn was not far off, which could be seen in the sky's ever more watery, bluish appearance. Two wearied attendants slept – one half-seated on a cot, the other hunkered down in a chair. In sleep their faces appeared greenish and very serious. Suddenly the one who was asleep in the chair wheezed and then jumped up. There was terror in his eyes.

"Do you see?" he cried out. "Do you see him?"

The other jumped up from the cot, his bug-eyes fixed on his comrade.

"What? What?"

"Did you see the poodle?" he asked in horror.

"What poodle? What the devil are you talking about? Losing your mind or what? I thought you heard a ring."

"A poodle I say, a black one, leaping outside the window. Gigantic . . . "[8]

"Go to hell," the second growled. "You scared me out of my wits. It's time to lock you up in the sixteenth."

The second groused a bit more and then stretched out to resume his interrupted sleep.

For a long time the first one . . . tried to settle down, his sad eyes wandering. The second had already begun . . . to drift off.

"Vasily!" the first attendant suddenly spoke up again. "I had a dream that someone in underwear . . . "

"Go back to sleep" . . . The first[9]

"Tell him that yourself," the voice ironically opined. "Say, 'I, Pavel Ivanych, inspired by the Lord God, do not agree with your conclusion.' He's going to give you quite a consultation! . . . "

The first sighed . . . and sadly . . . "Perhaps he doesn't have *mania furibunda*."

The second slept, whistling.

The first . . . shuddered from the cold and gazed around . . . he set out for the waiting room to see[10]

And this light was unexpected.

A shadow suddenly appeared in this light. It stood on four legs–legs long as telephone poles. The shadow rose out of . . . and bounded . . . A huge black poodle . . . became visible, inseparable from its shadow.

The attendant's heart sank in despair. He . . . his lips muttered . . . The poodle, flying . . . stopped, while its shadow . . . moved off . . . The poodle stared into the window to which the distorted face of the attendant was glued. Then it ran off . . . and it seemed to the attendant . . . that the poodle was glittering . . . as if with the deadly phosphorescent glow of a . . . streetlight. The dog's round yellow eyes stared directly at the attendant.

The attendant suddenly crossed himself. The poodle . . . darted, turned sharply, on his long dragonlike tail, turning his back to the attendant . . . and howled deafeningly.

"Why did he run into the garden?" the terrified attendant wondered. Could he believe his eyes? A fifteen-foot poodle? . . . there wasn't any such poodle, there never was and never could be. Then what was it, by God?! . . . from somewhere there swept . . . right through the attendant . . . Muttering . . . a distant howl. The poodle rushed toward the hospital windows . . . chasing after his shadow . . .

NOTES

1. Apparently this is the point in the novel at which Bulgakov definitively replaced "Bezrodny" with "Bezdomny." – M. C.

2. Ivan may be requesting wax here with a view to doing some divination in the time-honored Slavic manner, which involves dropping melted wax into water.

3. Bulgakov considered using this exclamation (in Russian, *On poiavilsia*) as the title for what became *The Master and Margarita.*

4. *Streltsy* were the first permanent, regular regiments of the Russian army, translatable as musketeers for the weapons they used.

5. In this early version Woland is identified as an engineer.

6. This Pelageia is the precursor to Annushka-the-Plague, whose jar of sunflower oil will figure so prominently in Berlioz's death.

7. An Igumen is an Orthodox ecclesiastical rank roughly equivalent to an Abbot.

8. In this version of the text Bulgakov has Woland, in the form of a poodle, jump into Ivanushka's room in order to continue the gospel story.

9. According to the editor, Marietta Chudakova, the rest of this manuscript page is torn.

10. Chudakova again notes a large rip in the manuscript here.

Mikhail Bulgakov and the Red Army's Polo Instructor: Political Satire in *The Master and Margarita*

J.A.E. CURTIS

In the mid-1930s the aristocratic game of polo was introduced to Stalin's Red Army. The man responsible for this improbable feat was Charles Thayer, a young diplomat at the new U.S. Embassy in Moscow. For many years after the 1917 Revolution no formal diplomatic ties existed between the USSR and the United States. In 1932, however, Franklin Roosevelt made it a plank of his presidential campaign that diplomatic relations should be restored, not least because of the need to coordinate resistance to the Nazi threat in Germany and to the apparently imperialist aspirations of Japan. Dialogue was officially resumed at the end of 1933, and arrangements were made to open an American Embassy in Moscow. A spectacular building on Spaso-Peskovskaia Square, known by the Americans as Spaso House, was allocated to the ambassador for his official residence. Everyone admired its imposing staircase and the domed ballroom with its white marble pillars and glittering chandeliers.

Charles Thayer, bored with life in the U.S. Army Academy, had already made his way to Russia to start learning Russian, at the same time hoping to obtain a job at the new embassy.[1] When William Bullitt, who was to be the first ambassador, arrived in Moscow in December 1933 to present his letters of credence, Thayer talked his way into Bullitt's hotel bedroom to plead his case. When he arrived, a rather bald and plump figure, dressed, to Thayer's surprise, in a kimono, invited him in and handed him the script of a play he was to attend that evening at the Moscow Art Theater, requesting that Thayer translate it. An appalled Thayer, whose knowledge of Russian did not at that point extend much beyond capital letters, recognized the play's title and realized it was Mikhail Bulgakov's *Days of the Turbins*. With great presence of mind, he offered to summarize the plot as he pretended to read, which he was able to do because he had already seen the play several times on stage. Bullitt gave him a job, for which Thayer may therefore in a sense be said to have Bulgakov to thank.

One of the tales Thayer tells of this period in his memoirs is of a dreary dinner attended by Marshal Voroshilov and General Budyonny, at which Thayer served as interpreter. Wearying of the usual social inanities between the ambassador and his guests, Thayer began to engage in a conversation of his own, asking the two military leaders why no polo was played in Russia. After a while, he turned to a startled Ambassador Bullitt to inform him that the Russians were delighted that he and Bullitt had apparently offered to teach them the game. So it was that Charles Thayer, with Ambassador Bullitt as referee, took part in regular matches near the women's nude bathing beach on the Moscow River, against a crack team from the Red Army mounted on a string of sixty-four perfect polo ponies conjured from nothing in a matter of weeks. Bullitt later reported to President Roosevelt that "the polo has brought not only myself but our military men into the closest relationship with the Red Army leaders and has proved most useful."[2] Only the worsening international situation later in the decade brought these encounters to an end, and Thayer remained the Red Army's one and only Senior Polo Instructor.

This was typical of the kind of scrapes Thayer got into. In 1934 he organized a Christmas party for the embassy, with performing seals who went berserk in the ballroom after their trainer drank too much and passed out. Despite that fiasco, Bullitt commissioned Thayer to organize another party in April 1935 – something really stunning designed to impress the Soviet establishment. Egged on by the counselor's wife, Irena Wiley, Thayer once again went for animals: a miniature farmyard with baby goats, roosters, and a baby bear, as well as golden pheasants, parakeets, and a hundred zebra finches in a gilded net (that escaped at the end of the party, much to Ambassador Bullitt's annoyance). They had chicory carpeting the tables, birch trees bursting into leaf after being kept in the embassy's bathrooms for a week or so, tulips flown in from Finland, and pictures of roses and camellias projected, on the advice of a director of the Kamerny Theater, onto the ballroom walls. There was a Czech jazz band, a Gypsy orchestra, and Georgian sword dances. Some five hundred guests were present, including Litvinov, Voroshilov, Kaganovich, Bukharin, Yegorov, Tukhachevsky, and Radek – all the Soviet elite except Stalin himself. It was deemed the most sensational party in Moscow since the Revolution.

Among the Russian guests at this occasion were Mikhail Bulgakov and his wife Elena Sergeevna. Bulgakov's play *The Days of the Turbins* had served to effect an introduction not only between Charles Thayer and Ambassador Bullitt but also, as it turned out, between the ambassador and its author. In December 1933 Elena Sergeevna records in her diary a newspaper cutting reporting Bullitt's attendance at *The Days of the Turbins* and his comments – presumably on the strength of Thayer's summary – "Splendid play, splendid performance."[3] In March 1934 Bullitt requested Bulgakov to send him a copy of the text; in August of the same year the Bulgakovs were introduced to Thayer at a reception; and in September 1934 they made the acquaintance of Bullitt himself at a performance of the play, which Bullitt said he had now seen five times.

By 1935 Bulgakov was entering a period of relative ease despite the political tensions of the day – the murder of Kirov in December 1934 had recently signaled the beginning of an extreme phase of Stalin's Terror. But several of Bulgakov's plays were in production or being staged, which seemed a more hopeful sign after the catastrophic banning of four of his plays in 1929. Not only had he at long last married his great love, Elena Sergeevna, but he had also been allocated a new apartment; he had begun to overcome the psychological condition which, for a period of six months in 1934, had made it impossible for him to leave the house alone; and now here was the U.S. ambassador himself acclaiming his work and drawing the Bulgakovs into the glittering social circles of embassy life. During this period the Bulgakovs would be driven to and from the embassy in American cars to attend receptions, meals, cocktail parties, and film screenings, and be introduced to the French, Turkish, and Romanian ambassadors and their families. In October 1934 Bulgakov spent an agreeable day at Thayer's dacha, discussing the theater. The Americans in turn accepted invitations to the Bulgakovs' apartment and would arrive bearing flowers and whiskey, to eat meals of caviar, salmon, and fried mushrooms. Always present on these occasions, of course, were Soviet "interpreters" who were patiently writing reports on every word spoken; but Bulgakov would nevertheless take advantage of the occasions to talk provocatively in front of these foreigners about his plans to travel abroad (a dream that was never to be realized). George Kennan, a future ambassador himself, came one day in 1936 to discuss a biography of Chekhov that he was planning to write, while Chip Bohlen – like Kennan, a third secretary – declared his intention of translating Bulgakov's play *Zoika's Apartment* into English.

The invitation to the midnight ball in April 1935 caused quite a stir in the Bulgakov household, and Elena Sergeevna has left an ecstatic account of the event in her diary:

> I was dressed by the seamstress and Tamara Tomasovna. My evening dress was a rippling dark blue with pale pink flowers; it came out very well. Misha was in a very smart dark suit.
>
> At 11:30 we set off . . . Never in my life have I seen such a ball. The ambassador stood at the top of the stairs to greet his guests. . . . Bohlen and another American, who turned out to be the military attache, . . . came down the stairs to meet us and received us very cordially.
>
> There were people dancing in a ballroom with columns, floodlights shining down from the gallery, and behind a net that sepa-

rated the orchestra from the dancers there were live pheasants and other birds. . . . There were masses of tulips and roses. Of course there was an exceptional abundance of food and champagne. . . . And we left at 5:30 in one of the embassy cars, having first invited some of the Americans from the embassy to call on us.[4]

Six days after the ball, Thayer, Irena Wiley, and Bohlen spent an evening with the Bulgakovs, and no doubt the preparations for the ball and the event itself formed a hilarious topic of conversation. Throughout the rest of 1935 and well into 1936 these social contacts continued, confirming Bulgakov's status as a member of the cultural elite. However, the frail hopes Bulgakov had in 1935 that his works would all finally get staged were soon dashed. After two devastating attacks on Shostakovich in the press early in 1936, Bullitt reported to Roosevelt that "Stalin's latest imitation of the Roi Soleil is to dictate in the field of music and drama."[5] On March 9, 1936, a leader in *Pravda* meted out the same treatment to Bulgakov with a denunciation of his newly opened play about Molière, *The Cabal of Hypocrites.* Soon Bulgakov's plays were all banned or canceled again, as they had been in 1929, and the years between 1936 and his death in 1940 were darkened by a pervasive sense of defeat. Contacts between the Bulgakovs and the Americans, for all the latter's sympathy, became more intermittent, especially after Bullitt left Moscow at the end of 1936.

It is obvious from the accounts of the April 1935 ball left by Thayer in his memoirs and Elena Sergeevna in her diary that the occasion proved a fertile stimulus to Bulgakov's portrayal of Satan's Ball in *The Master and Margarita.*[6] In earlier versions of the novel the occasion had been envisaged not as a ball but as a witches' sabbath, with scandalous erotic scenes (Chudakova describes as "Rabelaisian" a moment in the 1933 third redaction when a vase in the form of a golden phallus grows erect, to Margarita's laughter, at the touch of her hand).[7] In the later, rather more decorous version of the ball, Margarita arrives at the apartment and is astounded by the magnificence of the staircase and the vastness of the enormous colonnaded ballroom. Satan's retinue are dressed in tails, and even the cat Behemoth has donned a white tie, hung mother-of-pearl binoculars around his neck, and gilded his whiskers. During the ball itself, an explosion of light and sound, Margarita is impressed by the vegetation – here a tropical forest with lianas rather than chicory and birch trees – as well as the wall of tulips, the ballroom festooned with roses and camillias, and the loud jazz band – all details recalling the embassy party. Earlier, walking through the darkness, Margarita had been alarmed by something brushing against her head, which turns out to be one of the parrots that Behemoth, who is organizing the ball, has laid on. Woland grumbles about them just as Bullitt did about Thayer's escaped zebra finches. Perhaps there is indeed, at least for the duration of this episode, something of the buccaneer Charles Thayer in the cat Behemoth?

During the ball episode in the novel some striking remarks are made about the guests. Koroviev explains to Margarita, "We shall see people who commanded enormous authority in their time. But when you reflect on how infinitesimal their powers were in comparison to the powers of the one in whose retinue I have the honor to serve [Woland, the devil], then in my opinion they come to seem laughable, even pathetic."[8] Margarita endures the torment of receiving Woland's guests, until "she felt as little interest in the Emperor Caligula and Messalina as she did in any of the rest of the kings, dukes, knights, suicides, poisoners, gallows-birds, procuresses, gaolers, card-sharpers, hangmen, informers, traitors, madmen, detectives, and seducers." Korov'iev is notably "unable" to name the very last two guests to arrive, evidently the recently dead. As Piper and Lamperini have shown, their story, which involves one of them obliging the other to spray the walls of his successor's office with poison, is an anecdote that would have been immediately recognizable to a contemporary audience. The same charge was made against Yagoda, one of the perpetrators of Stalin's Terror, when he was accused in 1938 of getting his subordinate to spray with poison the office of his successor, Yezhov.[9]

In Bulgakov's re-creation of the ball, the final guest is the unfortunate Baron Maigel, an official "guide for foreign visitors," notorious as an eavesdropper and a spy whose death by shooting forms part of the ceremony conducted by Woland at the culmination of the ball. His character too can easily find a prototype in a man well known to Charles Thayer: a certain Baron Steiger who was well connected in the Soviet establishment. Every week Thayer used to deliver to him a tin of Edgeworth pipe tobacco to be passed on to Stalin himself. Thayer recalls having a conversation with Steiger shortly before he was arrested and shot in December 1937.[10] That he would have been associated in the Bulgakovs' minds with the American ball is indicated by Elena Sergeevna's description of their drive home afterward in an embassy car:

> We were joined in the car by a man we hadn't met, but who is known throughout Moscow and who is always to be found where foreigners are – I think he's called Steiger. He sat with the driver and we sat in the back.[11]

Several conclusions begin to emerge here. First, Bulgakov's experience of being taken up by the Americans and lionized during a span of barely eighteen months between 1934 and 1936 represented an astonishing contrast with the fears, oppression, and restrictions of his everyday life in Moscow. The ball at the U.S. Embassy figured as the peak of a golden, almost unreal phase in Bulgakov's increasingly grim life. The Americans arrived, seemingly out of the blue, in 1933; they offered him worldwide recognition, and they also brought with them a fantastical degree of glamour and luxury, a whiff of the life of the elite in pre-Soviet Russia, perhaps. They were free agents, able to travel wherever and whenever they wished; their powers must have seemed miraculous in the prison, as Bulgakov perceived it, of the USSR. As the hosts at the U.S. Embassy ball in 1935 they provide recognizable prototypes for the characters of *The Master and Margarita*, for if Charles Thayer has certain crazy and endearing features reminiscent of Behemoth, then Ambassador William Bullitt equally contributes to certain aspects of Woland.

Bulgakov could hardly fail to be struck by the personality of Bullitt, who was no less colorful a figure than Thayer. A diplomat who had for many years received treatment from Freud and who went on to write a biography of Woodrow Wilson in coauthorship with Freud, Bullitt had good contacts with Lenin in his day. He later married Louise Bryant, widow of John Reed, author of *Ten Days That Shook the World.* Clearly, Bullitt was someone who must have communicated to his Russian friends his intense and possibly sympathetic interest in the consequences of the 1917 Revolution, some of whose notable protagonists he had known personally. He was clearly dismayed with much of what he found. At a time of constant arrests – Mandel'stam was arrested from the apartment block where Bulgakov lived in May 1934 – Bullitt was helpless to intervene:

> The terror, always present, has risen to such a pitch that the least of the Muscovites, as well as the greatest, is in fear. Almost no one dares have any contact with foreigners and this is not unbased fear, but a proper sense of reality. . . . I can, of course, do nothing to save anyone. . . . The Russians still dare to come to my house for large entertainments, when there can be no possibility of private conversation.[12]

This report Bullitt sent to Roosevelt, written within a week of the embassy ball, emphasizes just how great a risk Bulgakov was taking in mixing with the Americans. But with his belief in the enduring significance of art ("Manuscripts don't burn," insists Woland [703]), Bulgakov cherished this recognition afforded him by the representative of a Western nation at a time when he could expect nothing but vilification from his fellow countrymen. Just before the Molière play was canceled, Bullitt, like their other embassy friends, attended a performance: "Bullitt spoke extremely favorably about the play and about Mikhail Afanas'evich in general, and called him a master," records Elena Sergeevna proudly.[13]

The Americans emerge, then, as partial prototypes for the hosts at Woland's ball. And what of the guests? The procession of murderers and pimps received by Margarita at the top of the stairs is, by implication, to be equated with the leading members of the government whom Thayer listed in his memoirs; people who, as he observes, went on over the next few years to eliminate one another as Stalin's Terror turned into a deadly struggle for survival among rivals in the elite.

However, we must beware of extending the interpretation of Woland and Behemoth as Bullitt and Thayer to the rest of *The Master and Margarita*. It would be a mistake to impose an overly allegorical and specifically political interpretation on a novel that achieves its impact largely through its mercurial and shifting generic identity. Indeed, no single generic categorization has ever seemed adequate to reflect the intricacy of the purposes of *The Master and Margarita*. The text contains a solemn and realistic "novel within a novel" that enters into dialogue with the Gospels themselves. When this is set alongside the blend of broad comedy and poignant romance in the Moscow chapters, a unifying allegorical interpretation becomes unthinkable.

But if it is not allegorical, the novel is certainly satirical in the sense that it is a comic work informed by a moral purpose that has topical relevance. The first of the various levels on which the novel's satire functions is that of universal satire, the mockery of perennial human failings as they manifest themselves in the Moscow of the 1920s and 1930s. The showing up of human weaknesses seems to be the primary purpose of Woland and his retinue in their visit to Moscow: they provoke and then punish the vices of vanity, greed, hypocrisy, and lying which characterize the Muscovites as they do humankind in general. "Altogether, they remind me of the people here before. . . . It's just that they've been warped by the housing crisis," concludes Woland.

A second level of satire is directed at certain institutions. Woland and his retinue wreak particular havoc among the administrators of the theatrical world and the membership of MASSOLIT, the fictional writers' organization whose headquarters at Griboedov House are eventually destroyed by fire. Clearly Bulgakov had particular reasons for selecting these targets for Woland's wrath. Having savaged the overbearing, bureaucratic, and exploitative attitudes he encountered while working in the Moscow Art Theater in his play *The Crimson Island* and his unfinished *Theatrical Novel*, in *The Master and Margarita* he aims his pen squarely at the groups that exercised control over literature – the Russian Association for Proletarian Writers (RAPP), which hounded his friend Eugene Zamiatin out of the country, and its successor, The Writers' Union, which imposed monolithic controls after 1932–34 through its theory of socialist realism. Nothing could have been more abhorrent to Bulgakov than the rule of the philistines in literature: "Surely you don't have to ask Dostoevsky for his membership card in order to be sure that he's a writer?" asks Koroviev disingenuously when challenged at the entrance to Griboedov House, that temple of material, as opposed to aesthetic, values. It is fitting that the culmination of Woland's visit to Moscow should be the moment at the ball when he awards Berlioz his just desserts and consigns him to oblivion for his "friendly" but unforgivable attempt to censor Bezdomny's poem because it is insufficiently atheistic.

In addition to the universal and the institutional, *The Master and Margarita* offers varying levels of political satire. Here we must disagree with Andrew Barratt's assertion that "very little of the satire has a specifically 'Stalinist' target."[14] The text brims over with allusions to the police state – some discreet, others less so. References to the pervasive suspicion of foreigners, Bezdomny's unthinking retort that Immanuel Kant should be dispatched to Solovki (a notorious labor camp in the White Sea), the "inexplicable" disappearances of people from Berlioz's and Likhodeyev's apartment, the latter's anxiety about his "unnecessary" conversation and article, many actual arrests, and Bosoy's "show trial" dream all reveal that Moscow is obsessed with the threat of repressions. "How jumpy people are nowadays!" exclaims Woland. The dominating presence of the OGPU is indicated largely through euphemism: "Take the telegrams personally. Let them sort it out," Rimsky tells Varenukha (525). Varenukha needs no further instructions about where to go, and when he does not return, Rimsky's only question is, "What on earth for?" (i.e., "Why have they arrested him?") (534). The OGPU headquarters are continually characterized with elliptical phrases such as "there," or "another place," as when Bosoy is summoned to the headquarters before being transferred to the asylum. When Azazello approaches Margarita in the Kremlin Gardens she immediately assumes she is being arrested, and he complains, "What is this – you only have to open your mouth for people automatically to think you're arresting them!" (641). At the entrance to Griboedov House, visitors' names are all "for some unknown reason" recorded (769). Indeed, this atmosphere of a police state pervades even the "neutral" omniscient narrative of the Moscow chapters, some of which appears to be couched mockingly in the form of a police report: "It is impossible to say . . . and nobody knows either . . . we are also unable to say, although we do know that . . . " (762). In a slippage characteristic of the novel's underlying and unifying poetics, such phrases even creep into the Yershalaim chapters: "No one knows . . . although we do know . . . " (733). Here it reinforces our sense of the authoritarian Roman regime, where figures such as Afranius constantly report on the thoughts and action of the citizens of Yershalaim. In Moscow the "police report" is, we may presume, compiled by the members of "a certain Moscow organization overlooking a large square" (747) – an unmistakable reference to the Lubyanka.

The Master's fate is alluded to in equally circumspect terms. His persecution at the hands of the critics is capped by Aloisy Mogarych's self-interested denunciation of him for harboring illegal literature. The very indirectness with which this dramatic event is told (we learn of a tapping at the window in October, of the Master's being released in January with no buttons on his coat, and of Margarita's hypothesis that he may have been sent into internal exile) evokes once again the fearfulness people felt about even alluding to these things out loud. When, in the asylum, the Master tells Ivan his story, this all-pervasive fear is underscored by the fact that a noise in the corridor causes him to describe his experiences with the OGPU in a whisper as inaudible, it seems, to the narrator as it is to the reader. We are left to infer the truth about his treatment from Woland's remarks ("They did a good job on him" [701]), that of the Master himself ("They have broken me," [708]), and that of Margarita ("They have laid waste to your soul . . . Just look at your eyes! They are empty, and look at your shoulders, bowed under their burden . . . They have simply crippled you." [782]). Bulgakov, although he himself escaped actual arrest, was aware that it was a threat that constantly hung over him. In his novel, however, he postulates a hopeful scenario, where the tragedy of persecution and parting can be healed by the forces of ultimate justice, thanks to the power of faithful love.

In the Yershalaim chapters no obvious direct references are made to Stalin's Russia, although perennial problems of tyranny, the courage required to withstand the forces of evil, and the destruction of innocence are raised. They do not need to be reduced to an allegory of the present to strike a chord in the mind of any modern reader, particularly since they belong to a historical moment that sets up paradigms of ethical dilemmas for all subsequent European culture. Pilate's vision of Tiberius with his ulcerated face; his fear of what might happen to him if he were to allow Yeshua's words about the transience of earthly power to go unpunished; the absolute nature of his own authority; and his remorse about his moment of cowardice – all these speak to us in their own right.

In identifying the episode of Satan's Ball as the only passage in the novel actually based on specific prototypes, we are not suggesting that the passage is inconsistent with the rest of the novel. The text elsewhere occasionally makes transparent allusions to real people or literary forebears. Although Gasparov's reading of the poet Riukhin as Mayakovsky, Bulgakov's bête noire in his attitudes toward culture, may be overstated,[15] it nevertheless picks up one of those elusive threads of reference in *The Master and Margarita* that contribute a shade to the novel's meaning but do not dominate the design of the tapestry as a whole. A similar technique has been observed with regard to Bulgakov's use of literary and operatic references, as, for example, his playful use of motifs from *Faust* in Goethe's and Gounod's renderings. Gasparov himself rightly observes of the novel that "any link you establish turns out to be partial and fleeting, it carries an association rather than a direct likening or equation."[16] This holds true equally for the episode of Satan's Ball.

Woland has other, much more important roles to play in the novel than that of the American plenipotentiary: a supernatural force that complements the unadulterated goodness embodied in Yeshua; a judge and tempter who sets people back on a righteous course; an emissary from the other world sent to observe whether individuals have changed, and how they behave in the militant atheism of the Soviet state (a theme already broached in *The Heart of a Dog*). This is one reason why the guests featured at the ball seem so incongruous – why does Woland receive the perpetrators of evil at his feast if his role in the rest of the novel is to punish them? It marks the passage as one that may contain additional layers of meaning. Bulgakov's treatment of the ball, although ultimately appropriate given Woland's major purposes (damning Berlioz and enabling Margarita to win back her lover), nevertheless contains certain features that have something of the private joke about them. For the entertainment of his family and friends, Bulgakov here recalls the spectacular party thrown by Bullitt and Thayer for Stalin's henchmen by inserting into the text a satirical allegory he dares not risk elsewhere in *The Master and Margarita*.

NOTES

1. The material in this essay on Charles Thayer is derived from his memoirs, *Bears in the Caviar* (London, 1952). This essay is based on talks originally given in London, Oxford, and Cambridge, beginning in May 1991.

2. Letter of August 5, 1934, cited in *Franklin D. Roosevelt and Foreign Affairs*, vol. 2, ed. E. B. Nixon (Cambridge, Mass.: Harvard University Press, 1969), 171 (hereafter referred to as *Franklin D. Roosevelt*).

3. Some of the entries from Elena Sergeevna Bulgakova's diary are quoted from the first version held in the Manuscript Section of the Lenin Library, Moscow (F 562, 29.5). Other extracts are quoted from my *Manuscripts Don't Burn. Mikhail Bulgakov. A Life in Letters and Diaries* (London: Bloomsbury, 1991) (hereafter referred to as *Manuscripts Don't Burn*). The

text of the diary in its edited version is published by V. Losev and L. Ianovskaia, *Dnevnik Eleny Bulgakovoi* (Moscow: Knizhnaia palata, 1990).

4. *Manuscripts Don't Burn*, 198–99.

5. *Franklin D. Roosevelt*, vol. 3, 207 (letter of February 22, 1936).

6. M. Chudakova drew attention to the links between the embassy ball and the version in the novel in her *Zhizneopisanie Mikhaila Bulgakova*, *Moskva* 12 (1988): 48–50, although discussion of it is for some reason passed over in her book published under the same title (Moscow: Kniga, 1988), 419. A. Etkind in "Kem byl Voland, kogda on ne byl Satanoi?" *Vremia i My* 116 (1992): 202–34, addresses some of the issues raised in this essay, although he argues that Bulgakov's rendering of Satan's Ball has little connection with the event at the embassy.

7. See M. Chudakova, "Tvorcheskaia istoriia romana M. Bulgakova *Master i Margarita*," *Voprosy Literatury* 1 (1976): 235–36; also her *Zhizneopisaniia Mikhaila Bulgakova* (Moscow: 1988), 389; and the publication of the early draft in M. Bulgakov, *Velikii kantsler* (Moscow: Novosti, 1992), 150.

8. *Master i Margarita* in M. Bulgakov, *Romany* (Moscow: 1973), 667–68. References to this edition will henceforth be given directly after quotations in the text.

9. D.G.B. Piper, "An Approach to *The Master and Margarita*," *Forum for Modern Language Studies* 7, no. 2 (1971): 146; M. P. Lamperini, "Glosse al 23ismo capitolo del *Maestro e Margherita* di M. A. Bulgakov," *Atti del Convegno "Michail Bulgakov"*, (Milan, 1986), 281–86.

10. Thayer, *Bears in the Caviar*, 155–56.

11. *Manuscripts Don't Burn*, 199.

12. *Franklin D. Roosevelt*, vol. 2, 493–94 (letter of May 1, 1935).

13. *Manuscripts Don't Burn*, 221 (diary entry for February 21, 1936).

14. Barratt, *Between Two Worlds: A Critical Introduction to The Master and Margarita* (Oxford: Clarendon, 1987), 88.

15. Gasparov, "Iz nabliudenii nad motivnoi strukturoi romana M. A. Bulgakova *Master i Margarita*," *Slavica Hierosolymitana* 3 (1978): 198–251.

16. Ibid., 203.

Correspondence Relating to *The Master and Margarita*

TO PAVEL POPOV[1]

March 24, 1937 (Moscow)
I haven't written to you before this because our life is always frantically busy and full of difficult and disagreeable problems. Many people told me that 1936 had been a bad year for me supposedly because it was a leap year – there's some sort of superstition about it. But now I can see that, as far as I am concerned, 1937 is going to be in every way a match for its predecessor.

Among other things, I am going to court on April 2 – some sharks from a theater in Kharkov are making an attempt to extract money from me by playing on my misfortune over *Pushkin*. Nowadays I cannot hear the name "Pushkin" without a shudder, and hourly I curse myself for having had the ill-fated thought of writing a play about him. Some of my well-wishers have adopted a rather strange way of consoling me. More than once I have heard their suspiciously unctuous voices: "Never mind, it will all get printed after your death!" I am very grateful to them, of course!

I would like to have a break. Elena Sergeevna and I invite you and Anna Ilyinichna[2] to come round on the twenty-eighth at 10:00 P.M. to drink tea. Drop me a line or ring to say whether you can come. (jaec)

TO ELENA SERGEEVNA IN LEBEDYAN (SOUTH OF MOSCOW)

June 1–2, 1938

Today, dear Lyu,[3] your letter of the thirty-first arrived. I wanted to get down to a long letter of my own as soon as I had finished dictating, but I don't have the energy. Even Olga,[4] with her unique powers of endurance as a typist, has run out of steam today. The letter will be for tomorrow, but now – into a bath, a bath.

We've done 132 typed pages. Roughly speaking, that's about a third of the novel (if you include the trimming down of overlengthy passages). (Here several lines were blackened out by E.S.B.)

In my dreams I shall endeavor to see the sun (of Lebedyan) and sunflowers. I send you a big kiss. (jaec)

June 2, 1938

My dear Lyu!

First, you will see glued into a corner the image of a lady, or rather a portion of that lady, which I have saved from being destroyed. I think constantly of that lady, and in order to think about her more conveniently, I keep such fragments in front of me . . .

Let's start with the novel. About a third, as I said in my postcard, has been typed. And you have to give Olga her due; she works very well. We compose for several hours at a time, and my head is filled with a quiet moan of weariness, but it's a good weariness, not a torment.

And so everything, you might think, is fine, and suddenly from the wings one of the evil geniuses emerges onto the stage . . .

With your typical shrewdness you will instantly exclaim, "Nemirovich!"

And you are quite right. It's him, precisely.

The thing is that, as I knew and said, all your sister's tales about how ill he was, and how the doctors were concealing . . . and so on, were complete rubbish, just typical Karlsbad-Marienbad trivial codswallop. He's as healthy as one of Gogol's coach builders, and is just pining in Barvikha with nothing to do and pestering Olga with all sorts of nonsense.

Feeling thoroughly at a loose end in Barvikha, where there's no Hotel Astoria, no actors and actresses or anything, he has begun threatening to arrive in Moscow on the seventh. And your sister has already declared triumphantly that from now on there will begin to be disruptions to our work. And that's not all: she also added, glowing with happiness, that perhaps he would "whisk her off to Leningrad on the fifteenth"!

It would be a good thing if Woland were to fly down over Barvikha! Alas, that sort of thing happens only in my novel!

A break in the typing would be the end!

I will lose the thread of the correcting and all the connections. Whatever happens the typing must be completed.

My mind is already working feverishly on the problem of where to find another typist, but of course it will be impossible to find one anywhere.

He's already dragged your sister off to Barvikha today, and I'm losing the day.

I think I should know today whether he's going off to Leningrad or not.

The novel must be finished! Now! Now!

Oh dear, I wrote to you that you shouldn't think about the theater or about Nemirovich, and here I am writing about him. But whoever would have thought that he would manage even to do some damage to the novel! But never mind, never mind, don't upset yourself – I will finish the novel. (jaec)

June 13, 1938

I'm dictating the twenty-first chapter. I'm buried under this novel. I've thought it all through, and it's all clear to me. I've completely withdrawn into myself, and I would be able to unlock myself only to one person, but she isn't here! She's growing sunflowers!

I kiss them both – the person and the sunflowers. (jaec)

June 14–15, 1938

Lyu! You shouldn't bathe three times! Sit in the shade and don't wear yourself out going to the market. They'll manage to buy eggs without you . . .

Sit and admire the landscape all around, and think of me. Don't walk too much. So your health is good? Write and tell me! (. . .)

Sist. (joyfully, triumphantly): "I wrote to Vladimir Ivanovich to say that you were terribly flattered that Vladimir Ivanovich had sent his respects to you."[5]

There ensued a huge scene made by me. A demand that she should not dare to write in my name things I had not said. I informed her that I wasn't flattered, and reminded her of how I had been included without warning in the Turbins' letter of congratulations sent to Nemirovich from Leningrad.

S.'s total stupefaction that for the first time in her life someone was creating a scene and it wasn't her. She muttered that I "hadn't understood!" and that she could "show me a copy."

Sist. (in businesslike tones): "I've already sent Zhenya (her husband) a letter saying that I couldn't see the main direction in your novel yet."

I (in a strangulated voice): "Oh, why's that?"

Sist. (not noticing my look): "Well, yes; that is, I'm not saying that it won't emerge. After all, I haven't got to the end yet. But I can't see it for the moment."

I (to myself): "..........!" (. . .)

In front of me lie 327 typed pages (about twenty-two chapters). If I remain in good health, the typing will soon be finished. Then the most important thing remains – my revision of it, which will be considerable and lengthy and painstaking, and might involve retyping some pages.

"And what will come of it?" you ask. I don't know. In all probability you will put it away in the writing desk or in the cupboard where the corpses of my plays lie, and from time to time you will remember. However, we cannot know our future.

I have already formed my judgment on the work, and if I can lift the end a little as well, then I will consider that the piece is worthy to be revised and to be put away into the darkness of a drawer.

For the moment I am interested in your judgment, and no one can tell whether I shall ever know the judgment of the reading public.

My esteemed copyist has particularly helped me to reach the sternest possible judgment on the work. In the course of 327 pages she smiled once, on page 245 ("Glorious sea"). Why that precisely should have amused her, I do not know. I am not confident that she will ever succeed in discovering any sort of main direction in the novel, but on the other hand I am certain that utter disapproval of the work on her part has been guaranteed. This found expression in the cryptic remark "This novel is your own private affair." (?!). Presumably she meant by this that she was not to blame. (. . .)

Ku! I kiss you tenderly for your invitation and for your concern. My only joyous dream is of seeing you, and I will try to do all I can to achieve it. But I can't promise that I will succeed. The thing is, Ku, that I have begun to feel unwell, and if it's going to be like today and yesterday, for example, then I am unlikely to get away. I didn't want to write to you about it, but I can't not. But I hope I will feel better all the same, and then I'll try. (. . .)

Oh, dear Ku, you can't see from a distance what this last sunset novel has done to your husband at the end of his dreadful life in literature.

I send you a big kiss. (jaec)

19 June, 1938

Dear Liu, let me know, how is your precious health? I think of you tenderly.

Is it true, what Sania[6] tells me, that the river is up to his knees? Can one really swim? Let me know.

I am exerting all my strength in order to get to Lebedyan sometime in the third week of June. If it's not too complicated (and if it involves distance and difficulty, don't bother), find out – is there a train with a first-class car? There must be. Well, if not – it's no problem. I can travel in a second-class car.

By the date on your postcard I established that you were watching a thunderstorm at exactly the same time I was dictating about the golden statues. The twenty-sixth chapter (Niza, the murder in the garden) is being written. Stop running out to the market for eggs and cucumbers! Sit in the shade! (. . .) (Last lines were blackened out by E.S.B.) (ldw)

June 22, 1938 (the night of June 21–22)

Dear Liuksi!!

Today I received the very seductive telegram about the boat and the sunflowers. I send you a big kiss.

I feel poorly, but I'm working. The twenty-eighth chapter is being dictated. (ldw)

June 22, 1938 (in the morning)

Dear Luisi, also known as the very charming and beautiful Helen, your letters and cards have been received. Of course, if I come to visit you, toward which I'm taking preparatory steps, I'll bring some money. Today I'll go to the theater to find out when they'll pay [our] salaries and when the season ends.

If Olga comes a bit early today I'll try to dictate a large chunk and then the end of the rewriting will be in sight. The only bad thing in all this is that I'm not feeling well. But that's all right! I kiss you. Greetings to your library in the paradise of Lebedyan, and especially to Radishchev! (ldw)

TO THE WRITER VIKENTY VERESAYEV[7]

March 11, 1939 (Moscow)

Not infrequently I have a great desire to talk with you, but I am somehow shy of doing that because, as with any writer who has been destroyed and persecuted, my thoughts are all the time directed toward one gloomy subject, my situation, and that becomes wearisome for those around me.

Having become convinced over the last few years that not a single line of mine will ever be printed or staged, I am trying to develop an attitude of indifference toward this fact. And it seems as though I have achieved some significant success.

One of my recent endeavors has been a *Don Quixote* based on Cervantes, written to a commission from the Vakhtangov Theater. And it's now lying there and will lie until it rots, despite the fact that they received it with enthusiasm and that it is furnished with a stamp from the Repertory Committee.

They have inserted it into such a distant corner of their plan that it is perfectly clear that it won't be put on. Nor will it be put on anywhere else. This causes me no grief at all, since I have already become used to considering each of my works from just one angle – how great will the unpleasantness be that it will bring me? And if I cannot foresee any major unpleasantness, then I am heartily grateful even for that.

At the moment I am engaged on a job that is entirely senseless from the point of view of everyday life – I am doing a final revision of my novel.

All the same, however much you might try to throttle yourself, it's difficult to stop seizing your pen. I am tormented by an obscure desire to settle my final accounts in literature.

What are you working on? Have you finished your translation?

I would like to see you. Are you ever free in the evenings? I will give you a ring and drop in.

Keep well, and I wish you fruitful work. (jaec)

NOTES

The letters have been compiled from two sources, the primary source being J. A. E. Curtis's *Manuscripts Don't Burn. Mikhail Bulgakov. A Life in Letters and Diaries* (London: Bloomsbury, 1991). Because the intent was to focus strictly on the progress of the novel, I interpolated the texts of some postcards and letters which Curtis had not included, using the most comprehensive (to date) edition of Bulgakov's correspondence: Mikhail Bulgakov, *Pis'ma. Zhizneopisanie v dokumentakh*, ed. Lossev and Petelin (Moscow: Sovremennik, 1989). In preparing her translations, Curtis had access to the original diaries in the archives at the Lenin Library. My translations have been made from the published version. The translator's initials follow each entry; J. A. E. Curtis's previously published text has been amended somewhat by the editor.

1. Pavel Popov (Patia): Bulgakov's long-time friend and biographer.

2. Anna Il'ichna: Popov's wife.

3. Liu, Liuksi, Liusen'ka, Helen, Ku: Fond nicknames Bulgakov gave his wife.

4. Olga Bokshanskaia (Ol'ga, Olia): Elena Sergeevna's sister, personal secretary to the director of the Moscow Art Theater Nemirovich-Danchenko, who also appears in correspondence. Married to Eugene (Evgeny) *Kaluzhsky*, an actor at the Moscow Art Theater.

5. As the personal secretary and right arm of the second most powerful figure at the Moscow Art Theater, Olga Bokshanskaia frequently took a superior attitude toward her "politically wayward" brother-in-law. Their conversation is easily visualized as an exchange of repartees from a comedy, and in fact comes complete with stage directions.

6. Zhenia (Eugene) and Serezha (Sergius) Shilovsky: Elena Sergeevna's sons by her second husband, Eugene (Evgeny) Shilovsky.

7. Vikenty Veresaev: An eminent writer who, like Bulgakov, began as a doctor. He is famous for his research on the great Russian poet Alexander Pushkin. He collaborated with Bulgakov on the play *Last Days* (*Pushkin*).

Selected Entries from Elena Sergeevna Bulgakov's Diary

September 27, 1993

Misha read to Kolia Liamin[1] some new chapters from the novel about the devil written over the last few days, or rather nights. (jaec)

October 10, 1933

This evening we had Akhmatova, Veresaev, Olia and Kaluzhskii, Patia Popov with Anna Il'ichna. A reading from the novel. Akhmatova was silent for the whole evening. (jaec)

October 12, 1933

In the morning a call from Olia: Nikolai Erdman[2] and Mass have been arrested. Apparently for some kind of satirical fables. Misha began to frown. (. . .)

During the night, Misha burned a portion of his novel. (jaec)

November 8, 1933

M. A. slept through almost the entire day. – he's had a lot of sleepless nights. Then he worked on the novel (Margarita's flight). He's been complaining of headaches. (jaec)

January 23, 1934

What a night. M. A. felt under the weather. While lying down, he dictated to me a chapter of the novel – the fire in Berlioz's apartment. The dictation finished at two o'clock in the morning. I went into the kitchen to see about supper – Masha was doing the laundry. She was in a foul mood and jerked the basin off the kerosene stove. It went flying off the table into the corner where there was a container-and-a-quarter of kerosene left uncovered. Flames shot up. I screamed, "Misha!!" He came running just as he was, in a nightshirt, barefoot, and found the kitchen already on fire. Masha, the idiot, didn't want to leave the kitchen because she had money sewn into her pillow.

I woke up Serezha, dressed him, and led him out into the yard, or rather I opened the window and jumped out, then took him. Then I went back into the house. M. A., standing up to his ankles in water, with singed hands and hair, was throwing everything he could onto the fire: bedspreads, pillows, and all the clean laundry. Finally, he put out the fire. But there was a moment when his assurance wavered, and he yelled, "Call the firemen!"

The firemen came when it was all over. And with them the police. They filled out a report. The firemen offered to soak the entire apartment with the hose. Misha, pressing his hand to his breast, declined.

We lay down at seven in the morning and we had to get right up so M. A. could go in to the theater. We ate breakfast in the Metropol', to Serezha's inexpressible delight – cafe glace in the morning. (ldw)

September 16, 1934

In the evening, Liamin. Misha read him several chapters of the novel. After he left we had a conversation until seven in the morning all on the same subject – M. A.'s situation. (jaec)

November 8, 1934

In the evening we sat surrounded by all the mess. M. A. was dictating the novel to me – the scene in the cabaret. Sergey was right there, sleeping on the ottoman. (jaec)

May 9, 1937

(. . .) In the evening we had the Villiamses[3] and Shebalin. M. A. read the first chapters of his novel about Christ and the devil. (It doesn't yet have a title, but that's how I describe it to myself.[jaec]) They liked it enormously and are begging him to come to their place on the eleventh and read further. (ldw)

May 11, 1937

(. . .) In the evening we went to the Villiams'. Petia says, "I can't work. I must know what happens in the novel." M. A. read several chapters. The response – a work of enormous strength, interesting for its philosophy as well as for its entertaining plot, and brilliant from a literary point of view. (ldw)

May 13, 1937

(. . .) In the evening we were alone. M. A. sat and revised the novel from the very beginning ("About Christ and the devil").

May 17, 1937

Everyone talks about one and the same thing: now, as a result of all the events in the literary world, M. A.'s situation has to change for the better.

In the evening M. A. worked on the novel about Woland. (ldw)

June 17, 1937

In the evening we had the Villiamses. M. A. read chapters from the novel ("The Consultant with the Hoof"). (ldw)

October 23, 1937

(. . .) Because of all this work on his own and others' libretti, M. A. is beginning to think of leaving the Bolshoi, revising the novel ("The Master and Margarita") and presenting it to the authorities. (ldw)

December 26, 1937

(. . .) In the evening we had Dmitriev,[4] the Villiamses, Boris,[5] and Nikolai Erdman. M. A. read them chapters from the novel: "Never Talk to Strangers," "The Golden Spear," and "Circus." (ldw)

January 1, 1938

(. . .) This evening we were at the Villiams'. Kolia Erdman was there too. They asked M. A. to bring the novel and read. M. A. read "An Incident at the Griboedov." (ldw)

February 9, 1938

M. A. is revising the novel about Woland in spurts, between "Minin" and the impending arrival of Sedoi. (ldw)

March 1, 1938

Misha was at Angarskii's[6] today, and they have arranged to read the beginning of the novel. It looks as though Misha has now settled for the title "The Master and Margarita." There is of course no hope of getting it published. Misha is now correcting it at night and is forging ahead with it; he wants to finish it in March. (jaec)

March 6, 1938

All his free time M. A. spends on the novel. (ldw)

March 9, 1938

The novel.

M. A. read me a scene – the buffet proprietor at Woland's. (ldw)

March 17, 1938

(. . .)In the evening the Villiamses came over. M. A. read them the new version of the chapters "Hail to the Rooster," "The Buffet Proprietor at Woland's." (ldw)

March 18, 1938

M. A. is sick; he's sitting – in his bathrobe, and in his little grey cap – over the novel. (ldw)

March 19, 1938

The flu. The novel. In the evening – Dmitriev. He wore M. A. out. (ldw)

March 24, 1938

Yesterday we had Erdman and the Villiamses. M. A. read bits of the novel. Today M. A. has work at the Bolshoi again. He came home at one in the morning, exhausted from a migraine. (ldw)

April 7, 1938

Today in the evening – a reading. M. A. long ago promised Tseitlin[7] and Arendt that he would read them some chapters (concerning Ivanushka and his illness). Today the Tseitlins, Arendts, Leontievs,[8] and Ermolinskiis will come over. (ldw)

April 8, 1938

(. . .)The novel produced a strong impression on everyone. Tseitlin offered many valuable observations. He somehow understood the entire novel from these chapters. He particularly praised the chapters from antiquity and was amazed at how masterfully M. A. transports us into that epoch. (ldw)

April 27, 1939

Yesterday we had the Faikos, both of them, Markov and Vilenkin.[9] Misha read *The Master and Margarita* from the beginning. Enormous impression. On the spot they insistently begged [him] to name a date for a continuation [of the reading]. After the reading Misha asked, "And who is Woland?" Vilenkin said he had guessed but wouldn't tell for anything. I proposed that he should write it down; I would also write it down and we would exchange notes. So we did. He wrote Satan, I – the devil. After this Faiko also felt like playing. And he wrote on his note, "I don't know." But I took the bait and wrote for him – Satan.

In the morning Lidia Aleksandrovna, all agitated, called and said, "We almost didn't sleep all night – we talked about the novel the whole time. During the night I guessed and told Alesha. We can't wait for the continuation." (ldw)

May 2, 1939

Yesterday we had the agreed on continuation of the reading to the above-mentioned company plus the Villiamses, who, having heard about the reading, announced they would come.

Once again, it was very nice. A wonderful audience. M. A. read very well. Colossal interest in the novel.

At supper Misha said, "Soon I'll submit it and it will be published." Everyone giggled with embarrassment. (ldw)

May 3, 1938

Angarskii asked M. A. to read the novel (*The Master and Margarita*). M. A. read the first three chapters. Angarskii immediately said, "Well, you can't publish that." "Why not?" "You can't." (jaec)

May 5, 1939

(. . .) In the evening – the continuation of the reading. Olia begged herself on – said she absolutely wanted to hear it. The Viliamses couldn't make it, Anusia is sick. Petia recounted how Samosud keeps exclaiming about the novel, "Genius!" (ldw)

May 15, 1939

Yesterday we had a reading – the end of the novel. Both Faikos, Markov, Vilenkin, Ol'ga, Anusia, my Zhenia. At suppertime Petia and Zhenia came.

For some reason they listened to the final chapters silent and numb. Everything scared them. In the corridor Pasha fearfully told me that under no circumstances should it be submitted – terrible consequences might ensue. (ldw)

January 15, 1940

Misha is correcting the novel (*The Master and Margarita*) as much as his strength will allow, and I am copying it out . . . (jaec)

January 16, 1940

(. . .)Work on the novel. A fuss over the phone with Vilenkin about the contract for "Pushkin" (the question of Veresaev).

(. . .) Misha's sister Elena came and read the novel (*The Master and Margarita*) avidly.

Ermolinskii came in felt boots and read aloud a bit of the novel. (ldw)

January 24, 1940

A bad day. Misha has unremitting headaches. He took four extra-strength tablets – it didn't help. Attacks. Nausea.

(. . .) Now it's eleven in the evening – I called Zakharov. Having found out Misha's condition, he agreed to a house call – he'll be here in twenty minutes. We're living these last days badly: almost no one comes or calls. Misha made corrections in the novel. I wrote [them down].

January 25, 1940

A walk to the Post Office (a telegram to Ruben Simonov) and to the Ermolinskiis. (. . .)

Dictated a page (about Stepa – Yalta). (ldw)

January 28, 1940

Work on the novel. (ldw)

March 10, 1940.

16.39. Misha died.

NOTES

The diary entries have been compiled from two sources, J. A. E. Curtis's *Manuscripts Don't Burn. Mikhail Bulgakov. A Life in Letters and Diaries* (London: Bloomsbury, 1991) and the diary kept by Elena Sergeevna Bulgakov, which appeared in book form in 1990 (*Dnevnik Eleny Bulgakovoi* [Moscow: "Knizhnaia Palata," 1990]). In preparing her diaries for publication, Elena Sergeevna, ever mindful of her role as the widow of a great man, made a number of revisions. Some of these amount to no more than a cosmetic touch-up of syntax, whereas others are more substantial. Among other things, there seems to be conflicting information as to the date when Bulgakov "finally settled" on the novel's title. In preparing her translations, Curtis had access to the original diaries in the archives at the Lenin Library. My translations have been made from the published version. The translator's initials follow each entry; J. A. E. Curtis's previously published text has been amended somewhat by the editor.

1. Nikolai Liamin (Kolia): Like Pavel Popov, a longtime friend.

2. Nikolai Erdman: famous satirical playwright and brother of Boris Erdman.

3. Villiams: A set designer at the Moscow Art Theater.

4. Dmitriev: A set designer at the Moscow Art Theater.

5. Boris Erdman: A set designer and close friend of the Bulgakovs.

6. Angarsky: An editor whom Bulgakov first met in connection with submitting pieces for the almanac *Nedra*.

7. Arendt: A doctor, related to Leontiev by marriage. After the onset of Bulgakov's fatal illness, Elena Sergeevna would call him in to consult on her husband's condition.

8. Iakov Leontiev: A member of the management of the Bolshoi Theater.

9. Aleksei Faiko: Bulgakov's friend and neighbor, himself a talented playwright.

A Note on Translations

Until very recently, the question of obtaining a superior translation of *The Master and Margarita* in English was complicated by the novel's somewhat bizarre publication history. The text as it originally appeared in the journal *Moskva* turned out to be heavily censored. The omitted passages were published subsequently by Einandi (*Master i Margarita. Neizdannye otryvki i epizody* [Berne, 1967]), and a text that included these passages in italics (and was at the time considered a complete text) was published by Possev Verlag in 1969. In the meantime, however, translators had already produced two English editions based on two different versions of the novel. Mirra Ginzburg's translation was published by Grove Press in 1967, and Michael Glenny's translation was published by Harper and Row in the same year. Ginzburg's source was the text as published by *Moskva*; Glenny's source was a text presumed to be identical to the Possev text, but has proven to vary considerably from it. As to the quality of the respective translations, Ginzburg's is the more accurate, as Glenny tends to gloss over difficult points and smooth out Bulgakov's syntax considerably.

The censored passages, which amounted to more than a hundred pages, presented an eclectic picture: some were clearly politically motivated, but not all. One notable episode that had been cut in full was the chapter "Nikanor Ivanovich's Dream," which deals with the touchy topic of show trials and foreign currency. Another crucial episode that did not appear either in the *Moskva* or the Possev texts was the Master's account of his neighbor Aloisy Mogarych, who, as it turns out, was responsible for turning the Master in to the authorities in order to obtain the Master's cozy basement flat. The absence of this passage left a palpable gap in the reader's understanding of the Master's fate. For Russian readers, many of these problems were solved by the appearance of the *Romany* text (Moscow: Khudozhestvennaia literatura, 1973), which represented a major textological advance. The differences between the two Russian texts were tabulated by Donald Fiene ("A Comparison of the Soviet and Possev Editions of *The Master and Margarita*," *Canadian-American Slavic Studies* 15, nos. 2–3 [1981]: 330–54). Nonreaders of Russian, however, were still left with the two existing translations.

Against this background, the world of Bulgakov afficionados greets with pleasure the publication of a completely new translation of the novel by Diana Burgin and Katherine O'Connor (Ann Arbor, Mich.: Ardis, 1995). This translation can be recommended for a number of reasons. Based on a version of the novel "compiled" from two current editions (Mikhail Bulgakov, *Sobranie Sochineniia v Piati Tomakh*, vol. 5 [Moscow: Xudozhestvennaia Literatura, 1989–90], ed. Lidiia Ianovskaia, and the earlier *Master i Margarita* edited by Anna Saakiants for the 1973 *Romany* Moscow edition), it faithfully reproduces Bulgakov's syntax, while at the same time devoting attention to key leitmotivs and repeated phrases crucial to the novel's structure. The translators have also devoted a great deal of effort to clarifying various details of clothing, food, and architecture, which feature so prominently in Bulgakov's universe. A good example is Berlioz's infamous "hat like a meat pie" (*pirozhok*) which turns out to be, in the coinage current in Bulgakov's day, simply a "fedora." Finally, this is the first annotated version of the novel in English, with the annotations done by the foremost Bulgakov scholar in America, Ellendea Proffer.

IV SELECT BIBLIOGRAPHY

This bibliography has been compiled almost exclusively with an English-speaking audience in mind, and is confined to the last ten years of Bulgakov scholarship (1985–95). For earlier references, readers are urged to turn to the bibliography in the *Transactions of the Association of Russian-American Scholars in the U.S.A.* listed below, as well as to Nadine Natov's "Bibliography of Works by and about Mikhail A. Bulgakov," *Canadian American Slavic Studies* 15, nos. 2–3 (Summer–Fall 1981): 457–61; and Ellendea Proffer's *An International Bibliography of Works by and about Mikhail Bulgakov* (Ann Arbor, Mich.: Ardis, 1976). For an excellent listing of Soviet texts since 1984 that reflect the enormous outpouring of archival material since glasnost, see Riitta Pittman's bibliography in *The Writer's Divided Self*, listed below.

Avins, Carol. "Reaching a Reader: The Master's Audience in *The Master and Margarita*." *Slavic Review* 45, no. 2 (1986): 272–85.

A seminal article. Examines in depth the status of the Master's text, the modes of its transmission, and its failure to reach the designated audience.

Barratt, Andrew. *Between Two Worlds: A Critical Introduction to "The Master and Margarita."* Oxford: Clarendon Press, 1987.

The most thorough, coherent, literate reading of *The Master and Margarita* to date. Especially important for its discussion of Woland's identity as the central riddle of the novel, its presentation of the gnostic worldview, and its exegesis of the Faust theme in the novel.

Bethea, David. *The Shape of Apocalypse in Modern Russian Fiction*. Princeton: Princeton University Press, 1989.

One of the most important recent contributions to Bulgakov criticism. Invaluable for placing Bulgakov's vision of history in its proper context. Traces the significance of the horse as a cultural artifact symbolizing at different times Russia, the Russian people (narod), and the course of Russian history (often symbolized as a runaway horse), and contrasts it to the image of the man on horseback symbolizing retributive judgment (as in Falconet's statue of Peter the Great). Also demonstrates the influence of Pavel Florensky on the novel's metaphysics.

Bushnell, John. "A Popular Reading of Bulgakov: Explication des Graffiti." *Slavic Review* 47, no. 3 (1988): 502–11.

Analyzes the graffiti on the wall of stairway 6, apartment building No. 10, Bolshaia Sadovaia, where Bulgakov lived briefly during his first years in

Moscow (later transformed into the "sinister apartment" inhabited by Woland and his suite), and draws some interesting conclusions about Bulgakov's influence on popular culture. Includes some fascinating photographs.

Cornwell, Neil. *The Literary Fantastic from Gothic to Postmodern.* New York: Harvester, 1990.

Places Bulgakov's novel in the context of the fantastic as defined by Todorov.

Curtis, J.A.E. *Bulgakov's Last Decade: The Writer as Hero.* Cambridge: Cambridge University Press, 1987.

A major contribution to Bulgakov studies, crucial for understanding the quixotic nature of Bulgakov's heroes and ultimately Bulgakov himself. Traces the theme of the writer in Bulgakov's later works as he becomes increasingly obsessed with the unhappy fates of Pushkin, Molière, and finally the Master. The final (and finest) chapter portrays Bulgakov as an anachronism, a man firmly entrenched in the nineteenth-century Romantic tradition exemplified by E.T.A. Hoffmann.

———. *Manuscripts Don't Burn. Mikhail Bulgakov: A Life in Letters and Diaries.* London: Bloomsbury, 1991.

A wealth of "marginal" material (archival material, diaries, correspondence) arranged chronologically, detailing six crucial periods in Bulgakov's life. Each section preceded by a brief summary of people and events in his life during this period. A fascinating look into Bulgakov's private and professional worlds.

Davies, J.M.Q. "Bulgakov: Atheist or Militant Old Believer? *The Master and Margarita* Reconsidered." *Australian Slavonic and East European Studies* 8, no. 1 (1992): 125–33.

Ericson, Edward E., Jr. *The Apocalyptic Vision of Mikhail Bulgakov's "The Master and Margarita."* Lewiston, N.Y.: Edwin Mellen, 1991.

Essential reading for understanding the theological context of the novel. Especially fine in covering the Russian Orthodox tradition (chapter three), the figures of the Master and Margarita (chapters six and seven) and the apocalyptic figures woven into the final chapters of the novel (chapter nine).

Haber, Edythe C. "The Lamp with the Green Shade: Mikhail Bulgakov and his Father." *The Russian Review* 44. no. 4 (1985): 333–50.

Establishes the influence of Bulgakov's father on the moral and philosophical framework of the novel. Examines in detail the father's attitude toward civilization embodied in the word "enlightenment" and elaborated in his monograph "On the Enlightenment of Peoples." His ideas of true and false enlightenment (material and intellectual progress with no corresponding spiritual illumination) find resonance in his son's artistic universe.

Kejna-Sharratt, Barbara. "The Characters in *The Master and Margarita.*" In *Atti del Convegno "Michail Bulgakov,"* edited by Eridano Bazzarelli and Jitka Kresalkova, 523–40. Milan: Universita degli Studi di Milano, 1985.

Analyzes the various hierarchies of characters in the novel, from the crowds or "masses" to the flat (in Forrester's terms) characters to the main protagonists, who function pivotally in each of the overlapping narratives to reproduce the thematic pattern of victim and disciple vs. a trio composed of a traitor, an authority figure and a cabal.

Krasnov, Vladislav. "*The Master and Margarita* in Light of Bakhtin's *Problems of Dostoevsky's Poetics.*" *Russian Language Journal* 41, nos. 138–39 (1987): 85–113.

Pursues the original definition of the novel as Menippean satire in greater detail. Examines the relationship between Menippean satire and Bakhtin's broader concept of polyphony.

Krugovoy, George. *The Gnostic Novel of Mikhail Bulgakov. Sources and Exegesis.* Lanham, N.Y.: The University Press of America, 1991.

The most sustained reading of the novel as a gnostic puzzle. Presents a much darker picture of Woland and his powers than is usual, and a much starker view of the cosmic conflict between the higher spiritual plane and the inferior, material plane of existence.

Longinovic, Tomislav Z. *Borderline Culture: The Politics of Identity in Four Twentieth-Century Slavic Novels.* Fayetteville: University of Arkansas Press, 1993.

A rich and rewarding reading of *The Master and Margarita* that deliberately blurs the usual categories for viewing certain issues. Under the hybrid rubric of psychopolitics, the Master becomes not simply a persecuted writer in Stalininst Russia, but rather Dostoevsky's underground man, subverting the dominant cultural mode. He is the antipode of the Stalinist Socialist Realist hero. Margarita represents the nexus of the most deeply held visions of Slavic womanhood, from the myth of Damp Mother Earth to the gnostic concept of Pistis Sophia. She is the quintessential mother figure, and their love is "the longing of the borderline writer for imaginary union with the maternal element."

Mann, Robert. "The Path of the Bronze Horseman in *The Master and Margarita.*" In *Proceedings of the Summer Intensive Workshop in Chinese and Russian,* edited by Albert Leong, 136–50. Eugene: University of Oregon, 1987.

Identifies Pilate as the avenging horseman astride Falconet's statue of Peter the Great, and establishes resemblances between the Yershalaim setting and Senate Square in St. Petersburg. Focuses on equine motifs and the use of floodwater as retribution to create the atmosphere of apocalypse. Gives evidence for the novel as the apocalyptic vision of Ivan (John) Bezdomny.

Mills, Judith M. "Of Dreams, Devils, Irrationality and *The Master and Margarita.*" In *Russian Literature and Psycholanalysis*, edited by Daniel Rancour-Laferriere, 303–28. Philadelphia: John Benjamins, 1989.

Valuable psychoanalytical reading of *The Master and Margarita.* Sees the entire novel as Ivan's creative dream vision engendered as he tries to cope with the eruption of the creative irrational (Woland) in Stalin's Russia.

Milne, Lesley. *Mikhail Bulgakov. A Critical Biography.* Cambridge: Cambridge University Press, 1990.

Excellent, highly readable account of Bulgakov's life and works. Presents a balanced account of Bulgakov and makes good use of the archival revelations that accompanied the advent of glasnost.

Natov, Nadine. *Mikhail Bulgakov.* Boston: Twayne Publishers, 1985.

Solid and thorough account of Bulgakov's life and work, with good select bibliography. Topics arranged not chronologically but by genre.

———. "On the Supernatural in Bulgakov and Gogol." In *The Supernatural in Slavic and Baltic Literatures: Essays in Honor of Victor Terras*, edited by Amy Mandelker and Roberta Reeder, 246–60. Ohio: Slavica, 1988.

Catalogs the techniques used by both writers to depict the supernatural (dream states, stock fairy-tale elements, etc.). Concludes with a surprising explanation of the double deaths of the Master and Margarita.

———, guest editor. *Transactions of the Association of Russian-American Scholars in the U.S.A.*, vol. 44. Richmond Hill, N.Y.: Association of Russian-American Scholars, 1991.

An extremely valuable collection containing a wealth of important articles as well as an excellent bibliography. In addition to Haber's article "The Lamp with the Green Shade," contains articles by Boris Pokrovsky, "The Conversation between Woland and Berlioz: Philosophical Issues in Bulgakov's *The Master and Margarita*"; Colin Wright, "Christ Interrogated: Bulgakov and Others"; David Bethea, "Bulgakov and Nabokov: Toward a Comparative Perspective"; and Katherina Filips-Juswigg, "Mikhail Bulgakov's *The Master and Margarita* and Oscar Wilde's *Salome:* Motif-Patterns and Allusions." Of special interest is the article "Future Prospects" ("Griadushchie perspektivy"—the text is in Russian), an article Bulgakov wrote very early in his career and published in the newspaper *Grozny* (November 13, 1919). The article gives a most gloomy prognosis for the future of Soviet society which turned out to be oddly prophetic.

Oja, Matt. "Bulgakov's Ironic Parallel Between Margarita and Afranius." *Slavic Review* 50, no. 1 (1991): 144–49.

Details structural parallels between Margarita's service to Woland and her reward after the ball, and Afranius's service to Pilate and his reward after the execution. This parallel then stood on its head by the moral qualities of conscience and free will.

Pittman, Riitta. *The Writer's Divided Self in Bulgakov's "The Master and Margarita."* New York: St. Martin's Press, 1991.

Uses Jungian terminology to analyze the split psyches of the novel's protagonists, each of whom appears paired with his "shadow" side. Ivan's and the Master's inability to defend the existence of the shadow leads to an unsuccessful resolution of the problem of schizophrenia.

Rzhevsky, Nicholas. "Magical Subversions: *The Master and Margarita* in Performance." *Modern Drama* 30, no. 3 (1987): 327–38.

Describes the ingenious methods used by Liubimov in adapting *The Master and Margarita* for the stage.

Sakharov, Vsevolod. "The Master's Behest: On the Novel *The Master and Margarita.*" *Soviet Literature* no. 7 (1988): 171–74.

Sokolov, B. V. "The Sources for Mikhail Bulgakov's *The Master and Margarita.*" *Soviet Review* 30, no. 4 (1989): 76–96.

Draws some interesting parallels between the biography of Immanuel Kant and that of the Master, which emerges as a "negative variant" of the great philosopher's. Offers convincing evidence that in the 1936 version of the novel, the Master's life mimicked Kant's daily regimen, and that the figure of Fesya was modeled on Pavel Florensky.

Testa, Carlo. "Bulgakov's *Master i Margarita*: Post-Romantic Devil Pacts." *Canadian-American Slavic Studies* 24, no. 3 (1990): 257–78.

Compares Bulgakov's Woland with the fragmented inner demons of late nineteenth- and early twentieth-century literature, and concludes that Bulgakov's novel is a return to a premodern relationship of the self with desire. The ever-problematical reward granted to the Master and Margarita is seen as a return to the Romantic universe of the first half of the nineteenth century.

Tumanov, Vladislav. "Diabolus ex Machina: Bulgakov's Modernist Devil." *Scando Slavica* 35 (1988): 48–81.

Vozdvizhensky, Vyacheslav, editor. *Mikhail Bulgakov and His Times: Memoirs. Letters.* Moscow: Progress, 1990.

Although marred by stilted translation and some "overly artistic" reminiscences, provides a resource for English-speaking readers to sample a variety of prose portraits of Bulgakov by various associates and each of his three wives. The sketches by his friends Fayko and Yermolinsky are well worth reading.

Weeks, Laura D. "In Defense of the Homeless: On the Uses of History and the Role of Bezdomny in *The Master and Margarita*." *The Russian Review* 48, no. 1 (1989): 45–65.

Posits that the novel's central argument is the interpretation of history. Key episodes in the novel are represented as the collision of profane, secular history and sacred History, or Great Time in Eliade's terms. Ivan Bezdomny is seen as the pivotal figure who retreats from the realm of history to become the chronicler of History, and the author of *The Master and Margarita*.

Williams, Gareth. "Some Difficulties in the Interpretation of Bulgakov's *The Master and Margarita* and the Advantages of a Manichaean Approach, with Some Notes on Tolstoi's Influence on the Novel." *Slavonic and East European Review* 68, no. 2 (1990): 234–56.

Finds many elements of Manichaean worldview in Bulgakov's polarized universe (light-darkness; good-evil; sun-moon). Especially effective in describing the function of the moonlight in the novel.

Wright, A. Colin. "Female Characters in Bulgakov." In *Atti del Convegno "Michail Bulgakov,"* edited by Eridano Bazzarelli and Jitka Kresalkova, 553–62. Milan: Universita degli Studi di Milano, 1985.

Divides Bulgakov's female characters into recognizable types. Interesting discussion of Margarita as a confusion of the pure mother/sister image and the more erotically charged image of mistress.

———. "Animals and Animal Imagery in Bulgakov." *Zeitschrift fur Slawistik* 36, no. 2 (1991): 220–28.